"Derek Tidball has successfully achieved something few have attempted. He has written a theological overview of the New Testament that maintains both its unity and diversity. But here—and this is key—his approach is completely innovative: we get to listen in as a 'seminar leader' directs a conversation on the major themes of the New Testament. And his conversation partners are none other than the writers of the New Testament! A question is launched—So what about Jesus as Son of God?—and suddenly we can listen to Luke, Mark, John, Paul and others weigh in from their distinctive perspectives. The approach is at once richly entertaining and deeply insightful. This book is a masterpiece written by a highly skilled teacher and theologian, and it will win high praise from students and teachers alike."

Gary Burge, professor of New Testament, Wheaton College, author of *Mapping Your Academic Career*

"Imagine attending a panel discussion on New Testament theology. Derek Tidball invites us to imagine that the panelists are the writers of the New Testament. Instead of a theology volume with a section on, for example, the sinlessness of Christ, we have a discussion by New Testament writers on the subject. Can such an artificial scenario really help? Yes, I think it can. This is not novel theology but well-vetted theology presented in a fresh, novel way. In the end it may be less artificial, less speculative than many traditional New Testament theologies. My students will find it more accessible and certainly more engaging."

E. Randolph Richards, dean and professor of biblical studies, Palm Beach Atlantic University

"Are you tired of seeing your students' eyes glaze over when you teach theological method? Do you long for a creative resource that helps your students discern the difference between systematic theology and the theological content of the New Testament? Would you appreciate a fresh approach to introducing biblical theology that takes seriously the different voices within Scripture while at the same time values coherence? Get this book. Derek Tidball has done a great service to the academy and the church by organizing an imaginative conversation between the heroes of our faith, helping us celebrate the theological diversity and unity of the New Testament. A joy to read."

Rodney Reeves, dean and Redford Professor of Biblical Studies, Southwest Baptist University

The Voices
of the
New Testament

INVITATION TO A
BIBLICAL ROUNDTABLE

DEREK TIDBALL

IVP Academic
An imprint of InterVarsity Press
Downers Grove, Illinois

InterVarsity Press
P.O. Box 1400, Downers Grove, IL 60515-1426
ivpress.com
email@ivpress.com

InterVarsity Press® is the book-publishing division of InterVarsity Christian Fellowship/USA®, a movement of students and faculty active on campus at hundreds of universities, colleges and schools of nursing in the United States of America, and a member movement of the International Fellowship of Evangelical Students. For information about local and regional activities, visit intervarsity.org.

Cover design: Cindy Kiple
Interior design: Beth McGill
Images: the apostles: ©DEA / A. DAGLI ORTI/Getty Images
    speech bubbles: ©Cagisha/iStockphoto

ISBN 978-0-8308-5148-5 (print)
ISBN 978-0-8308-9447-5 (digital)

Printed in the United States of America ∞

Library of Congress Cataloging-in-Publication Data
A catalog record for this book is available from the Library of Congress.

| **P** | 23 | 22 | 21 | 20 | 19 | 18 | 17 | 16 | 15 | 14 | 13 | 12 | 11 | 10 | 9 | 8 | 7 | 6 | 5 | 4 | 3 | 2 | 1 |
| **Y** | 35 | 34 | 33 | 32 | 31 | 30 | 29 | 28 | 27 | 26 | 25 | 24 | 23 | 22 | 21 | 20 | 19 | 18 | 17 | 16 |

Contents

Preface

When George Mallory was asked why he climbed Everest, he famously replied, "Because it's there." Writing a book that seeks to convey the message of the New Testament is a bit like climbing Everest. The New Testament is wonderfully rich, complex, and diverse, and also, precisely because it is not a systematic textbook, it can appear untidy. So it's quite a challenge to bring unity to it without doing it a disservice—but it is a challenge any Bible teacher is likely to welcome, at least after teaching it for some years. Yet that in itself is not an adequate answer. There are some excellent theologies of the New Testament already available (see the bibliography for the details), so why another?

The short answer is that none has adopted the approach of this book, which arises from a suggestion made some years ago by the scholar George Caird, as explained more fully in the opening chapter. I imagine the writers of the New Testament sitting around and having a conversation with each other about what they have written. Hopefully this makes it all the more personal and enables us to see more easily where they agree and why they write with different emphases from different perspectives. Imagining a conversation that, as far as we know, never took place is quite a challenge, especially if you want to let the authors speak for themselves without supplementing their words for the sake of the conversation. I am aware how much more could have been said about the topics they discuss, how much more by way of background and interpretation could have been added, and how many other doctrines or themes could have been covered. However, many New Testament theologies are too long to be useful, and they spend time on academic questions that can divert attention from the message itself. It is hoped that both the approach and the level of this book will introduce the one but varied message of the New Testament to those who will never pick up the heavier tomes.

The book developed as a result of teaching a New Testament course at Colombo Theological Seminary in 2014. I dedicate this book to the staff and students of Colombo Theological Seminary, Sri Lanka, and to South Asia Institute of Advanced Christian Studies, Bangalore, India, where it has also been my privilege to teach in recent years. They will know the need to take the revealed gospel of Jesus Christ and faithfully translate it into an Asian context.

Writing a book is always a team effort. On this occasion I am particularly grateful to Chris Brown, who checked the many references in an earlier version of this document, and to Phil Duce and Suzanne Mitchell for their excellent editorial skills, which have improved the manuscript greatly. As always, however, I bear the responsibility for any errors that may remain and for the views and interpretations given in the book.

Paul wrote of "the boundless riches of Christ" that he was called to preach (Eph 3:8). In using the word *boundless* he was not saying that the gospel is boundary-less, in a postmodern, anything goes type of way. Rather he meant that the gospel of Jesus Christ is so rich and deep, and can be expressed in so many ways and understood from so many angles, that no one can ever say, "That's it. I don't need to look at it further. I've understood it all. I've reached the summit." The gospel is "too vast to explore completely and too deep to fathom."[1] It's like Everest—except Everest is too high to fathom! Which of us, though, would miss out on at least climbing the foothills, if we could, and beginning to grasp the "unsearchable" gospel? Let the climb—or to mix one's metaphors, the conversation—begin.

---

[1]Peter T. O'Brien, *The Letter to the Ephesians*, Pillar NT Commentary (Grand Rapids: Eerdmans, 1999), 242.

Introducing
the Conversation

What is the message of the New Testament? Behind this deceptively simple question lies an assumption that there is one coherent message in the New Testament, which many have doubted. So this book asks, how far is it possible to speak of *the* message or theology of the New Testament? Is there just one message of good news or several? And what does that good news look like?

The Background

New Testament theology seeks to bring coherence to the diverse teachings and approaches found in the New Testament. This is no simple task. While the writers are clearly all concerned with the story and significance of Jesus, the New Testament is a collection of twenty-seven books written by at least nine different authors and addressed to individuals or groups in several different locations over a number of years. Some of the readers are evidently Jewish, others belong to mixed Jewish-Gentile churches, while some audiences are predominantly Gentile.

The books adopt very different styles, or, more technically, different genres. The Gospels form a distinct genre of their own, with some similarities to ancient biographies. Much of the New Testament consists of letters, but one book, Acts, is a work of history; at least one other, Hebrews, is a sermon (some people think 1 Peter was also a sermon, preached at a baptism); and at least one other, Revelation, is apocalyptic in form (with apocalyptic passages in other writings as well). How do you integrate stories, narrative teaching, and apocalyptic with doctrinal propositions?

The New Testament documents were also written over a period of time. While the precise dating of the documents is a happy hunting ground for New Testament specialists, it is obvious that some of the writings belong to the very start of the New Testament period while others belong to the time when the original apostles were disappearing from the scene. For example, 1 Thessalonians is a short follow-up letter from an early stage in Paul's missionary career, whereas 2 Timothy comes from the end of his life. Mark's Gospel is a very early account of Jesus' life, whereas John's Gospel is a later and mature reflection on it. Given this, some argue that we should not expect to find any tight unity in the teaching of the New Testament but should look instead for the way its theology develops and changes over time to meet new circumstances and answer new questions. Are the different voices to be explained, at least in part, as coming into the conversation at different times? Are we in danger of imposing a false unity on these writings if we ignore the time frame?

Another obvious difficulty in seeking to understand the united message of the New Testament is that the books often appear, at least on the surface, to be talking about different issues. To take some obvious examples: the central message of the Synoptic Gospels (Matthew, Mark, and Luke) is "the kingdom of God" (or "kingdom of heaven," as Matthew terms it); for John it seems to be "eternal life"; whereas for Paul many would say it is "justification by faith." And that refers only to the main players. Once we add in Hebrews, which perceives the gospel through Jewish lenses, Peter, with his emphasis on hope, and James, who writes as a typical wisdom writer, the question becomes even more complex. How do these connect to each other?

A related and important issue highlights the significance of the question further. The New Testament is not a systematic textbook in theology and doesn't seem concerned to present itself as such. Some documents may have been composed with the idea of producing a comprehensive account of things. Luke, for example, "carefully investigated everything from the beginning" and sets out to write "an orderly account" of the life of Jesus (Lk 1:3). Even so, he doesn't tell us everything, as a comparison of his Gospel with the others shows. Some claim Romans is Paul's systematic statement of his theology, and in a sense it is probably the nearest we get to a systematic approach; but even Romans is written because Paul wants to explain to his readers his personal mission and plans (Rom 15:14-33), and it certainly does not provide a comprehensive account of his theology. Romans focuses on the relationship between the Jewish people and the Gentiles who are now included in the gospel, but there are many other topics Paul addresses for which we have to read his other letters. So the New Testament documents are quite unlike the systematic theologies produced later by such giants as John Calvin or Karl Barth. They are documents written in the heat of the missionary activity of the early church, on the job, and they deal with the living and ever-changing context of the young church.

All this diversity adds richness to our understanding of the Christian faith and its fundamental beliefs. It is far more exciting, lively, and instructional to read such documents than it is to read systematic textbooks. (Believe me, I've read enough of those to know the truth of that claim!) Their diversity resonates with the real world in which we live rather than the ivory towers inhabited by some academics. Of course, some might object that there are dangers involved in this "occasional" approach. How do we know everything is covered? Wouldn't such an informal approach lead to some aspects being overemphasized at the expense of others? Might not something important be missed because it wasn't thrown up by a question in the church at the time?

There are several answers to these questions. First, anyone setting out to write systematically is quite capable of missing something important, and systematic textbooks are quite capable of distorting issues to fit their system while conveniently ignoring anything that doesn't seem to fit it. A systematic approach is not necessarily a safeguard against such liabilities, while having disadvantages of its own. Second, while the New Testament shares much in common with other humanly written documents, it is at the same time in a class of its own. The writing, editing, and collecting of the New Testament documents were superintended, or inspired, by the Holy Spirit who as the Spirit of truth (see Jn 14:17, 26; 15:26; 16:13) guarantees not only the trustworthiness and reliability of what is written but also that it is sufficient for our needs. The New Testament is "useful for teaching, rebuking, correcting and training in righteousness, so that the servant of God *may be thoroughly equipped* for every good work" (2 Tim 3:16-17).[1]

THE APPROACH

Given the challenges outlined above, how might we go about the task of discovering coherence in the teaching of the New Testament without imposing

---

[1] All emphases in Scripture quotations are mine.

a false synthesis on it, squashing its diversity, or distorting the emphasis of any individual writer? The approach adopted here is to imagine a conversation between the New Testament authors that both reveals how much they have in common and equally permits them to emphasize their distinctive or even unique contributions.

Our news headlines periodically inform us that world leaders are meeting in a summit conference. They're holding crucial talks with a view to finding unity about a world crisis or ongoing challenge, even though their politics and the needs of their separate countries are very different. Imagine, then, a conference not of world leaders but of New Testament authors, seeking to do the same about the Christian faith. They have much more in common than world leaders. Without presupposing anything we shall later discover, we know that they share a common devotion to Jesus as Christ and Lord, and a commitment to getting the message of what God has done through him to rescue the world from its mess out to the whole of humankind. Furthermore, they are not about building their own empires, protecting their own backs, or defending their own positions (not even in the fierce argument we will encounter in Galatians!). They are all servants on a level with each other, committed to furthering the interest of the Savior, Jesus.

As in any such conference, some voices are more dominant in the conversation than others, but all can find their voice and contribute appropriately. So we might expect Luke, as the author of a two-volume work about the origins and beginning of the church, or Paul, as the author of the majority of New Testament letters, to contribute more fully than, say, Jude or James; but no voice would be stifled. This will, I believe, lead us to find a genuine meeting of minds and spirit in the New Testament and a common set of beliefs that coherently form the original teaching of the apostles. Unlike world leaders meeting in summit, their agreement will be no equivocation, no clever playing with words that covers over the real cracks and disagreements that remain underneath the surface.

The idea of the New Testament authors engaging in conversation in this way is not new. George Caird suggested it in his magisterial *New Testament Theology* in 1994.[2] He argued that there was precedence for the approach and that it was modeled on what the early church itself did at the so-called

---

[2]George Caird, *New Testament Theology*, ed. L. D. Hurst (Oxford: Oxford University Press, 1994), 18-26.

Jerusalem Conference of Acts 15 and in the "discussion" Peter and Paul had that is recorded in Galatians 2. However, although he occasionally used the idea in the rest of his book, he did not develop it as fully as he might have done and seems content to let the texts lie side by side rather than engage with each other.[3]

To imagine such a conversation is a delicate task, and I am aware of its pitfalls. To help the conversation along I have introduced an imaginary person who presides over the discussions. The chair's role is to introduce the topic, invite the relevant participants to contribute, and summarize the discussion. The chair is not designed to "steer" the conversation in a particular direction but to enable the various voices to be heard. The participants speak for themselves, but unless we are merely to hear them cite texts from their writings, there will be an unavoidable element of interpretation involved in weaving their voices into a conversation. Care has been taken to ensure that any interpretation is both minimal and characterized by integrity.

I have also introduced an imaginary observer. This device gives us the freedom to expand on features of the conversation and especially to make brief comments about the way theologians later dealt with issues such as the Trinity, the atonement, and eschatology. By using this technique there should be no confusion between the original teaching of the New Testament and later developments.

The participants who sit around the table are listed at the end of this chapter.

ALTERNATIVE APPROACHES

Others have approached the writing of New Testament theology differently. Four major approaches have been adopted, each of which has strengths and weaknesses.

Authorial approach. Several theologies start by outlining the theology of the different writers of the New Testament—of Paul, John, Peter, the Gospel writers, and so on—before seeking to relate them to one another. The danger is that while this does justice to the distinctive emphases of the individual authors, it is more difficult to identify what they have in common, and it can result in *theologies* of the New Testament rather than a unified *theology* of the New Testament.

---

[3]I. Howard Marshall, *New Testament Theology: Many Witnesses, One Gospel* (Downers Grove, IL: InterVarsity Press, 2004), 25.

Howard Marshall provides us with an example of this type of approach—one that avoids the fragmentation just mentioned—in his *New Testament Theology: Many Witnesses, One Gospel*.[4] He adopts a step-by-step approach, first exploring the theology of individual documents, then identifying any central point or assumed framework of an author, and next tracing any development in thought between them, before attempting a synthesis. He acknowledges that there may be "a conceivable further stage" which involves constructing a "dogmatic theology" for the church. The result is essentially a description and analysis of the theology of New Testament books and authors, in the order of the New Testament itself.[5]

In asking what binds the diverse writings together, he comments, "The obvious answer is that they are all concerned with Jesus and the repercussions of his activity," developing out of Judaism. It is, he stresses, "helpful to recognize them as the documents of a mission." They are essentially "missionary theology."[6]

As a result of his exploration of the individual writers, Marshall concludes that there is an essential unity expressed through the diversity.[7] The main theme of the New Testament, he suggests, is a religion of redemption, which unfolds in four stages: first, humans as sinners under divine judgment; second, the saving act of God through Jesus Christ, the incarnate Son of God, which occurs through his death and resurrection; third, the new life that those who have faith in the (trinitarian) God experience, individually and in community; and fourth, God's bringing "his redemptive action to its consummation with the *parousia* of Christ."[8]

Developmental approach. Marshall claims the route more commonly taken by recent travelers through the terrain of New Testament theology is that of a developmental approach.[9] The maps come in many different forms, from the historical skepticism of the influential Rudolf Bultmann[10] to the

---

[4]Marshall, *New Testament Theology*. Note also his shorter version, *A Concise New Testament Theology* (Downers Grove, IL: InterVarsity Press, 2008).

[5]Marshall, *New Testament Theology*, 46-47.

[6]Ibid., 34.

[7]Ibid., 731.

[8]Ibid., 717-18.

[9]Ibid., 27.

[10]Rudolf Bultmann, *The Theology of the New Testament* (London: SCM Press, 1956). Many such theologies were concerned to establish which sayings of Jesus could be trusted as authentic before constructing any theology. See, for example, Joachim Jeremias, *New Testament Theology*, trans. John Bowden, vol. 1 (London: SCM Press, 1971), 1-41.

conservative writings of George Eldon Ladd.[11] Ladd saw the task as essentially a descriptive one that would lay foundations on which systematic theologians would build.

A prime example of this variegated approach is found in the writings of James Dunn, especially in his *Unity and Diversity in the New Testament*,[12] but also in many of his other works. Indeed, in a recent work Dunn has argued for combining a historical-critical approach to the New Testament documents with recognition that they demonstrate not a unified theology so much as an ongoing (and so incomplete?) theologizing about the significance of Jesus.[13]

In his seminal *Unity and Diversity in the New Testament*, Dunn distinguished four streams of early Christianity. First, there is Jewish Christianity, which is seen in John, Matthew, Hebrews, and James. Second, there is Hellenistic Christianity, which is illustrated by Acts 6–7 and some of Paul's writings, such as the letters to Corinth, with their concern about proto-Gnosticism, and his concern with other opponents like those described in Colossians. The pastoral letters in part and Jude also fall into this group. Third, there is Apocalyptic Christianity. Mark 13, 1 and 2 Thessalonians, 2 Peter, and Revelation are prime examples of this strand. And then, fourth, there is Early Catholicism, which marks "the fading of the *parousia* hope"[14] and the growth of institutionalization of the church, as seen, it is argued, in Ephesians and the pastoral letters. Dunn agrees that these are "not mutually exclusive segments of first-century Christianity."[15]

Is there a "unifying core" to these four streams? The answer is a definite yes. It is "the affirmation of the identity of the man Jesus with the risen Lord,"[16] by which he means there is "a unity between the historical Jesus and the kerygmatic Christ":[17] the before and after Easter proclamation about Jesus is diverse but one.[18] However, he states, "This unifying core is

---

[11]G. E. Ladd, *A Theology of the New Testament*, ed. D. A. Hagner, 2nd ed. (Grand Rapids: Eerdmans, 1974).

[12]James D. G. Dunn, *Unity and Diversity in the New Testament: An Inquiry into the Character of Earliest Christianity* (Philadelphia: Westminster Press, 1977).

[13]James D. G. Dunn, *New Testament Theology: An Introduction* (Nashville: Abingdon Press, 2009).

[14]Dunn, *Unity and Diversity*, 344-51.

[15]Ibid., 236.

[16]Ibid., 227.

[17]The "kerygmatic Christ" refers to the Christ preached and taught by the apostles with a view to evoking faith among those who heard them.

[18]Dunn, *Unity and Diversity*, 228.

an abstraction," and the particular expressions of the faith are always bound
to be much fuller than this general core.[19]

The general difficulty with this approach (as distinct from Dunn's particular example of it), as Marshall argues, is that it is "complex and
speculative"[20] and is in danger of producing not so much a New Testament
theology as "an archaeological dig."[21] It also tends, on the one hand, to over-
systematize messy trends found in the living documents, and, on the other
hand, to underplay the unity involved.

Thematic approach. The best example of the third approach, the thematic
one, is Donald Guthrie's *New Testament Theology.*[22] Guthrie was concerned
to recover the unity of the New Testament in the face of the increasing fragmentation evident in the writings of contemporary scholars. The book is
comprehensive and divides its discussion into the major areas of God, man
and his world, Christology (Christ's person and mission), the Holy Spirit,
the Christian life, the church, the future, ethics, and Scripture itself. In each
case the background to the topic is considered before the Synoptic Gospels,
John, Acts, Paul, Hebrews, the rest of the New Testament, and Revelation
are scoured to see what they might say about it.

Thomas Schreiner's criticism[23] that this leads to a work of systematic theology has some merit, although it depends on your understanding of systematic theology, since it is in no way concerned to relate its review of the
biblical material to the contemporary world or philosophy. It is perhaps
better to class Guthrie as writing a thematic New Testament theology than
a systematic one. It is fair to say that the approach lacks a center or focus and
is content to explore what the New Testament teaches about individual subjects rather than trying to find coherence between them. While recognizing
this weakness, we can at least absolve Guthrie from falling into the trap of
distorting the individual strands of the New Testament in a desire to com-
press them all into a system. The approach is perhaps more characteristic
of "older conservative works of systematic theology that are basically

---

[19]Ibid., 229-30.

[20]Marshall, *New Testament Theology*, 29.

[21]Ibid., 27.

[22]Donald Guthrie, *New Testament Theology* (Downers Grove, IL: InterVarsity Press, 1981).

[23]Thomas R. Schreiner, *New Testament Theology: Magnifying God in Christ* (Grand Rapids: Baker
    Academic, 2008), 10.

compilations of biblical material" than of more contemporary approaches.[24] Wayne Grudem's *Systematic Theology*,[25] which covers the Old and New Testaments, is an unashamed example of this approach and is primarily a review of the texts that are relevant to a particular topic or doctrine.

Systematic approach. Thomas Schreiner's own *New Testament Theology*, subtitled *Magnifying God in Christ*, might, to my mind, be even more guilty of being a systematic theology than Guthrie's. True, the system is a doctrinal system, influenced by Reformed theology, rather than a contemporary systematic theology, but it is highly systematic nonetheless. Schreiner correctly asserts that a true New Testament theology must have a center. Caird cautioned that "the music of the New Testament choir is not written to be sung in unison."[26] While that is true, the music was not written to produce disconnected or discordant notes either, and we legitimately strive to bring out its harmony because this brings depth, variety, and unity to the singing.

Schreiner accepts that no one center "will ever become the consensus" and that since "the subject matter of New Testament theology is God himself" the subject will never be exhausted.[27] Nonetheless he ventures to have a twin focus: "First, God's purpose in all that he does is to bring honor to himself and to Jesus Christ." This involves "the supremacy of God and the centrality of Christ," which can easily be taken as so obvious that we miss it. The second focus is "the history of salvation [and] the fulfillment of God's promises," which incorporates themes such as the "already/not yet" experience of Christians, judgment, and the completion of the promises.[28] So he begins, "The thesis advanced in this book is that New Testament theology is God-focused, Christ-centered, and Spirit-saturated, but the work of Father, Son and Spirit must be understood along a salvation-historical timeline; that is, God's promises are already fulfilled but not yet consummated."[29]

His theology is constructed in four parts. The first concerns the fulfillment of God's saving promise and the theme of already/not yet. Second,

---

[24]Marshall, *New Testament Theology*, 25n11. The approach is of great value for those who preach and teach the Bible in a local church setting.

[25]Wayne Grudem, *Systematic Theology: An Introduction to Biblical Doctrine* (Grand Rapids: Zondervan, 1994).

[26]Caird, *New Testament Theology*, 24.

[27]Schreiner, *New Testament Theology*, 13.

[28]Ibid., 14-15.

[29]Ibid., 23.

he explores the God of promise: the saving work of Father, Son, and Spirit including the nature and work of Christ. The third part is about experiencing the promise: believing and obeying, with a fairly heavy emphasis on sin, faith, obedience, and law. Finally, he turns to the people of the promise and the future of the promise, which includes topics such as church, the social worlds of God's people (which involves a discussion of ethics), and the consummation of all that God has promised.

The clear and unapologetic focus of Schreiner's approach is welcome. It is good to read a theology that is so clearly God-focused. However, questions remain as to whether it does not suffer from some distortion and whether it overplays certain themes, such as sin and judgment, because of an already presupposed framework, rather than letting each element of the New Testament speak in its own right.

Each of these approaches has strengths and weaknesses, and all of them are profitable if used with discernment. But the discussion approach to composing a New Testament theology has much to commend it as well and is worth exploring more fully than has been undertaken so far.

RETURNING TO THE DISCUSSION: WHO'S WHO?

One more introductory matter needs clarifying before the discussion can begin. As with any conference we need to know who the participants are. New Testament scholars dispute the identity of several of them and indeed their identities do throw up some interesting and complex questions; but this is not the place to explore them. Most introductory textbooks on the New Testament or commentaries delve into the issues involved. For our purposes the main participants, in alphabetical order, are as follows:

Luke: a Gentile doctor, historian, superb storyteller, and occasional companion of Paul who authored two books, the Gospel that bears his name and the Acts of the Apostles. Together they make up around a quarter of the New Testament.

James: the half brother of Jesus and leader of the church in Jerusalem who wrote a short letter "to the twelve tribes scattered among the nations" (Jas 1:1), which sits within the Jewish wisdom tradition.

John: traditionally thought to be the apostle John and seen as the author of the Gospel, three letters, and the book of Revelation. In 2 and 3 John he refers to himself as "the elder" and is associated in later years with the church at Ephesus. We will assume the common authorship of the books that bear his name.[30]

Jude: the author of a short letter in which he "contend[s] for the faith that was once for all entrusted to God's holy people" (Jude 3). He identifies himself as "a brother of James" and on that basis was also a brother of Jesus. Older views identified him as one of the apostles, but this cannot be right if we correctly understand his place in Jesus' family.

Mark: son of Mary who hosted the church of Jerusalem in her house. He was an early follower of Jesus and companion of both Peter and Paul. He is frequently referred to as John Mark. An early church document by Papias suggests his Gospel was based on Peter's testimony about Jesus.

Matthew: a converted tax collector who became an early disciple of Jesus. Mark and Luke know him by the name of Levi. He has a special interest in the relation between the Christian faith and its Jewish heritage. Many question for several reasons whether the Gospel, which is unattributed, was written by the apostle.

Paul: the converted Pharisee who became "the apostle to the Gentiles." His name is attached to thirteen letters in the New Testament. The majority of these (Romans and Colossians are exceptions) are follow-up letters to churches he founded or personal letters to colleagues in ministry. For various reasons many recent scholars think that only eight letters were actually written by Paul himself. The others belong to his school of thought and make use of his name to enhance their authority. We will assume all are genuinely from his hand.

Peter: the early disciple of Jesus who, after denying Jesus, became "the rock" and chief among the apostles. The apostles were the foundation of the Christian church and exercised authoritative and formative influence over what it was correct to believe and the nature of a Christian lifestyle. While some doubt he wrote the second letter that bears his name, we shall assume he wrote 1 and 2 Peter.

The Hebraist: Hebrews is anonymous, giving rise to all sorts of speculation as to who wrote it, with the names of Apollos, Priscilla, and Barnabas frequently among the suggestions. Known to the original readers, the author is unknown to us and so we will refer to him or her as the Hebraist.

---

[30]Many scholars dispute the common authorship of these works, but for a recent defense see Paul A. Rainbow, *Johannine Theology: The Gospel, the Epistles and the Apocalypse* (Downers Grove, IL: InterVarsity Press, 2014), 39-53.

Matthew, Mark, and Luke are sometimes referred to as "the Synoptic Gospels" because of the similarity between them.

To these genuine characters we add two more:

Chair: an imaginary person who introduces the topic and brings in the speakers. The chair seeks to relate them to each other with a light touch and without imposing her own views on the discussion. She provides occasional summary statements.

Observer: the observer does not take part in the discussion as such but has freedom to comment on it. This enables some contemporary reflection to be included. It often takes the form of a background comment, clarifying the way the church subsequently developed the issue or adding a recent quotation or summary which throws light on it.

A couple of further comments might be helpful. First, the approach inevitably leads to some repetition, but this has been kept to a minimum and cross-references have been employed wherever possible. Second, the danger of composing any New Testament theology is that it can get swamped in references and the truth buried in a string of texts. For this reason, although the principal texts are mentioned in the course of the discussion, additional and supporting texts will be found in textboxes in order to provide a more expanded picture.

Having set out the background, let's eavesdrop on the discussion.

2

THE COMMON THREAD OF THE NEW TESTAMENT

The Good News

Chair: Since we must start somewhere, is it possible to identify a theme that we can all agree on as the thread that runs through all the writing of the New Testament? Without wishing to prejudge the discussion or to impede any of the rich diversity I know we'll discover as the conversation unfolds, we might ask nonetheless what it is that holds us together. Any ideas?

Mark: Perhaps I might boldly jump in and suggest that the very first verse of my Gospel, which serves as a title for what follows, identifies such a theme: "The beginning of the good news about Jesus the Messiah, the Son of God" (Mk 1:1). What we have in common is the *good news*, or *gospel*—it's the same thing—of Jesus. I summarize his very first sermon just a few sentences later when he himself said as much: "The time has come. . . . The kingdom of God has come near. Repent and believe the good news!" (Mk 1:15). Jesus himself spoke of "the good news" several times, using it as shorthand for his message and mission.

Paul: I would certainly agree with Mark on this. I think I can claim to be the one

> ### "GOOD NEWS" OR "GOSPEL"
> in Mark: 8:35; 10:29; 13:10; 14:9; 16:15.

who chiefly established the term *gospel* as at the heart of the Christian faith. It's a central plank of my theology. I'm told I use the word sixty times, and in twenty-three of those I don't even qualify it in any way as it speaks for itself. The *gospel* is well understood as the good news that God acted through the life, death, resurrection, and exaltation of his Son, Jesus Christ, to save the world.

My writings are soaked in the concept of the gospel.[1] It's what shapes my worldview and determines my mission. My personal calling as "a servant of Christ Jesus" was to be "set apart for the gospel of God" (Rom 1:1), and I have focused solely on preaching that gospel rather than engaging in other tasks such as baptizing people (see 1 Cor 1:17). I didn't learn of the gospel through human messengers but received it by direct "revelation from Jesus Christ" (Gal 1:11-12). Astonishingly, I have been "approved by God to be entrusted with the gospel" message (1 Thess 2:4). This gospel is more than words and is conveyed with "power, with the Holy Spirit and deep conviction" (1 Thess 1:5). I've devoted my whole life to preaching this gospel. Indeed I feel under an obligation to do so: "Woe to me if I do not preach the gospel!" (1 Cor 9:16). I'll do everything "for the sake of the gospel, that I may share in its blessings" (1 Cor 9:23). It has not always been easy, and I've suffered for preaching it. In fact, I've described myself as "an ambassador in chains" (Eph 6:20; cf. Philem 13) because of my activity in "defending and confirming the gospel" (Phil 1:7).

Chair: Paul, why is the gospel so important to you?

Paul: First, because it totally revolutionized my own life. I can never forget the experience of encountering the risen Jesus on the way to Damascus, where I was going to persecute his followers (see Acts 9:1-19; 26:1-32). It was a light shining in my heart that displayed God's glory in the face of Jesus (see 2 Cor 4:6). Through the gospel I experienced the Lord's grace "poured out on me abundantly" even though I did not deserve it (1 Tim 1:12-14).

Yet it is not only personal. I'm passionate about the gospel because it is "the power of God that brings salvation to everyone who believes" (Rom 1:16). It is the means by which people are "saved"—rescued, in other words (1 Cor 15:2). It is a revelation of "the righteousness of God" (Rom 1:17). It is "the

---

[1]For a brilliant summary of this see N. T. Wright, *Paul and the Faithfulness of God* (London: SPCK, 2013), 410-11.

true message" (Col 1:5; cf. Gal 2:5, 14) and the source of hope (see Col 1:23) for humanity.

The gospel was never God's plan B, but always his plan A to bring salvation to the world, reconciling Jews and Gentiles in the same way by means of faith (see Gal 3:8; Eph 1:13; 2:11-22). The gospel we now believe is the same one as was announced to Abraham "in advance" of others (Gal 3:8; Rom 4:1-25). The heart of the gospel is that "Christ died for our sins according to the Scriptures, that he was buried, that he was raised on the third day according to the Scriptures, and that he appeared to Cephas" and then to a host of others (1 Cor 15:3-5; cf. 2 Tim 1:10; 2:8). To benefit from it we need to have faith in the gift of salvation that came through the Lord Jesus (Eph 2:8) and "obey the gospel" (2 Thess 1:8). Doing so removes us from facing God's wrath (see 2 Thess 1:8; Rom 1:18-32; Col 3:6).

Let me add one other note before I yield the floor to others. This gospel is all we need. It is both the basic message we preach through which people are reconciled to God initially and a message that is sufficient to enable them to continue and mature in their Christian lives. You don't begin with the gospel and then graduate to something else (Gal 3:3-4; Col 2:6-7). All believers need to do is to "continue in your faith, established and firm, and . . . not move from the hope held out in the gospel" (Col 1:23). It's an exciting message: "Christ in you, the hope of glory," and it is more than sufficient for all our needs (Col 1:27). Christian living and ethical decisions are about conducting ourselves "in a manner worthy of the gospel of Christ" (Phil 1:27).

> **Observer:** The term *gospel* or *good news* is often said to have come from the context of the Roman Empire and to be associated with the birth of a ruler, an enthronement, or the announcement of a military victory. It was especially associated with oracles from the gods and with the emperor cult. For example, the birthday of Augustus, celebrated circa 9 BC, is recorded as follows: "It is a day which we justly count as the beginning of everything . . . inasmuch as it has restored the shape of everything that was failing and turning into misfortune. . . . The birthday of the God [Augustus] was the beginning of the world of the glad tidings [in the Greek, the Evangel] that have come to men through him." U. Becker comments: "The proclamation of the *euangelion* (gospel) does not merely herald a new era: it actually brings it about.

The proclamation is itself the *euangelion*, since the salvation it pro-
claims is already present in it."[2]

Mark shares this sense of a decisive change occurring with the
coming of Jesus. Yet we don't need to look to the Roman world to explain it, since it has an Old Testament background as well, especially in
terms of heralding glad tidings in the Psalms (see Ps 40:9; 96:2) and in
Isaiah 40:9, "You who bring good news to Zion"; Isaiah 41:27, "I gave
to Jerusalem a messenger of good news"; Isaiah 52:7, "How beautiful
on the mountains are the feet of those who bring good news"; and
Isaiah 61:1, "The Spirit of the Sovereign LORD is on me, because the
LORD has anointed me to proclaim good news to the poor": all speak
of proclaiming the gospel.

Chair: Thank you, Paul. I wonder, to what extent would others share our
view that the key message is about the gospel?

Matthew: Early on in my Gospel I say, "Jesus went throughout Galilee,
teaching in their synagogues, proclaiming the good news of the kingdom,
and healing every disease and sickness among the people" (Mt 4:23). I offer
a very similar summary in 9:35 and have no doubt that the message to be
announced to the world is "this gospel" (Mt 24:14; 26:13).

Luke: I agree, although I use the noun the *gospel* (*euangelion*) only a
couple of times (Acts 15:7; 20:24) for the apostles' preaching. Don't be misled
by that, though, because I'm more interested in the activity of spreading the
good news, so I use the verb *to gospel*
(*euangelizomai*) twenty-five times in
Acts. I also tend to use the alternative
phrase "the word of God" as my way of
talking about the gospel.

"THE WORD"

Acts 4:31; 6:2, 7; 8:14; 11:1;
12:24; 13:5, 7, 46; 17:13.

Chair: John, you seem to be some-
thing of an exception here because, remarkably, you don't use the word in
your writings, with one exception.

John: You're right. The one exception is in Revelation 14:6, where I mention
an angel "flying in midair, and he had the eternal gospel to proclaim to those

---

[2]U. Becker, "Gospel," in *Dictionary of New Testament Theology*, ed. Colin Brown, vol. 2 (Grand
Rapids: Zondervan, 1976), 108.

who live on the earth—to every nation, tribe, language and people." Otherwise I don't use the word, and that both is and is not significant. It's not significant because my theme of "eternal life" highlights the purpose and achievement of the gospel, and I speak frequently about that. Most famously I wrote, "For God so loved the world that he gave his one and only Son, that whoever believes in him shall not perish but have eternal life" (Jn 3:16). I've included many sayings like this. Yet that also highlights something of the difference. Note that I wrote "have eternal life": that is to say, they possess it already through believing in Jesus. I remember Jesus saying, "Whoever hears my word and believes him who sent me has eternal life and will not be judged but has crossed over from death to life" (Jn 5:24). Note the "has . . . has" he used. The other Gospel writers talk about eternal life in the sense of the life of the age to come. I was more interested in stressing that this future life has already begun in the here and now. It's not something we have to wait for sometime in the future, but it is realized now.

> ## "ETERNAL LIFE"
>
> in John: Jn 3:15, 36; 4:14, 36; 5:39; 6:27, 40, 47, 54, 68; 10:28; 12:25, 50; 17:2-3; 1 Jn 2:25; 3:15; 5:11, 13, 20. in the other Gospels: Mt 19:16, 29; 25:46; Mk 10:17, 30; Lk 10:25; 18:30.

Chair: Let's bring the others in. Is the gospel significant enough for you to agree that it is the central theme of the New Testament as a whole?

The Hebraist: I think so, even though I develop the good news in a very different way from the others. I'm concerned to explain it in relation to the former covenant God had with his people, so I delve into several features of Old Testament faith and worship and draw some comparisons and contrasts between that and the covenant inaugurated by Jesus. What I'm talking about, though, is still the gospel—just the gospel from a different angle. Indeed, in 4:2 I speak about our having "had the good news proclaimed to us," which shows how much I'm in agreement with what the others are saying.

Peter: Similarly, I don't use the word much (1 Pet 1:12; 4:6) but the gospel is what it's all about. My couple of uses of it show how much I assume it. When I warn, for example, that judgment will "begin with God's household," I add, "if it begins with us, what will the outcome be for those who do not obey the gospel of God?" (1 Pet 4:17). The gospel underlies everything.

Chair: That just leaves James and Jude. Jude, while you don't use the word *gospel* in your short letter, you do write about "the faith." Am I right in thinking that is virtually the same as writing about "the gospel"?

Jude: You're right.

James: And my agenda in writing is somewhat different, so I don't connect directly with the concept of the gospel, but nor am I in any way in conflict with it either.

Chair: So there's still a lot more to say, but we can agree that our discussions will revolve around the good news and will explore in depth its contents, its significance, and its implications and application.

Observer: The chief question about this focus is whether the concept of "the gospel of Jesus Christ" is sufficient and comprehensive enough to embrace the whole of New Testament theology. The answer is surely yes. This central focus compels us to consider God, three-in-one, the person and work of Christ, sin and salvation, conversion and ongoing growth in the Christian life (usually called sanctification), belief and conduct, individual spirituality and the church, and the past, present, and future of both humans and creation. It all naturally unfolds from the seed of the gospel, just as a flower naturally blossoms from a small bud. We do not need to add to the gospel or supplement it. We need to understand it.

3

What Is the Source of the Good News?

Chair: The good news is "the good news about Jesus the Messiah, the Son *of God*" (Mk 1:1), and Paul describes himself as having been "set apart for the gospel *of God*" (Rom 1:1). So perhaps the right starting point is to consider God himself.

The Good News Originates with God

Paul: That sounds good to me since God is the author and source of the gospel. I set this out in the opening passage of my letter to the Ephesians (1:3-14). He is the source of all the blessings we have received through Christ. The gospel was no afterthought but God's plan and pleasure from the very beginning, even before creation itself. It is all about God's grace being made known to us through Christ, so that we are set free—*redemption* is the word I use—at the cost of his blood, which provides us with forgiveness and a good deal more besides. Through Christ we become set apart for God, blameless, and members of his family. And it doesn't stop with us. God worked all this out and brought it about so that "all things in heaven and on earth," currently out of joint with him, could be brought back into harmony and their rightful place through Christ.

The gospel arises from "the riches of God's grace," and when it has had its effect leads to "the praise of his glory." It is really all about him.

THE NATURE OF GOD

Chair: Let's take a step back. Paul's opening statement assumes we know about this God who is the source of the gospel. What, though, are the fundamental beliefs we hold about him?

God as Creator

John: Perhaps the first thing should be that God is the Creator and life-giver. I begin my Gospel where the Bible itself begins. John 1 echoes Genesis 1 and sketches out the parallels between God and "the Word"—that is, Jesus, God's "one and only Son" who was none other than God embodied among us (Jn 1:14). Let me mention a few connections. First, you can't get more ultimate than God. You can never get behind him to something else. He is "in the beginning." God was (and is). And since "the Word was God," "the Word" was also without beginning (Jn 1:1). Second, Genesis 1 tells us God made the world and everything in it by his word. Therefore I say, "Through him [that is, the Word] all things were made; without him nothing was made that has been made" (Jn 1:3). Third, both God and the Word have life in themselves and are the source of all life (see Jn 1:4; cf. 5:26). We derive our life from others, our parents, but God and the Word are not dependent on others for life. Fourth, their life is communicated to others. It is in their nature to be life-givers or life-donors. Light plays a crucial role in bringing about life. So just as God's first words were "Let there be light" (Gen 1:3), with the result that creation sprang to life, so the Word was the light that brought about life (Jn 1:5).

It's at this point I begin to follow something of a new trajectory. The world that God had made to be good and unblemished (Gen 1:31) had sadly become a place where darkness reigned, robbing people of life. The Word shone as light in that darkness, defying all attempts to extinguish it (see Jn 1:5, 9). That light was the light that led not only to the original gift of life itself—that is, to physical existence—but also to new, full, and re-created life (see Jn 10:10), which I generally refer to as "eternal life." This eternal life has been made available through "the light of the world" (Jn 8:12) to all who believe in him (see Jn 1:9-13). I call it "eternal" not because it is unending, though it is, but because it partakes of the life to come when all of creation will be restored to a right relation with God. We don't have to wait for that to occur, however, since this is a life that we can already begin to experience today.

But that's getting ahead of ourselves a little. The point is that God is the Creator, the source of all life, and it's characteristic of him to give life to others. God's creation is good and to be enjoyed to the full, and it would have been if sin hadn't spoiled it. The same claim is made of Jesus as well as God. He is the Creator and life-giver, and he is also the re-creator and life-restorer of darkened lives.

Chair: The belief that God is the Creator seems a fundamental assumption on which everyone else builds. Is that so?

Mark: Yes, it is assumed. For example, Jesus just slips it into his address about the future "days of distress," which he said would be unparalleled since "the beginning, when God created the world" (Mk 13:19), and he affirms the view that God made humans as male and female (see Mk 10:6; Mt 19:4).

Luke: Interestingly, when Paul was preaching to Gentile audiences, he thought it important to assert, rather than just assume, that God was the Creator. So when preaching the gospel in Lystra, he contrasted "the living God, who made the heavens and the earth and the sea and everything in them," with the worthless idols they worshiped (Acts 14:15). Similarly at Athens he spoke of "the God who made the world and everything in it [as] Lord of heaven and earth" (Acts 17:24).

Paul: Luke's right. Additionally, in my writings I speak of all things coming from God (see 1 Cor 8:6; 11:12; Eph 3:9). Creation itself is imprinted with God's fingerprints (see Rom 1:20) and made for humans to enjoy (see 1 Tim 4:3). As John was saying, though, sadly creation has been spoiled by sin, so much of my focus is on the way it will one day be restored (see Rom 8:19-21; 1 Cor 15:27-28; Eph 1:10; Col 1:20).

The Hebraist: Like the others I believe God is the Creator but I go beyond them a little in saying, "the universe was formed at God's command, so that what is seen was not made out of what was visible" (Heb 11:3; cf. Ps 33:6-9).

God as Savior

Chair: The second fundamental aspect of God's character we need to address is that he is a savior. Having had his creation corrupted by sin, he reaches out to rescue sinful people and the broken creation itself, to renew his image in human beings and heal his ruined world. So creation and salvation are intimately connected. The fallenness of his creation leads to him taking the initiative in salvation, and salvation leads not to escape from the world but to the restoration of God's original purpose for it.

We'll spend a great deal of time discussing the salvation we have in Jesus Christ, so we'll be brief here, but I wanted to draw out that God didn't reinvent himself as a savior when Jesus came, but was always a savior, wasn't he? I'm thinking of the most remarkable event in Israel's history, when he delivered them from slavery in Egypt. A whole glossary of salvation words is used to describe it: God "rescues" (Ex 3:8), "redeems" (Ex 6:6), "brings out" (Ex 13:3), "delivers," and "saves" his people (Ex 14:30).[1]

Equally, when Israel returned from their exile in Babylon, they rejoiced that God had been their Savior. God said of himself, "I, even I, am the LORD, and apart from me there is no savior" (Is 43:11). Looking back on their experience of exile, Israel responded to the claim by saying, "Truly you are a God who has been hiding himself, [but you are indeed] the God and Savior of Israel" (Is 45:15).

GOD AS SAVIOR

in the Psalms: 18:46; 24:5; 25:5; 27:9; 38:22; 42:5, 11; 43:5; 51:14; 65:5; 68:19; 79:9; 85:4; 89:26.

In the light of these historical experiences, Israel regularly acknowledged God as their Savior, both in their praises and in their petitioning of him.

Paul: That's a very helpful summary, Chair. I'm sure all those themes will come out later as we explore the way we all write about the salvation we have in Jesus Christ.[2]

Other Attributes of God
Chair: There is so much more we could say about God. Let me briefly invite you to draw attention to some other aspects of his character we've not yet mentioned. Let's be very selective in doing so.

Uniqueness
Paul: In a world that seemed to be populated by a multitude of gods in the eyes of most people, we took it as absolute that the God of Israel, the God and Father of Jesus Christ, is unique. He alone is living and genuine while other "so-called gods" are the products of human imagination or manufacture. The reality is

[1] I owe this to Walter Brueggemann, *Theology of the Old Testament* (Minneapolis: Fortress Press, 1997), 174-76; see his work for fuller details.
[2] See, for example, chap. 5, 77, and chap. 7, 141.

that "there is no God but one" (1 Cor 8:1-6; cf. Deut 6:4). He alone, though invisible, is the immortal "King of kings and Lord of lords" (1 Tim 6:15-16).

Glory

John: Most obviously for me, God is a God of glory—that is, of magnificent beauty, majestic splendor, and awesome power. The world had glimpsed his glory on a number of occasions (e.g., Ex 19:1-25; Is 6:1-5) but never as fully, continually, or amazingly as in the life of Jesus (see Jn 1:14; cf. 5:41-44).

Matthew: We Synoptic Gospel writers—that is, Mark, Luke, and I—also speak much about God's glory, but we witnessed it most in the transfiguration of Jesus (see Mt 17:1-13; Mk 9:2-13; Lk 9:28-36).

Peter: Just to add, I never forgot that episode and mention in my writing that I was an eyewitness "of his majesty" when "he received honor and glory from God the Father" that day (2 Pet 1:16-17).

Paul: I often speak of "the glorious Father" (Eph 1:17), especially when attributing glory to him in my doxologies (see Rom 16:27; Phil 4:20; 2 Tim 4:18).

Sovereignty and Power

Chair: His unique glory closely relates to his sovereign rule over his creation.

Luke: I think we all constantly allude to this, but it was explicitly mentioned in the early days of the church. Times and dates were determined by God's own authority (see Acts 1:7). The death of Christ for which human beings bore responsibility was nonetheless part of "God's deliberate plan and foreknowledge" (Acts 2:23; cf. 3:17-21). The early Christians prayed to God who was their "Sovereign Lord" (Acts 4:24). Nothing, perhaps, revealed their deep belief in God's rule over history so much as Stephen's speech to the Jewish council prior to his execution (see Acts 7:2-53). He credits God as the active agent and true disposer of events throughout his lengthy account of Israel's story.

Paul: Without stopping over the details here, since we'll return to them later,[3] my exposition of the future of Israel in Romans 9–11 is an illustration of the strong belief we held of God as absolutely sovereign in making choices and determining the course of history.

Holiness and Righteousness

Chair: The danger with power, as we all know, is that it corrupts people. God's power, however, in no way corrupts him because of his other

---

[3]See chap. 8, 197.

attributes—that is, his holiness and righteousness. They're not quite the same, but we'll treat them as one in this brief introduction. Who wants to chime in first?

Peter: Those of us who enjoyed the privilege of a Jewish religious upbringing believed firmly that God was holy. Essentially this meant he was altogether different from human beings. One aspect of this comes close to the idea of glory and picks up on his transcendent majesty; but another element is his moral purity and ethical incorruptibility. Therefore I quote from Leviticus, a book that reveals the holiness of God in many different ways, where God commands his people: "Be holy, because I am holy" (1 Pet 1:15-16; cf. Lev 11:44-45; 19:2). That aspect of holiness comes close to the idea of God's righteousness.

John: I recall Jesus addressing his Father as "Holy Father" (Jn 17:11), and so I myself speak later of God as "the Holy One" (1 Jn 2:20) and mention his holiness several times in Revelation (see Rev 3:7; 4:8; 6:10; 15:4; 16:5).

Paul: My stress is a little different. I don't use the word *holy* of God himself, although I do use it of people and things associated with God, especially his Holy Spirit and holy people, the church. My concern lies more with his righteousness and justice. John records Jesus as speaking to God not only as "Holy Father" but also as "Righteous Father" (Jn 17:25), and it is that aspect I reflect on a lot. I believe the gospel is a revelation of "the righteousness of God" (Rom 1:17), which is the theme that runs throughout Romans. God will hold people to account for their lifestyles, but unlike human judges God will always judge them in an absolutely "righteous" way (Rom 2:5). It is also true that Christ's sacrifice was a demonstration of God's righteousness, and a better one than his judgment (see Rom 3:21-26). People may then be brought into a right standing with God by having faith in Christ.[4] The way he is dealing with Israel, spelled out in Romans 9–11, is all an outworking of his righteousness.

Chair: All this leads to there being a problem between human beings and their holy Creator, which needs solving. This is why there is need for the gospel.

Compassion and Mercy
Chair: From the beginning God revealed himself to be "the compassionate and gracious God, slow to anger, abounding in love and faithfulness"

---

[4]See further on justification in chap. 7, 139-41.

(Ex 34:6). Those qualities continue into the New Testament and may be said to be its major theme, demonstrated and taught in a whole host of ways throughout its writings. Perhaps we can just highlight some key sayings.

Luke: Jesus said that God "is kind to the ungrateful and wicked. Be merciful, just as your Father is merciful" (Lk 6:35-36).

> ## REPETITION OR VARIATIONS OF EX 34:6
>
> in the Old Testament: 2 Chron 30:9; Neh 9:17; Ps 86:15; 103:8; 111:4; 112:4; 145:8; Joel 2:13; Jon 4:2; Nahum 1:3.

Matthew: In our day, these divine qualities become associated with Jesus, who has "compassion" on people (Mt 9:36; 14:14; 20:34; Mk 6:34).

Paul: Yes, but the "compassion and grace" of God are often mentioned in terms of related ideas such as "his kindness, forbearance and patience," which are intended to lead people to repentance (Rom 2:4; cf. 2 Pet 3:9). I speak time and again about the mercy of God, such as in Romans 9:14-18, and describe God as "rich in mercy" (Eph 2:4). It was through "the kindness and love of God" and because of his mercy that Christ appeared among us to bring us salvation (Tit 3:4-5). I speak of God's love and grace being poured into our lives whenever I get the chance.

The Hebraist: Yes, the heart of the gospel might be said to lie in giving us confidence to approach God's throne of grace "so that we may receive mercy" (Heb 4:16).

James: I affirm Exodus 34:6 when I say, "The Lord is full of compassion and mercy" (Jas 5:11)—but more from me in a moment.

John: I, of course, say it most succinctly of all when I state, "God is love" (1 Jn 4:8).

Jude: Even my somewhat severe letter is not devoid of presenting God as a God of love. I refer to God's love for those who are called by him twice in the opening greeting (see Jude 1-2) and encourage my readers to keep themselves in that love. God's love, compassion, grace, and mercy are never far away from our thinking.

Chair: So there's no disagreement about God as the compassionate one, then.

Another Voice: James

James: Our approach here might be in danger of making God a little too abstract. References to God abound in my short and practical letter, so I wonder if I might contribute from a different angle. Just let me rattle things off.

God is one, and demons tremble before him (see Jas 2:19). He is "the Father of the heavenly lights" (Jas 1:17), who is Creator and life-giver (see Jas 1:18), and who has created human beings in his own image (see Jas 3:9). He is impervious to temptation, being altogether pure (see Jas 1:13) and trustworthy because he is unchangeable (see Jas 1:17). He is "the Lord Almighty" (Jas 5:4), and men and women will one day encounter him as Judge (see Jas 2:12; 4:12; 5:1-9). He makes his will known (see Jas 2:8-11). Being "full of compassion and mercy" (Jas 5:11), as mentioned above, he treats religious practice as authentic only if it looks after the vulnerable and poor in our communities (see Jas 1:27). He hears the prayers of the oppressed (see Jas 5:4). In response to faith-filled prayer, he heals and forgives (see Jas 1:5-6; 5:15). He will keep his promises and reward those who are faithful to him, no matter what they go through in this life (see Jas 1:12; 2:5). Above all, he longs to enter into friendship with human beings (see Jas 4:4-10).

That's quite a God, one worthy of worship and service.

JESUS AS THE REVEALER OF GOD

Chair: How do we come to know this God, since he is an invisible spirit?

John: The God who had been invisible to human eyes was made visible before our very eyes in Jesus through his incarnation and in his life and death. As I freely confess, "No one has ever seen God," but the difference now is that "the one and only Son, who is himself God and is in the closest relationship with the Father, has made him known" (Jn 1:18). He spent his life making the invisible God visible, and revealing him more fully. The revelation occurred through his signs, in his teaching, and as he both demonstrated and spoke of his integral relationship with God. This is why, at a crucial moment in his ministry, he could say to Philip, "Don't you know me, Philip, even after I have been among you such a long time? Anyone who has seen me has seen the Father. How can you say, 'Show us the Father?'" (Jn 14:9). All this will be discussed more fully in the conversation that follows, but we need to note that anything we knew about God up to the coming of Jesus has been brought into a much sharper focus, and presented in much more glorious color than it was, by his unique Son.

ONE GOD, TWO TESTAMENTS

Chair: Many people seem to think there are two Gods, not one. The God of the Old Testament, they say, is holy, mighty, and angry, whereas the God of the New Testament is merciful, loving, and forgiving. There is, however, only one God. Jesus may have revealed him more fully, but he did not reveal a different God. The God Jesus served and in whom he believed is the God made known initially in the Old Testament. We find massive continuity between the two Testaments, even if the New Testament gives us a fuller picture and sheds some fresh light on various aspects of God's character. There's certainly no contradiction between them. Without going into more or greater detail, by way of conclusion I'm sure we can agree on the following summary of what we've been discussing. Here are ten things about the one God that I've supported with just a couple of choice references:

- God is self-existent (see Ex 3:14; Jn 5:26).

- God is one (see Deut 6:4; 1 Cor 8:6).

- God is the Creator and life-giver (see Gen 1:1–2:25; Acts 17:24-28).

- God is holy (see Lev 19:2; 1 Pet 1:15-16).

- God is King and Judge (see Ps 95:3; 99:4; 1 Tim 6:15-16).

- God is merciful, gracious, and forgiving (see Ex 34:6; Jer 31:34; Lk 6:35).

- God is Savior (see Ex 12:31-42; Tit 3:4-5).

- God is transcendent—that is, different (see Is 6:1-5; Rev 4:1-11).

- God is immanent—that is, near (see Deut 30:14; Phil 4:5).

- God is the covenant God of Israel (see Deut 29:1-28; Rom 9:1–11:36).

4

WHY IS GOOD NEWS NEEDED?

Chair: If the central thread of the New Testament is good news, it assumes that we need good news. This may simply be because there has been no news for some time, whether good or bad; but it might also be needed because there's bad news that needs overturning. So it's reasonable that our next question should be "Why is good news needed?" I think we'll find that there are several different layers involved in answering that question.

PERSONAL SIN

Paul: That's true, but the root problem is sin. Every human being is caught up in the problem of sin, "for all have sinned and fall short of the glory of God," whatever our background or heritage (Rom 3:23). The glory God intended us to display when he made us in his image has been corrupted and tarnished.

Luke: The preaching of the apostles would support that. On the day of Pentecost Peter told his audience to "repent and be baptized . . . for the forgiveness of your sins," bluntly warning them to save themselves from their "corrupt generation" (Acts 2:38, 40). While their preaching doesn't give us a deep analysis of sin—but you probably shouldn't expect that in the sermon summaries I record—they assume sin is the basic problem to which humans need to find an answer (see Acts 3:19; 17:30). Stephen claimed it was in Israel's bones to reject God's grace, to be "stiff-necked" and to "resist the Holy Spirit"—they'd always done it (Acts 7:39, 51). Their long-standing practice of rejecting God's messengers, he said, reached its climax in their murder of "the Righteous One" (Acts 7:52-53). No wonder they didn't like it and killed him.

I detected something of a change in emphasis when the preaching was directed to Gentile audiences. The primary characteristic of their sin, according to Paul, was that of idolatry (see Acts 14:15-16; 17:16).

Matthew: Such preaching is a natural follow-up of Jesus' own life and teaching. The clue for me lay in his name. The angel instructed Joseph to call his surprise child Jesus, which means "deliverer," "because he will save his people from their sins" (Mt 1:21).

Luke: The same point could also be made from the song Zechariah sang to celebrate the birth of his equally unexpected son, John. John was to open up the way for Jesus, who would "give his people the knowledge of salvation through the forgiveness of their sins" (Lk 1:77). Sin becomes a running thread throughout my Gospel, which

> ## JESUS AND SINNERS
> Lk 5:8, 20, 32; 7:34, 36-39, 47-49; 15:1-2, 7, 10, 18, 21; 17:4; 18:13; 19:7.

culminates in Jesus' resurrection appearance to his disciples and his announcement of his plan going forward: that "repentance for the forgiveness of sins will be preached in his name to all nations" (Lk 24:47). Even more than the theme of sin itself I remember how Jesus was accused of mixing with "sinners." That was a label commonly used to describe people in all sections of society who for some reason were unacceptable to the religious leaders and the respectable establishment, and, since they didn't measure up, they were deemed in need of forgiveness, whether poor or rich, prodigal or otherwise. The only answer for any of them, and for us, lay in the kindness and mercy of God (see Lk 6:35-36).

Mark: I think Matthew, Luke, and I are of one mind here. A story we all tell is the way in which in one of his early miracles Jesus made a connection between physical healing and forgiveness of sins. A paralyzed man had been lowered down to him through the roof, and Jesus announced that his sins were forgiven. That created quite a stir, since only God could forgive sins. But in order to justify his authority to make such a pronouncement, he went on to say to the man, "Get up, take your mat and go home," which is exactly what he did (Mk 2:1-12; Mt 9:1-8; Lk 5:17-26). I tell you, accusations of blasphemy quickly turned into shouts of praise. That may have been a very memorable occasion, but it was far from unique.

Matthew: There are a couple of things I would add. Although I frequently use the general word for sin, *hamartia*, and recognize, as Mark and Luke do, that people are by nature evil, *ponēroi* (see Mt 7:11; cf. Mark 7:14-23; Lk 11:13), we might also say they are on the wrong side of God's law, transgressors of it, wicked, and trespassers. Sin can be described in various ways, but whatever word is used, it highlights how much we are out of sync with God.

> *ANOMOS*, A PERSON
> OUTSIDE THE LAW
>
> Mt 7:22-23; 13:41; 23:28; 24:12.

> **Observer:** The most frequent word for sin is *hamartia*, used 173 times in the New Testament, of which Paul is responsible for sixty-three. Donald Guthrie explained that "its basic meaning is failure to hit the mark."[1] In other words, it is to fall short of God's intentions for us as human beings made in his image, and of his declared pattern for our living.

Chair: John, you usually have a different take on the gospel. Do you agree with this emphasis that humanity's basic problem is sin?

John: Absolutely. I may bring some different elements to the discussion of sin, but not contradictory ones. I signal the importance of the problem of sin right at the beginning of my Gospel by recalling, not what was sung about Jesus' birth, but that amazing claim made by John the Baptist, who pointed to Jesus one day and said, "Look, the Lamb of God, who takes away the sin of the world!" (Jn 1:29). He probably had the Passover lamb (see Ex 12:1-51) or the lamb of Isaiah 53 in mind. Either way, it put the focus on Jesus dealing with the problem of sin. Like others, I often use the word *hamartia*—seventeen times, in fact—but I've other things to say as well.

I use a lot of imagery, so I picture sin as ignorance rather than knowledge (see Jn 1:10); living in darkness rather than in the light (see Jn 3:19-20; 9:1-41); basing life on a lie rather than on the truth (see Jn 3:21; 8:44); and leading to death rather than to life (see Jn 5:24; 8:21, 24). At heart, sin is about unbelief and mistrusting Jesus (see Jn 3:18, 36; 6:29; 8:42-47; 16:9).

---

[1]Donald Guthrie, *New Testament Theology* (Downers Grove, IL: InterVarsity Press, 1981), 188.

Sin is endemic in the world. I use "the world" fifty-six times to describe humanity as organized in opposition to God (see Jn 7:7; 12:46-47; 15:19), and in that world sin enslaves people (see Jn 8:34). They're subject to an evil power, that of "the prince of this world" (Jn 12:31; 14:30; 16:11). Even so, since the coming of Christ people cannot excuse themselves; they are accountable for their own beliefs and actions and so are guilty before God (see Jn 15:22). God's judgment is already at work, and those who refuse to believe "are condemned already" (Jn 3:18). However, we should not mistake that for the popular belief that suffering is always God punishing us for our sins. On occasions he may use suffering as a means of disciplining us and calling us to our senses, but sometimes we suffer simply because we live in a fallen world and God has other motives in permitting it (see Jn 9:3).

James: I imply there may be a connection between sin and sickness when I'm advocating prayer for healing (see Jas 5:14-16).

John: Yes, and in my later writings I take essentially the same stance about sin. It remains an important issue. So, for example, in 1 John I mention it seventeen times and point out again that sin is universal (see 1 Jn 1:8), characterized by lawlessness (see 1 Jn 3:4), and that "the one who does what is sinful is of the devil" (1 Jn 3:8, 10). As for Revelation, no one should need persuading that the root of all the problems the world and the church face is universal sin, aggravated by Satan, which rightly provokes both God's judgment and his salvation into action.

Chair: Paul, I think you have a lot to say about sin.

Paul: Yes, I do. Traditionally, the Jewish people are not interested in speculating about how sin entered God's good creation, and neither am I. Our problem goes back to Adam, whose children we are (see Rom 5:12). His disobedience has caused us to be extremely vulnerable, with a built-in bias toward sin in our natures. We know this from the way in which our desires are so often skewed and distorted (see Eph 2:3; 4:22). I refer to this as "the flesh" or our "earthly nature." This is not to say that sin is to be identified with

FLESH

Rom 8:7-8; Gal 5:16-21; Col 3:5-11.

the physical dimension of our lives, as opposed to some disembodied spirit dimension. I use the word *flesh* mostly in an ordinary, neutral, sometimes even positive sense, but, as we well know, sin often does exploit our physical, especially sexual, natures. By using the term *flesh* or *earthly nature*, though, I mean the corruptible aspect of our makeup, our life when we are out of touch with God, when we are indifferent to him or even rebellious against him. It's no light thing, since we are "all under the power of sin" (Rom 3:9). Honesty compels us to admit we're very conscious of it (Rom 3:20), that it easily rules over us (see Rom 6:12), and even that we are slaves to it (see Rom 6:16-20).

We cannot pass the blame on to others but must personally take the responsibility for the wrong we do, the sinful actions in which we engage (see Rom 3:19). Sin makes us subject to God's wrath and brings us under his judgment (see Rom 1:18-20; 2:5, 8). Unlike the anger we sometimes display, God's anger is deserved, judicious, and righteous (see 2 Thess 1:5). It will be meted out by Jesus Christ (see 2 Tim 4:1). The sentence we experience as a result of our sin is "death" (Rom 6:23), which is a multidimensional experience. For one thing, giving place to sin in our lives means we are dead to God even while physically alive (see Eph 2:1; 4:18). It also means we die physically, not just as a biological fact but as a judicial penalty. Death stares the human race in the face as an enemy (see 1 Cor 15:26). And, unless we are delivered from it by God himself, after the initial death there is another, "second death," as John calls it (Rev 2:11; 20:6, 14; 21:8), to follow, which involves eternal separation from God.

> ### GOD'S WRATH
> Rom 5:9; 1 Cor 11:29, 34; Eph 2:3; 5:6; Col 3:6; 1 Thess 2:16.

Our urgent need, then, is to be forgiven for our sin (see Rom 4:7; Eph 1:7; Col 1:14).

Observer: The judgment of God is terrifying and real, made necessary as a response to the evil that would destroy his creation. He has scheduled "a day" when it will occur (Acts 17:31). However, we should not imagine he delights in it. The rabbis said, "When God is angry, he says to the sinner who has provoked him, 'You have caused me to take up a trade that is not mine.'" God is a creator and gracious life-giver. Therefore Martin Luther described judgment as his "alien work."[2]

---

[2]George Caird, *New Testament Theology*, ed. L. D. Hurst (Oxford: Oxford University Press, 1994), 86-87.

Chair: That's a robust analysis of our plight, Paul, but we haven't really defined sin. What is at the heart of it?

Paul: The heart of sin is a failure to worship God as God and to live in an obedient, joyful relationship with him. In a couple of places where I write about it, I see this arises because we suppress the truth (see Rom 1:18), which results in upside-down thinking so that we boast of the very things of which we should be ashamed. That was essentially written about Jews, but the same is true of the Gentiles. It makes no difference. Writing to the Ephesians, I mount an equally vigorous critique of the Gentile mindset; I accuse them of being futile in their thinking and point out that this leads to their being "darkened in their understanding and separated from the life of God because of the ignorance that is in them due to the hardening of their hearts" (Eph 4:17-18). So, while separation from God or alienation from him is at the heart of it—we are all ungodly and so are his enemies (see Rom 5:10), to which the Gentiles have the added disadvantage of being outside the covenant people of God (see Eph 2:12)—it is not easy to separate out the various elements of our complex humanity. The thinking, willing, feeling, and doing aspects of our being are all corrupted—whatever else sin is, it is unrighteousness.

Chair: Is this a picture others share?

Luke: Perhaps we should admit that, while the early apostles presumed the problem was sin, as we've already mentioned, the truth is that their sermons don't consider the theology of it deeply. They were, after all, preaching the gospel to very mixed audiences rather than engaging in the sort of in-depth exposition in which Paul later engaged in writing to the churches.

The Hebraist: I reflect on the issue somewhat differently. The problem of sin underlies everything I am writing about, so there is no disagreement there. However, I'm writing from the perspective of the story and religious practices of the Jews, in which sacrifices were central to making atonement with God— in other words, overcoming that

SACRIFICES

Lev 1:1–7:38; 16:1-34; Heb 2:17; 5:1; 7:27; 9:26, 28; 10:4, 12, 26; 13:11.

separation from God that Paul spoke about. There would be no need to make atonement through sacrifices except for sin having caused that alienation from God. Indeed I introduce my letter by talking about the uniqueness of Jesus and the way in which, "after he had provided purification for sins, he sat down at the right hand of the Majesty in heaven" (Heb 1:3; cf. 10:12). Making atonement for sin through sacrifice is what priests do, especially the high priest on the Day of Atonement, and that is how I present Jesus. So, yes, sin is the problem Jesus solves.

With others, I see the heart of sin as lying in not believing the word of the living God (see Heb 3:12), which leads to rebellion against him and a rejection of his law.

However, I think I have something distinct to add about the nature of sin. As I see it, it is really a failure to live up to our God-given destiny. In 2:5-10 I muse on the way in which Christ fulfilled humanity's destiny, as set out in Psalm 8, when the rest of us have not. We have exchanged the "glory and honor" of being made in God's image for something tawdry and dishonorable. Israel behaved in typical fashion when they failed to enter the land and rest God had promised them, choosing instead to disbelieve him, harden their hearts against him, and test his patience (see Heb 3:7–4:11). For me, the root of sin is a failure to listen to and believe God. Oh, and I too assert the reality of judgment (see Heb 9:27).

James: There's only one thing I'd add to this. I see our twisted desires as being the midwife of sin. It's my way of saying what Jesus said, according to Mark 7:14-23, when he taught that all sorts of evil things are expressions of what's in us. Remarking on the way in which "each person is tempted when they are dragged away by their own evil desire and enticed," I explain that, "after desire has conceived, it gives birth to sin; and sin, when it is full-grown, gives birth to death" (Jas 1:14-15). My reason for stating this is so that it is clear that no one can hold God, who only ever gives us good things, as responsible for our sin. He, indeed, provides an answer to it by giving us a new beginning "through the word of truth"—that is, through the gospel (Jas 1:17-18).

Like others I also see sin as breaking God's law (see Jas 2:9-10), a failure to do what is right (see Jas 4:17), and as having the capacity to deceive us (see Jas 1:22, 26; cf. Heb 3:13). Furthermore, I concur that God is the judge who alone "is able to save and destroy" (Jas 4:12).

BROKEN COMMUNITIES

Chair: So personal sin is clearly bad news and a major reason why we need to hear some good news. But is that the only problem, or is there more? If we stop at this point, are we not in danger of coming up with a gospel that is good news only for individuals? What about the wider problems of broken communities and a fractured world? Are they part of the problem that the gospel addresses?

Let's start with the broken communities first. As soon as Adam and Eve disobeyed God, we read that they lost the innocent intimacy they once enjoyed and that their relationship and the relationships of their heirs were disrupted (see Gen 3:7–4:24; 6:11).

Paul: Sin certainly does destroy good relationships. God clearly intended us to enjoy quality love and integrity in our close relationships and our wider communities, if we take the Genesis account of the creation of Adam and Eve seriously at all. And the evidence of our failure to experience that is found at every level of society and community.

At the most general level, our world is riddled with major divisions, the greatest of which is that between Jews and Gentiles. The former, who boast that they are circumcised, see themselves as elect insiders whom God favors. The latter are viewed as "uncircumcised," "unclean," "excluded," "outsiders," and "foreigners." That's bad news for all, not just for the Gentiles. The good news is, as I explain in Ephesians 2:11-22, that God has overcome that division through Christ Jesus, who through sacrificing his own body "has made the two groups one and has destroyed the barrier, the dividing wall of hostility," and brought about peace. The reconciliation of divided people can only truly take place as both sides put their hope in Christ. That same theme lies behind the letters I wrote to the Romans and the Galatians, who wanted to perpetuate the old distinctions in Christ's church. To have done so would have been to undermine a key element of the good news.

It's in that fierce letter I wrote to the Galatians that I also acknowledge there are other major divisions besides the great divide between Jews and Gentiles. In 3:28 I mention the way Christ has overcome not only that divide but also the social division between those who are slaves and those who are free, and the gender division of male and female. These divisions, so important to others, are entirely irrelevant to followers of Jesus. I mentioned something very similar to the Colossians. There the issues were slightly different, so I didn't mention males and females; but I did speak of another division in my world—that between barbarians and Scythians. When "Christ is all, and is in all" (Col 3:11), such cultural identities become entirely unimportant.

To tell the truth, the brokenness of our relationships is structured into our society through institutions such as slavery. Slavery and other hierarchical relationships are present social realities, and we're people who live with a foot in two camps. One foot is planted in the realities around us, while the other foot is firmly planted in the new community that has begun with Christ's coming but hasn't yet fully arrived. So we have to negotiate a little, transforming where we can, as the instructions about household living demonstrate. My letter to Philemon about Onesimus, his slave who had run away,[3] shows what I really think about slavery.

HOUSEHOLD CODES

Eph 5:21–6:9; Col 3:18–4:1; 1 Pet 2:18–3:7.

James: I make exactly the same point, from a different angle, when I rebuke the church for treating people differently according to their social or economic status (see Jas 2:1-13). I point out how this is a contradiction of the levitical law—just read Leviticus 19—which is summed up in the command to "love your neighbor as yourself" (Lev 19:18). In fact, God reveals himself as having a special concern for those who are vulnerable in our society, and so, if we want to be acceptable to him, we should demonstrate the same concern (see Jas 1:27). We dare not look at people through the conventional eyes of our status-riddled, stratified world.

GOD'S CARE FOR VULNERABLE PEOPLE

Ex 22:22; Deut 10:18; 14:29; 24:17-21; 26:12-13; 27:19; Ps 68:5; 82:3-4.

John: I make an almost identical point in my first letter (see 1 Jn 3:16-18) when I insist the love of God must lead to practical action and that we reveal we lack that love if we see people in need and don't do something to help them.

Paul: Too true. Your comments lead us to another level of fractured relationships, which is not that of the general cultural level or the structural level in society, but the personal level. You can detect my concerns when I rebuke the churches for reproducing divisions in their house groups, as they did in Corinth (see 1 Cor 1:10-17), or for their failure to "live in harmony with one another," or even "accept one another," and for their seeming eager still

---

[3]Some believe Onesimus, rather than being an absconder, had been sent by Philemon to help Paul in prison.

to "repay . . . evil for evil," as I mentioned to the Romans (Rom 12:16-17; 15:7). This failure can all too easily still plague the church, as is evident when dealing with issues where our background or context means we differ in our practice from fellow Christians about things that are not of the essence of the gospel. I have issues such as the observance of special religious days or special diets (see Rom 14:1-23), or how we handle meat that's been used in idol worship (see 1 Cor 8:1-13), in mind. Once (see Phil 4:2), when I knew the people well and knew it would be constructive, I even mentioned the names of two ladies who had joined in my evangelistic missions and yet were now at odds with one another. The answer to broken relationships between individuals is again only truly to be found in Christ and in his followers imitating his example of humility (see Phil 2:5-11).

Mark: I guess the role we play in this as Gospel writers is to document the encounters Jesus had with those whose relationships with others had broken down. One thing I was conscious of was the way religious purity regulations so easily divided people and even excluded some from their families and communities. I give several illustrations of this, such as when the lawyers criticized Jesus for forgiving the sins of the paralyzed man (see Mk 2:1-12) and for eating with "sinners and tax collectors" (Mk 2:13-17), people who were beneath contempt as far as the so-called respectable were concerned.

The disruption of relationships was both very evident and most distressing when Jesus encountered a demon-possessed man who "lived in the tombs" away from his family. That's why, when he was delivered from his demons, Jesus told him to go home rather than travel around with the rest of his disciples (see Mk 5:1-20). It was equally so when that poor woman who'd been hemorrhaging for twelve years was healed. She was considered contaminated goods according to the purity regulations of her day, which was probably why she didn't want to draw attention to herself in the crowd but tried to gain her healing secretly. And that's precisely why Jesus called attention to her—so that she could be restored to the worshiping community of Israel (see Mk 5:24-34). Matthew, Luke, and I tell many stories like that, but it's probably Luke who's most tuned in to this theme.

Luke: Thanks, Mark. Yes, incident after incident and story after story demonstrate the hallmarks of broken relationships. Just to pick up a couple: I mention ten lepers who were excluded from normal society because of their sickness. What epitomized their plight for me was where Jesus met them: "along the border between Samaria and Galilee. As he was going into a village . . ." They were outsiders who didn't belong anywhere (Lk 17:11-19). Then there was Zacchaeus, the tax collector who worked for the occupying power, who had to climb a tree to see Jesus because the crowd didn't exactly welcome him. That's why, after Zacchaeus had announced he was going to change his way of life—that's what many would call repentance—Jesus stressed that "this man, too, is a son of Abraham" (Lk 19:1-10).

The issue crops up in his teaching as well, such as when he replied to the man who wanted Jesus to tell his brother to divide the inheritance with him (see Lk 12:13-21). How often money and wills have been the cause of broken family relationships! Then one day, as he was eating a meal at a Pharisee's house, Jesus had to instruct his host as to who was on God's invitation list—which was a little different, I tell you, than the usual list of those who were "in" in Jewish society at the time (see Lk 14:15-24). Most famously, of course, there was his story of the broken relationships in the family of the man who had two sons (see Lk 15:11-32). It came to be known as the story of the prodigal son, but, as Jesus told it, it was hard to know which one was the prodigal. There, family members were alienated from one another even while under the same roof, an experience with which, sadly, many can identify. And so we could go on.

Chair: John, I'm not sure you paint exactly the same picture, do you?

John: Well, I overlap in many ways, but I also have my own take on it, as you might expect. I see darkness as pervasive, although unable to snuff out the light (see Jn 1:5). And I tell some different stories about people who experienced that darkness for several different reasons. They demonstrate how relations are disrupted in this fallen world. There's the most poignant story of the Samaritan woman (see Jn 4:1-42), and the one of the lonely

> **DARKNESS AND LIGHT**
> 2 Cor 4:6; Col 1:13; 1 Pet 2:9.

man at the pool of Bethesda who had "no one to help [him] into the pool" when the water that contained healing properties was stirred (Jn 5:1-15). For me, though, the alienation is seen in other kinds of darkness too. The darkness was sometimes moral and spiritual (see Jn 3:19; 9:35-41), sometimes the darkness of blindness (see Jn 9:1-14), once the darkness of death (see Jn 11:17-44), and supremely the darkness of betrayal (see Jn 13:18-30, esp. v. 30). Darkness meant people were lost in a world that God had designed to be their home (see Jn 12:35). I carry the theme over into my first letter, where I refer to people who "claim to be in the light" but whose hatred and harmful actions means they're really stumbling around, since "the darkness has blinded them" (1 Jn 2:9-11). Darkness spells death, but Jesus longs to bring people out of darkness into the light (see Jn 8:12). This is something I know Paul and Peter pick up in their writings too. After all, God is light, and in him is no darkness at all (see 1 Jn 1:5).

FRACTURED WORLD

Chair: Time to move on. The first reason we need good news is because we are a fallen humanity. The second is because we suffer broken relationships. But there's a third dimension too, and maybe even a fourth, depending on how you express it. The third dimension I have in mind is that of our living in a fractured world.

> **CREATION AS GOOD, THEN CURSED**
>
> Gen 1:4, 10, 12, 18, 21, 25, 31; 3:14-19.

Creation itself is out of line with its Creator, isn't it, and in need of healing? God made everything in creation to be "good," but that's not our experience of it, is it?

Paul: Too true. I presuppose that Adam and Eve's disobedience had a negative impact on the physical creation. The curse that followed affected the animal and plant creation. We experience the effect of this still. "Creation was subjected to frustration," and we often encounter it "groaning" in one way or another. This creation appears to be dying, or decaying at least (Rom 8:19-25). How it longs for the day when it will be liberated from all this and re-created, never to be corrupted again!

When I tackle this, I mostly do so from a positive angle. As Christians we may struggle now, but we have a sure hope for the future. We look forward to the day when creation will be liberated from its enemies, healed, and its original harmony restored. In one of my earliest writings I speak of this as the time when Christ will have defeated our ultimate enemy, death, and will make the creation subject to God's rule again (see 1 Cor 15:24-28). Nothing will then oppose his rightful and beneficial rule. Throughout my writings, though, I mention the same hope. I wrote to the Philippians about the way we "eagerly await a Savior from [heaven]" whose power will enable him "to bring everything under his control," so the chaotic and destructive elements that corrupt our world now will no longer be able to do so (Phil 3:20-21).

To the Colossians, writing about Christ's role in the physical creation, I spoke of the way he will reconcile—that is, bring into a harmonious relationship with himself—"all things, whether things on earth or things in heaven, by making peace through his blood, shed on the cross" (Col 1:20). I expanded that even more when writing to the Ephesians, when I talked about Christ bringing unity "to all things in heaven and on earth under Christ," "when the times reach their fulfillment" (Eph 1:10). The brokenness of our world will be healed, and its disjointedness overcome, when Christ returns.

One of the elements we must address here is the presence in our creation of spiritual powers that seem intent on destroying humans and the creation itself. This may explain why the chair thought there might be four reasons, rather than three, why good news is needed. Again, it's to the Colossians I write most explicitly about this because their culture and history made them

THE POWERS

Acts 16:16-18; 19:11-20;
Eph 2:2; 6:12; Heb 2:14-15.

very conscious of hostile cosmic powers that were out to harm them. These powers were sometimes visible but could also be invisible. They went under various titles: "thrones or powers or rulers or authorities" (Col 1:16), although I was never interested in working out the details of any hierarchy they belonged to. That was to miss the point, which was that Christ had unmasked and defeated them, so Christians need no longer be intimidated by them or live in any fear of them (see Col 2:15).

Observer: Two recent writers helpfully comment on this. W. T. Wilson has commented on the

> feelings of dislocation and loneliness among Hellenistic people. It seemed that the universe, in all its vastness and intricacy, was beyond human comprehension or control, being governed instead by a host of wrathful gods and indifferent supernatural powers. Human beings could do little more than struggle against the relentless tide of "Fate."

For them, personal and material insecurity, not to mention moral and spiritual indeterminacy, characterized the human condition, which often amounts to little more than a fruitless search for meaning that ends in death and oblivion . . . [and they held] the belief that the very fabric of the universe suffered from some sort of irreparable rift. The two fundamental realms of reality that make up the universe, the celestial and the terrestrial, are set in opposition to one another on account of some cosmic crisis variously described.[4]

In addition, N. T. Wright has shown how demons, whom he describes as "grubby backstreet swindlers," are deceivers who have no real authority but are "reliant on humans to give them such power as they still possess against the day of their abolition."[5] Christ has unmasked the emptiness of their power, and Christians, taking their stand on the cross of Christ, should do so too.

Chair: Let's bring in others.

Mark: As you might expect, we Gospel writers don't explicitly theologize on what lies behind the problems of creation, but we record plenty of examples of the creation gone wrong. When Jesus worked his nature miracles, it was because there was something wrong in the natural world. That goes for his stilling the storm as he crossed the Sea of Galilee. Interestingly, he commands the wind to "be still," which is personal, not impersonal, language,

FEEDING THE CROWDS

Mt 14:15-21; 15:32-38; Lk 9:12-17.

as if he knew there was a personal spiritual power behind the storm (Mk 4:35-41; cf. Mt 8:23-27; Lk 8:22-25). Also, when he feeds the great crowds, whether four or five thousand strong (see Mk 6:35-44; 8:1-9), he is implicitly recognizing the way in which food is not readily available to all the world's population or evenly distributed to all. John, of course, reflects more deeply on the meaning of the feeding of the five thousand (see Jn 6:5-13, 25-59).

His healing miracles and exorcisms are too numerous to mention. They, of course, relate to the hostile powers Paul has just talked about, and are all

---

[4]W. T. Wilson, *The Hope of Glory: Education and Exhortation in the Epistle to the Colossians* (Leiden: Brill, 1997), 3.

[5]N. T. Wright, *Paul and the Faithfulness of God* (London: SPCK, 2013), 378.

part of the same picture. They're all about the problems of a fallen world, which, among other things that harm it, has been illegitimately occupied by hostile spiritual powers.

Luke: We all agree that Satan's fingerprints are all over our world. I note several symptoms of our world being fallen, such as the collapse of the tower of Siloam (see Lk 13:4), which cost many lives. However, I also pay more attention to Satan and the way he especially targeted Jesus just after his baptism and plagued him, often through his demonic henchmen, throughout. I think the exorcisms Jesus performed are very significant, and so I mention them often. When driving out demons, it was clear that Jesus thought he was face-to-face with Satan himself, as the argument about where he got his power from shows (see Lk 11:14-20).

TEMPTATION OF JESUS

Mt 4:1-11; Mk 1:12-13; Lk 4:1-13.

Matthew: I fully agree, even if I don't tell as many stories about exorcisms as the others. I have my own special way of signaling that Christ's mission addressed the fractured nature of our world. Creation itself was no silent observer of his crucifixion. Supernatural signs occurred at that time, including an earthquake, and "holy people" were raised to life, stepped out of their tombs, and went into Jerusalem and showed themselves to many (Mt 27:52-53). That surely was a sign that the old creation, long damaged by corruption and death, was coming to an end.

SATAN'S "FINGERPRINTS"

Lk 4:33-37; 6:18; 7:21; 8:2, 26-39; 9:37-43; 11:14; 13:11, 32.

Luke: I should add that the healings and exorcisms of Jesus' day continued into the early days of the church. Peter, Philip, and Paul all experienced them, including bringing the dead back to life. They were signs of the healing of a fallen world that was coming into being through the work of Christ.

APOSTOLIC WONDERS

Acts 3:1-10; 5:12-16; 8:5-7; 9:32-43; 19:11-20; 20:7-12; 28:1-9.

John: I address the same problem. In terms of incidents, one of the key moments for me came when

Jesus visited the Feast of the Tabernacles (see Jn 7:14-44). The feast was partly about Israel's struggle to survive in a barren land and their total dependence on God to send water to irrigate their crops or else there'd be no harvest. The point of the water ceremony was to pray for that. In doing so it looked forward to the day when the Messiah would come and the barrenness that had plagued creation would be brought to an end. When Jesus preached at the festival that year, he invited the thirsty to come and believe in him, promising that by doing so "rivers of living water [would] flow from within them" (Jn 7:37-38). The healing of creation had begun.

Peter: Yes, I also look forward to the day when creation will be renewed, but I express it in the language of apocalyptic and speak about our present cosmos being destroyed by fire and its replacement by "a new heaven and a new earth, where righteousness dwells" (2 Pet 3:10-13). It may be dramatic, strong language that I use, but it points to the same problem: we live in a broken creation in need of fixing.

John: I can identify with that. Most of Revelation, which also adopts an apocalyptic approach, illustrates the corruption, disjointedness, and out-of-sortness of the current natural and political worlds. Yet I end with a very positive vision of a renewed creation. One day all the faults will be overcome, and Eden's original vision of God dwelling harmoniously with his creatures and people living securely and righteously with one another will be realized (see Rev 21:1–22:5).

Chair: So, to conclude, though we may express it differently, we all agree there are three major reasons why we need good news. We need it because we are sinners who face God's judgment, because we are entwined in networks of broken relationships and divided communities, and because our world is in need of healing and, in its fractured state, has opened itself up to the destructive powers of Satan and his evil minions.

Let's turn to the good news.

5

WHO IS JESUS,
THE MESSIAH?

Chair: If we go back to our lead text—"The beginning of the good news about Jesus the Messiah, the Son of God" (Mk 1:1)—we immediately realize that the answer to humanity's problems is not found in a plan but in a person. Jesus is the good news. Even in these few words we learn a lot about him. He is called Jesus, which means "deliverer," "rescuer," "savior" (see Mt 1:21). His title is that of Christ, which means "anointed" (Is 45:1). Messiah means the same thing and was the title for the long-awaited one who would rescue Israel from their woes. Mark also describes him as "the Son of God," a common enough phrase but one which here seems to mark him out as having a special relationship with God the Father. This is all very condensed. So before we look at anything he taught or did, perhaps we should explore more fully who he was.

If Jesus was to offer any real solution, rather than just a fictional one, to the problems we've identified, it would seem he needed to enter fully into our humanity and experience our lives from the inside, rather than as a distant onlooker. I imagine that's why many of you seem to emphasize that, whatever else he may have been, he was a real human being. Unlike the Greek and Roman deities that lived in fantasyland, Jesus lived a fully human life in the context of our fallen world, and in doing so he modeled what God's intention for humanity had been all along.

JESUS: THE TRUE HUMAN BEING

His Humanity

Chair: Is that how you see it? Let's begin by discussing his humanity.

Luke: When you listened to the apostles' early preaching, you were left in no doubt that Jesus was a man. At Pentecost, for example, Peter preached that "Jesus of Nazareth was *a man* accredited by God to you by miracles, wonders and signs." "This *man* . . . ," he continued (Acts 2:22-23). Moreover, they kept saying he was from Nazareth, as if they had a desire to locate him in a real town and not to associate him with those from Mount Olympus or some other imaginary location.

> **". . . OF NAZARETH"**
>
> Acts 3:6; 4:10; 6:14; 10:38; 22:8; 26:9.

This is entirely consistent with what I record in my first volume. We know nothing of his personality and we're not bothered about what he looked like—his height, weight, frame, and so on—but even so I recorded the way he developed like any other kid, being obedient to his parents and growing "in wisdom and stature, and in favor with God and man" (Lk 2:51-52).

All of us record Jesus doing ordinary things like eating, sleeping, getting weary, crying, going to the synagogue, paying taxes, demonstrating

> **JESUS' "ORDINARY" LIFE**
>
> Mt 8:24; 9:10; 11:19; 17:24-27; 24:36; 26:17-30, 37-38; Mk 2:15-16; 4:38; 5:31-32; 13:32; 14:12-26, 33-34; Lk 4:2, 16; 5:29-33; 7:34; 8:23; 14:1; 22:8-30, 44; 24:30, 42-43; Jn 4:6, 31; 11:11, 33, 35, 38; 21:12-15.

limits to his knowledge, being emotional and even distressed in Gethsemane.

John: Absolutely. People had no doubts about his humanity. They identified him as "the son of Joseph, whose father and mother we know" (Jn 6:42) and mostly addressed him respectfully as a rabbi, an ordinary teacher, one of many at the time. As I reflected on it I knew there was a mystery in that he was clearly from another world, but even so I was driven to the conclusion that in Jesus "the Word became flesh [that is, a human being] and made his dwelling among us" (Jn 1:14). Unlike other so-called deities, he didn't breeze in and out before people could examine him too closely. He made his home with us, so we could see him up close and personal.

Paul: To tell the truth, I don't approach his humanity in quite the same way, but that doesn't mean I doubted it in the least degree. I trace his human ancestry back to King David (see Rom 1:3) and the patriarchs (see Rom 9:4-6). My allusion to his birth, which speaks of him being "born of a woman, born under the law" (Gal 4:4), equally assumes his true humanity. Elsewhere I refer to his family (see Gal 1:19) and his poverty (see 2 Cor 8:9). In Colossians I stress the physicality of his death (see Col 1:22; 2:9-11). It was as a real human being that he suffered.

For me, his humanity was essential to the plan if he was to reconcile a fallen humanity to a holy God. That's why my approach is to present him as a second Adam—more on that later.[1] I'm guarded in my language and speak of him being "in the likeness of sinful flesh" (Rom 8:3) and "being made in human likeness" (Phil 2:7). The language of *likeness* doesn't suggest he wasn't a real human; in fact, it says the opposite. *Homoiōmati* means an exact duplicate of the original. Nonetheless, the language hints that, in spite of his being a human being, that is not all we can or should say about Jesus.

The Hebraist: For me, the humanity of Christ is absolutely crucial if he is to serve us as an effective priest. Priests have to be real humans if they are to represent us to God, and he certainly was. Only by being "fully human in every way" could he act as our priest (Heb 2:17; cf. 4:15; 5:7), and that included entering into our temptations and weaknesses. The one point at which he differed was that "he did not sin" (Heb 4:15). Psalm 8:5 describes human beings as made "a little lower than the angels," and that included Jesus himself "for a little while" (Heb 2:9)—that is, while bodily present among us on earth. His humanity can also be seen in the way he "learned obedience from what he suffered" (Heb 5:8-9; cf. 2:10). That's not saying he was disobedient beforehand, but rather that he underwent a normal process of human development toward maturity. Then, in comparing and contrasting Jesus' work to the Day of Atonement (see Lev 16:1-34), I quote Psalm 40:6-8, which points out that the sacrifices God really requires are not the bodies of dead animals but living obedient human beings. And in Jesus he found a human who did his will exactly (see Heb 10:5-10).

---

[1]See chap. 5, 49-50.

Peter: In my first letter I am at pains to emphasize the physical nature of Christ's death and suffering and to commend him as an example to us lesser humans as to how to handle suffering (see 1 Pet 2:21-25).

1 Pet 2:24; 3:18; 4:13; 5:1.

John: The purpose of my writing my first letter was to combat a heresy known as Docetism, which taught that Jesus didn't really suffer as a human being and his body only appeared to be real. So I stress over and over the *enfleshed* reality of the person of Jesus. So much hinges on this that I, who am usually gentle in disposition, call those who deny his true humanity "liars" and "the antichrist" (1 Jn 2:22).

1 Jn 1:1-2; 4:2-3; 2 Jn 7.

If asked why I don't mention it in Revelation, my answer is that my purpose there is different. I do refer once to Jesus as "someone like a son of man" (Rev 1:13). However, the greater need of my readers was to know the other side of him and to see him as the victorious, undefeated, and glorious Lord of lords and King of kings, rather than as a human being.

His Sinlessness

Chair: So we're agreed that he was a real human being who genuinely experienced the lives we ourselves enjoy (or is it endure?). Surely, though, there were some differences between him and us, weren't there?

The Hebraist: There certainly were, and we've already begun to point to them in what we've just said. I've mentioned that I view him from the perspective of the priesthood. Surely he was "a great high priest"; but the difference between him and all the others who've held that office is that though he "has been tempted in every way, just as we are—yet he did not sin" (Heb 4:15). We can't class him merely as one priest among many, because he is "holy, blameless, pure, set apart from sinners, exalted above the heavens" (Heb 7:26). He's the one human being who has done the will of God flawlessly (see Heb 10:9). He is in a class of his own.

Matthew: Agreed. He certainly seemed to distance himself from others, as when he said at one point, "If *you*, then, though you are evil . . ." rather than "If *we*, then, though we are evil . . ." (Mt 7:11). No one else could take this stance without it sounding hollow—but from him it rang true.

John: Another way he distanced himself from us was when he talked about God as Father. His words suggested he related to God as Father differently from us. So on the resurrection morning he said to Mary Magdalene, "I am ascending to my Father and your Father, to my God and your God" (Jn 20:17). Perhaps that's the prerogative of one who claimed always to do the will of God (see Jn 8:29; 14:31) and who found no takers when he threw down the challenge, "Can any of you prove me guilty of sin?" (Jn 8:46).

Mark: Yes, and I remember how, when a man addressed him as "Good teacher," Jesus didn't accept the courtesy but replied, "Why do you call me good? . . . No one is good—except God alone" (Mk 10:17-18). No one disagreed with that, but nor, on the other hand, did anyone say: so that means you aren't good either. Of course, when it came to his trial they could find only false witnesses to speak against him (see Mk 14:57-59). The truth would never have convicted him.

Luke: Picking up the fact that only God is good, Peter told Cornelius that "God anointed Jesus of Nazareth with the Holy Spirit and power, and [that] he went around doing good" (Acts 10:38). As a historian and Gospel writer, I may not make many explicit claims about his sinless life, but I record what people said and how they reacted. Not for nothing was he frequently called "the Holy One" or the "Righteous One."

> **HOLY AND RIGHTEOUS ONE**
>
> Acts 2:27; 3:14; 4:30; 7:52; 13:35; 22:14.

Paul: We who wrote to spell out the significance of what the Gospel writers record didn't hold back from making more explicit claims about the unblemished and sinless character of Jesus. I had no hesitation in stating that he "had no sin" (2 Cor 5:21), and it is because of this that I write about him being in "the *likeness* of sinful flesh" (Rom 8:3) rather than being actually sinful in his earthly life.

Peter: I don't hesitate to claim he was sinless either. I deliberately apply to Jesus Isaiah 53:9, which says of the suffering lamb, "He committed no sin" (1 Pet 2:22), and I explain that as a result, when he died, he "'bore *our* sins' in his body on the cross," not his own sin (1 Pet 2:24). We are unrighteous, but he was righteous (see 1 Pet 3:18).

John: In 1 John 3:5 I bluntly state, "In him is no sin." That's surely enough to settle this part of our discussion.

Observer: The New Testament writers are united in their claim that Jesus did not sin, but subsequent theologians have sought to delve more deeply into what this means. One question is whether this is a crunch argument for his divinity or not. Stanley Grenz was surely right to point out that, while it "has significance for the assertion of his deity," it has even more significance as "an indication of his perfect humanity."[2] Here was the one person who lived the quality of human life God had intended that all those born in his image should live. If we want to know what true humanity looks like, we see it in Jesus.

Another, more complex debate is whether the claim is simply that he did not sin or that he could not sin, because he was free from the "original sin" that inflicts the rest of humanity. Reformed theologians have argued he was free from the disposition to sin, while others say he must have been able to sin or else he could not redeem us. Some suggest the conundrum is resolved in that his being conceived by the Holy Spirit enabled him to adopt a precreation—that is, unfallen—human nature. This would put him in the same position as Adam before he fell. If so, the temptation to sin was a real one—and that's the important point. Jesus did not glide through life, Teflon-coated as far as temptation was concerned. He experienced the pressures we face.

The debate is ultimately irresolvable on the basis of Scripture itself, since it does not directly address the question. Jesus, in fact, must have felt the intensity of temptation more than we do, because we're liable to give in to it. He never did. As one recent writer has put it, his "were genuine struggles and temptations, but the outcome was always certain."[3]

Jesus as the Last Adam

Chair: Let's return to Paul, because in your writing you advance the discussion of the humanity of Jesus in a unique way that places him in the

---

[2]Stanley Grenz, *Theology for the Community of God* (Nashville: Broadman & Holman, 1994), 329.

[3]Millard Erickson, *Christian Theology*, 2nd ed. (Grand Rapids: Baker, 1998), 736. See further his discussion on pp. 735-37.

whole sweep of the history of salvation and that draws out its significance for our salvation.

Paul: You're referring to the way I write of Jesus as the second or last Adam. I use this insight in Romans 5:14-19 and in 1 Corinthians 15:21-22, 45-49. At every stage I am emphasizing that both Adam and Jesus Christ were real men. Adam was there at the beginning of the human race and responsible for it becoming trapped in sin. Jesus, by way of contrast, introduces the beginning of a new creation that human beings can enter through his death and resurrection. In writing this I'm building on the account of Genesis 1–3 and also on Psalm 8.

The best way to understand this is if I set it out in two columns:

Table 1. Christ as the second Adam

Adam	Christ
Romans 5:14-19	
many died	God's grace overflowed to many
one man's sin brought condemnation	brought justification
death reigned	life reigned
1 Corinthians 15:21-22, 45-49	
death	resurrection
in Adam all die	in Christ all will be made alive
the first Adam	the last Adam
a living being	a life-giving spirit
first man was of the dust of the earth	second man is of heaven
image of the earthly man	image of the heavenly man

Put this way, you can see how important it was for Jesus Christ to have become a human being so as to undo the grief brought about by the first Adam. Just as we're inevitably incorporated into the first Adam at birth and inherit from him our propensity to sin—with all that follows, such as death and judgment—so we can be incorporated into the life of the last Adam by faith, with all it results in by way of justification and eternal life. I may not say much about the earthly life of Christ in my letters, but this idea alone shows how fundamental it is in my thinking.

Observer: Gregory of Nazianzus (330–389), an early theologian of the church, pointed out that "what has not been assumed cannot be healed." So, if Christ had not become a true human being, he could not save humanity. It was only by assuming our nature and living our life that the God-man could save us completely.

Wayne Grudem, a contemporary theologian, has helpfully listed eight reasons why the humanity of Jesus is important.[4] They are as follows:

- For representative obedience (Rom 5:18-19)

- To be a substitute sacrifice (Heb 2:14-17)

- To be the one mediator between God and mankind (1 Tim 2:5)

- To fulfill man's original purpose of ruling over creation (Mt 28:18)

- To be our example and pattern (1 Pet 2:21; 1 Jn 2:6)

- To be the pattern for our redeemed bodies (1 Cor 15:42-44)

- To sympathize as high priest (Heb 4:15-16)

- To be a man in heaven (Acts 1:11; 7:56)

JESUS AND THE INCARNATION

Chair: John wrote, "In the beginning was the Word, and the Word was with God, and the Word was God. . . . The Word became flesh and made his dwelling among us" (John 1:1, 14). Accepting the importance of the humanity of Jesus, we need to explore further. Did he exist before becoming a human being, or did his life begin at his birth? And how exactly did he become a human being? These questions relate to the incarnation.

His Preexistence

John: Since you quote me, let me start. When I wrote about the entry of Jesus into the world, I found it necessary to go way back beyond his birth to explain him. My claim is that, just as God always was, so also was Jesus. This means he existed before he became a baby in Bethlehem. He existed

---

[4]Wayne Grudem, *Systematic Theology: An Introduction to Biblical Doctrine* (Grand Rapids: Zondervan, 1994), 540-43.

eternally. That explains some words from Jesus' lips that otherwise would sound very strange. In a debate with a Jewish crowd one day (Jn 8:39-59) he spoke about Abraham, who had lived centuries beforehand, rejoicing "at the thought of seeing my day; he saw it and was glad." He did little to clear up the mystery of how this could be, given the age difference between them, when he caused further puzzlement by saying, "before Abraham was born, I am!" (Jn 8:58). Given that he was using the sacred name, it almost got him stoned, there and then. It all points to what is called his "preexistence."

And in case there was any doubt about it, toward the end he said to his disciples, "I came from the Father and entered the world; now I am leaving the world and going back to the Father" (Jn 16:28). That seemed pretty clearly to indicate an existence prior to his birth.

> ### JESUS CAME "FROM HEAVEN"
> Jn 3:13, 31; 6:33, 38, 41-42, 50-51.

Paul: In Philippians 2:6-8 I use an early Christian hymn that makes exactly the same point as John does in the opening of his Gospel. I cite Jesus as "being in very nature God," making himself nothing and "being made in human likeness [and] being found in appearance as a man." The former speaks of what he always was ("God"), the latter of what he later became ("a man").

The other so-called hymn in Colossians 1:15-20 makes similar claims. There Christ is spoken of as "the firstborn over all creation," not meaning he was the first to be born after creation—indeed, the whole point of the early part of the hymn is that creation was made "in," "through," and "for" him—but meaning he is in the supreme place of honor in creation, as the eldest son was in the family. The claim that "he is before all things" pretty clearly indicates he existed before making an appearance as a human being on earth.

In a number of other places my wording hints at his preexistence. Sometimes it is because the identification of Jesus with the eternal God is so close that it is hard to escape that conclusion (see 1 Cor 8:6; 2 Cor 4:4-6); sometimes it is to do with God sending his Son, who by implication already existed, into the world (see Rom 8:3; Gal 4:4).

Observer: The reference to Christ "emptying himself" in Philippians 2:7 (translated as "made himself nothing" in NIV) has been the cause of much comment. Cutting a long discussion short, Walter Hansen has come to a sensible conclusion:

> Christ did not empty himself of his divinity, his divine form and equality with God, but he surrendered his divine rights and cloaked his divine glory by becoming a human in the form of a slave. His existence in the form of God was both manifested and concealed in the form of a slave. His act of self-emptying was the incarnation; the result of the incarnation was humiliation, suffering and death.[5]

A second area of discussion has involved how much the view of Christ there, and in Colossians 1:15-20, is built on the concept of a personified Wisdom that is found in Proverbs 8 and the writings of the extracanonical *Ben Sirach* and the *Wisdom of Solomon*. These writings suggest a similar role in creation for wisdom to that claimed for Christ. However, not all scholars are convinced Paul is dependent on this idea.

The Hebraist: The opening words of my "sermon" (Heb 1:1-4)—for that's what Hebrews really is—are a close parallel to John 1 and Colossians 1. Jesus was the one "through whom" God created the universe, and he holds it together still. Yet he who brought the cosmos into being is Jesus, the one who "in these last days" has spoken to us, and who temporarily was made "lower than the angels" (Heb 2:9).

Peter: I write that Jesus was "chosen before the creation of the world, but was revealed in these last times" (1 Pet 1:20). It's obvious he must have existed beforehand or else he couldn't have been "revealed" in our lifetime.

John: Just before we leave this, it's worthwhile pointing out that when I speak of Jesus in Revelation as "the First and the Last" (Rev 1:17; 2:8; 22:13), I'm not only identifying him with God, who is "the Alpha and the Omega" (Rev 1:8; 21:6; a title I use of Jesus himself in 22:13), but am also saying there was nothing before him and will be nothing after him. He is the beginning and the end. He was, and is, and is to come, the eternally existing one.

---

[5]G. Walter Hansen, *The Letter to the Philippians*, Pillar New Testament Commentary (Grand Rapids: Eerdmans, 2009), 151.

The Virgin Birth

Chair: If it is agreed that he was "in very nature God" before appearing on earth, how did that appearance come about? This leads us to think about what we call the virgin birth. I know views are somewhat more mixed on this.

Luke: I have no doubts about it, although it is more accurate to talk of a virgin conception than birth. When Mary asked the angelic messenger from God how she could possibly be pregnant because she was a virgin, the angel replied, "The Holy Spirit will come on you, and the power of the Most High will overshadow you" (Lk 1:35). In other words, this birth was not going to occur as a result of a young woman being impregnated by a man.

Matthew: There's more to the story than that, as I tell in my Gospel. Mary and Joseph didn't have sexual intercourse until after Jesus was born (see Mt 1:18-19), so it was a major embarrassment to poor law-abiding Joseph to find his bride-to-be already pregnant. He tried to handle the situation discreetly and must have been somewhat relieved when an angelical messenger appeared to him to explain what was going on. That messenger said that "what is conceived in her is from the Holy Spirit" (Mt 1:20).

Throughout my Gospel I have a particular interest in showing how what happened in Jesus fulfilled the promises and meaning of the Old Testament, so that the Christians could be assured about the continuity of their faith with God's revelation to Israel. So, typically, I linked the message Joseph received with the words of Isaiah 7:14: "the virgin will conceive and give birth to a son, and they will call him Immanuel" (Mt 1:23). *Virgin* originally meant a young woman of marriageable age whose virginity was assumed. The context in which I quote Isaiah makes it very clear that in Mary's case she was definitely a virgin.

Mark: Fascinating. I guess I was too impatient to get on and talk about Jesus' mission, so I don't give any attention to the circumstances of his birth.

John: I've already explained that in my introduction I go way back behind any birth that took place in Bethlehem to explain Jesus, and so I don't record the circumstances of his birth either. However, I do recall that in one heated discussion the Jews cast doubt on the legitimacy of Jesus' birth (see Jn 8:41), so gossip about his parentage was obviously circulating. Of course, that has to be balanced by the opposite comment made when, on another occasion, they replied to his claim that he was "the bread that came down from heaven" by the put-down remark that he was nothing of the sort, because he was the son of Joseph, and they knew his father and his mother (Jn 6:41-42).

Observer: The rest of the New Testament writings make nothing of the virgin birth, though some have thought Paul's comment that Jesus was "born of a woman" (Gal 4:4) hints that he was not born of a man—but that's probably reading too much into it. The fact that only Matthew and Luke make much of the virgin conception has meant that Christians have not always subsequently thought it to be a *primary* article of the faith. The concept, however, is important, since it might well be a way of explaining how the two natures of Jesus, as human and divine, could have combined so perfectly in him.

JESUS: HIS TITLES

Chair: Let's turn to a different area. What did people make of Jesus during his lifetime and immediately afterward? I know that to begin with, and for some time afterward, people were trying to work him out, but pretty soon they began to attribute names and titles to him that showed how they understood him. What did they call him?

Observer: We need to be a little cautious of basing too much on his titles. Michael Bird, for example, warns that the affirmation of the deity of Jesus Christ doesn't depend on his titles, but on the whole story, where "the narrative climax of the gospel points us toward Jesus as the full-blooded fullness of the divine person."[6] On the other hand, James Dunn argues that the titles are important, since they reveal how the early Christians understood him. Dunn argues that very quickly the title *teacher*, which was frequently used in the Gospels, proved "inadequate to express the significance of his person and work."[7] The same was true of the use of the title *prophet*. At Pentecost Peter announced that "God has made this Jesus, whom you crucified, both Lord and Messiah" (Acts 2:36), and it would seem that the claim "Jesus is Lord!" (Rom 10:9; 1 Cor 12:3; cf. 16:22) quickly became established as the basic Christian confession.

---

[6]Michael F. Bird, *Evangelical Theology: A Biblical and Systematic Introduction* (Grand Rapids: Zondervan, 2013), 460.

[7]James D. G. Dunn, *New Testament Theology: An Introduction* (Nashville: Abingdon Press, 2009), 54. See 53-65.

The Messiah/Christ

Mark: Well, I begin my Gospel by being quite open about who Jesus was: I'm writing "the good news about Jesus the Messiah" or "the Christ." One of the pivotal points in the story, as all three of us Synoptic Gospel writers make clear, is when Jesus asked his disciples who people thought he was and Peter replied, "You are the Messiah . . ." (Mk 8:27-30; Mt 16:13-20; Lk 9:18-21). "The Messiah" was the title for God's anointed one, the one whom people longed to come and deliver Israel from their oppressors and restore the throne of David to its former glory. And the crowds certainly saw him in that light as he entered Jerusalem, on a colt, toward the end of his life. They greeted him with the very words that spoke about the coming Messiah and king (see Mk 11:1-11; Mt 21:1-11; Lk 19:28-40).

> **Observer:** Views about the Messiah were still relatively fluid at the time, with the community at Qumran, for example, looking for the coming of two Messiahs. The popular view, however, coalesced around the idea that the Messiah was a political figure who would overthrow Israel's enemies, triggering a new golden age, and that he would be one "who like David of old would lead the armies of Israel to military victory."[8] As "Israel's true king" he would be God's agent of salvation, but at least to start with, he was not necessarily considered to be a divine figure himself.

Mark: One day, when teaching in the temple, Jesus raised an interesting question that went to the heart of this matter. People said the Messiah was "a son of David," but in Psalm 110:1 David calls him his "Lord." How could he be both a descendant of David and yet be honored as his "Lord"? Jesus was teaching people to expect something more surprising than their current ideas had ever led them to imagine.

> **THE COMMAND TO KEEP QUIET**
>
> Mk 1:34, 43-45; 3:12; 5:43; 7:36; 8:26, 30; 9:9.

This became apparent at his trial when the high priest bluntly asked him, "Are you the Messiah, the Son of the Blessed One?" (Mk 14:61; cf. Mt 26:63; Lk 22:67). Pilate also quizzed him as to whether he was the Messiah or not. Our sources remember his reply a little

---

[8]Richard Bauckham, *Jesus: A Very Short Introduction* (Oxford: Oxford University Press, 2011), 31.

differently, but mine told me that at long last Jesus shed the veil of secrecy to which he had been wedded and said, "I am" (Mk 14:62). That sent them into shock and was enough in itself to secure his condemnation on a capital charge. But that was the surprise: no one had ever thought that a genuine messiah would be crucified. Plenty of false ones had been executed, but their deaths served only to prove they weren't the genuine article. Jesus' crucifixion, and the resurrection that followed, was to prove that he was the Messiah and that God was going to destroy his enemies, not by force and military might, but by apparent defeat and death.

Matthew: That's a picture I agree with. I'd just add that at the start of my Gospel I'm interested in tracing the family line of Jesus. After all, one of the important things about those who claim to be kings is that they are legitimate heirs to the throne! As I researched it, I was driven to the conclusion that he was the Messiah, and so I unashamedly use the title four times in my introduction (Mt 1:1, 16-18).

Luke: I would add a couple of details to this. First, at his birth, the angel choir celebrated him as the Messiah, and not long after, the saintly Simeon was moved to go into the temple because the Holy Spirit had informed him that he would see "the Lord's Messiah"—that is, "his anointed" one (Is 45:1). There he encountered Mary and the infant Jesus and praised God that he had seen the one who would be the Savior of Israel and a light to the Gentiles (see Lk 2:25-32).

Most remarkable of all was when Jesus returned home, in the early days of his public ministry, and in front of everyone in the synagogue said that Isaiah's prophecy (Is 61:1) that "The Spirit of the Sovereign LORD is on me, because the LORD has anointed me" applied to him (see Lk 4:16-19). His explanation did nothing to cool things, and he only just stopped being thrown off the cliff in the end.

The other thing I recall is the way in which, after his resurrection, he and others freely used the term *Messiah* in reference to what had happened (see Lk 24:26-27, 46-47).

Chair: Is this a title that went on being used about Jesus?

Luke: The apostles certainly carried on using it in their preaching. What they

> **JESUS THE MESSIAH OR CHRIST**
>
> Acts 2:36; 8:5, 12; 9:22; 10:36-38; 11:17; 17:3; 18:5, 28; 24:24; 28:31.

proclaimed was the good news of Jesus the Messiah (see Acts 5:42). From
the beginning they had a very high view of Jesus, especially because his
resurrection made him a "heavenly Messiah," Lord and Judge over all, as well
as a unique Savior (see Acts 3:20-21; 4:12; 10:36-38; 17:31).

John: I'm writing later than the other Gospel writers, but I still thread
the title through my Gospel. I don't take it for granted that people will understand that *Messiah* means "Christ," so I actually make the connection
obvious (see Jn 1:41; 4:25). It was early on that Andrew announced to Peter
he had found "the Messiah" (Jn 1:41); then Jesus admitted who he was to the
woman of Samaria (see Jn 4:25-26); while later Martha declared it at Lazarus's grave (see Jn 11:27)—a confession that is of equal significance, and as
clear, as Peter's confession. His visit to the Feast of Tabernacles sparked a
vigorous debate as to whether or not he was the Messiah (see Jn 7:25-44). At
the end of the Gospel I come clean and say that my purpose in writing it was
to persuade readers to "believe that Jesus is the Messiah, the Son of God, and
that by believing [they] may have life in his name" (Jn 20:31).

By the time I wrote my letters, the title had become a common appel-
lation for Jesus. And while I use the title only three times in Revelation (Rev
1:1, 2, 5), partly because there are other fresh and exciting titles to use, there is
no doubt that the whole point of the book is about the triumph of Jesus at
the end of the age (see Rev 11:15; 12:10).

"CHRIST" IN JOHN'S LETTERS

1 Jn 1:3; 2:1; 3:23; 4:2; 5:6, 20; 2 Jn 7.

Paul: I'm not sure how to contribute usefully to this discussion because my
writings are peppered with the title *Christ* or *Messiah*. It is my favorite title
for the Savior. I often couple it with his personal name, Jesus, and sometimes
even with *Lord* as well. Two things may be of note. First, I used this title from
the start, so the title very quickly came into common currency among us.
Second, I used it even though the Gentile converts wouldn't have known the
Jewish background to it—at least, not to begin with; and yet the quest for a
Messiah still made sense to them.

Observer: The title *Christ* is used 531 times in the New Testament,
of which Paul is responsible for 383 uses.

Peter: While agreeing about how quickly the title became common, let me just add almost a footnote. It's noteworthy that I use it twenty-two times in my first letter, especially in connection with suffering.

Son of Man

Chair: So *Messiah* or *Christ* is not only a common title for Jesus of Nazareth but also gives us an insight into his mission. When he refers to himself, however, he usually uses another title, doesn't he? Doesn't he prefer the title *Son of Man*? Who's going to start?

Matthew: Yes, he certainly did prefer the title *Son of Man*. He used it frequently—I mentioned he did so on twenty-nine occasions—and in a whole range of situations, like when he was asserting his authority to forgive sins (see Mt 9:6) or as Lord of the sabbath (see Mt 12:8). When he wanted to know what people were saying about him, he asked his disciples, "Who do people say the Son of Man is?" (Mt 16:13).

Mark: Absolutely. Even in my shorter Gospel I record the title being used fourteen times. Matthew and I both record one key occasion, when he said, "For even the Son of Man did not come to be served, but to serve, and to give his life as a ransom for many" (Mk 10:45; Mt 20:28). That connected this title very closely to his role in suffering, as did some of his other sayings.

Luke: He seemed to me actually to use the title, which I also cite almost as much as Matthew, twenty-four times, in a number of distinct ways.

First, he uses it when talking of his life and ministry on earth. As Matthew mentioned, sometimes this was about his authority to do things (see Lk 5:24; 6:5; 11:30); but more often it was about the way he lived life, as one who enjoyed celebrating (see Lk 7:34) or didn't have a home of his own (see Lk 9:58). His mission as the Son of Man was clear: it was "to seek and to save the lost" (Lk 19:10). Several times he spoke about people not being ashamed of "the Son of Man" (Lk 9:26; 12:8, 10).

> **SON OF MAN AND SUFFERING**
>
> Mk 8:31; 9:9, 12, 31; 10:33, 45; 14:21, 41.

Second, he especially uses it in connection with his suffering, as Mark mentioned. His suffering, rejection, and crucifixion wasn't an unfortunate accident but something that as Son of Man he "must" endure (Lk 9:22; cf. 9:44; 18:31; 22:22). Mark perhaps especially draws this out.

Third, he uses it when he wants to point beyond his suffering to his glorification and coming again. Once he compared himself to Jonah (see Lk 11:30), not so much because Jonah was dispatched to certain death, as was Jesus, but because after three days Jonah was alive again. It was a great sign that Jesus would reproduce in his own unique way. More particularly, however, he often used it with apocalyptic language to speak of his vindication and coming to reign in power (see Lk 12:40; 17:24, 30; 18:8; 21:27, 36).

So the genius of the title is that it combines the future status, power, and judicial authority of Jesus with his present weakness and suffering. One of the reasons he preferred this title must be that it enabled him to distance himself from popular ideas of the Messiah, which overdosed on the militaristic-power axis but had no place for an axis of suffering. People could easily have gotten the wrong idea of him if he'd openly declared himself to be the Messiah from the start. There was enough evidence that they did exactly that in spite of his being careful how he presented himself. Though undoubtedly seen as the Messiah, his using this title let people know he was redefining the role and wouldn't easily fit their expectations, since they'd never have thought that the Messiah would suffer.

Matthew and Mark have parallels to all this.

Observer: The early church tended to see the title *Son of Man* as primarily a way of pointing to Jesus as a human being, perhaps drawing on its Old Testament roots, such as Numbers 23:19. However, as G. E. Ladd points out, if that was all it meant, we would expect other people to be called that in the Gospels—which they aren't. So to understand it merely as "man" is an "error."[9]

More recently, because of its connection with Christ's future coming in power, people have come to realize this is a title with a history. The background to it is found in Daniel 7:13-14:

> In my vision at night I looked, and there before me was one like a son of man, coming with the clouds of heaven. He approached the Ancient of Days and was led into his presence. He was given authority, glory

---

[9]G. E. Ladd, *A Theology of the New Testament*, ed. D. A. Hagner, 2nd ed. (Grand Rapids: Eerdmans, 1974), 144.

and sovereign power; all nations and peoples of every language worshiped him. His dominion is an everlasting dominion that will not pass away, and his kingdom is one that will never be destroyed.[10]

Daniel's purpose is to contrast the "man" who is given the kingdom with the four beasts of the earlier vision. The man has real God-given power and will preside over a lasting kingdom, as opposed to the beasts who have usurped their authority illegitimately and won't last. This "son of man" may have been a representative figure in Daniel's mind (cf. Dan 7:17-18, 27), but the title came to be seen as applying to an individual who enters God's presence and then establishes his kingdom on earth. The title connects suffering with glory and came to be understood to refer to the mission of the Messiah in writings such as the *Similitudes of Enoch*. The Gospel writers are drawing on all this when they report Christ's self-designation as "Son of Man."

John: For once I am glad to overlap with my fellow Gospel writers. It's not that we disagree on other things, but I usually write from a different angle, using somewhat different language. On this, however, we stand shoulder to shoulder. I mention the title twelve times, sometimes in connection with his suffering (Jn 3:14; 6:53; 8:28; 12:23, 34), twice of his vindication (Jn 5:27; 13:31), and otherwise just as a title (Jn 1:51; 3:13; 6:27, 62; 9:35). Naturally I put my own stamp on it, so, more than once, I describe his suffering as his being "lifted up." At one level this is an obvious reference to his being lifted up on the cross, but at another level it enables me to say that by being lifted up he becomes the means of our healing, just as the serpent in the wilderness was (see Num 21:4-9).

I don't use the title much in the rest of my writings, except twice in Revelation (Rev 1:13; 14:14). After the resurrection there were other titles, such as *Christ, Messiah,* and *Lord,* which were more appropriate.

Luke: That's true. The early apostles didn't use it in their preaching, although, significantly, Stephen had a vision of "the Son of Man standing at the right hand of God" as he was being martyred (Acts 7:56). The prophecies of his exaltation had obviously come true.

---

[10]See further, Joachim Jeremias, *New Testament Theology,* trans. John Bowden, vol. 1 (London: SCM Press, 1971), 276; Ladd, *Theology of the New Testament,* 156; and Thomas R. Schreiner, *New Testament Theology: Magnifying God in Christ* (Grand Rapids: Baker Academic, 2008), 225.

The Hebraist: The title seems to have dropped out of use almost entirely after the Gospels. It had served its purpose, and I'm the only one of the later writers even to mention it (Heb 2:6-8)—and only then when quoting Psalm 8:4-6.

Son of David

Chair: Let's turn to another title. Matthew, the opening words of your Gospel are, "This is the genealogy of Jesus the Messiah, the son of David, the son of Abraham." Let's explore the "son of David" bit. What was that all about, and why was it important?

Matthew: It was important because people were looking for the coming of a Messiah who would be a descendant of David. They didn't need a pretender to usurp David's throne but rather a genuine heir who had a legitimate right to reign and who in doing so would show that God had kept his promise to David that "Your house and your kingdom will endure forever before me; your throne will be established forever" (2 Sam 7:16).

When people saw what Jesus was doing, they had no difficulty in identifying him as this messianic figure who would be a "son of David." That was what two blind men called him, not once but twice (Mt 9:27; 20:30). Mark (10:47-48) and Luke (18:38-39) mention yet another blind beggar who addressed Jesus in this way. A Canaanite woman called him by that title too (Mt 15:22). And when he entered Jerusalem in that final, fatal week of his life, the crowds had no hesitation in greeting him as the king who had come to establish David's throne once more (Mt 21:9). The authorities, of course, were very nervous about the political implications of such a greeting and tried to get Jesus to calm them down; but he simply quoted Psalm 8:2 to them, suggesting that they were right to praise God in this way.

> **OTHER RELEVANT DAVID TEXTS**
>
> Jer 23:5; 30:9; 33:15; Ezek 34:23; 37:24; Hos 3:5; Amos 9:11.

Mark: That was an exciting day indeed. The crowds were in a fervor of expectation, thinking the kingdom of David was about to be restored there and then. "Blessed is the coming kingdom of our father David!" they sang (Mk 11:10).

Luke: Let me take a step or two back, because it was evident from the start that this was a suitable way of understanding who Jesus was. The angel had told Mary that "The Lord God will give him the throne of his father David" (Lk 1:32). Yet in spite of such a clear promise, the way it was to work out wasn't altogether clear. To begin with, his kingdom wasn't like any kingdom that people had encountered up to now. And there was the riddle Jesus himself picked up on, about who was the greater, David or David's son? If the Messiah is genuinely a son—that is, a descendant—of David, why does David call him "Lord," as he does in Psalm 110:1? It's a puzzle we all note (see Mt 22:41-46; Mk 12:35-37; Lk 20:41-44). It was a way of saying that Jesus truly was heir to David's throne but that he would be far greater than David ever was, both because he was a unique Son of God and because he exercised an even more magnificent rule.

This argument may not mean much to the Gentiles to whom I directed my writings, but it certainly mattered to Jews. So, on the day of Pentecost, Peter made much of it as a way of persuading his Jewish, or at least God-fearing, audience that Jesus was superior to David and that God had acknowledged him now as both "Lord and Messiah" (Acts 2:36).

David got mentioned quite a bit in those early sermons, although usually merely to refer to his history. Paul, though, might remember preaching in Antioch—the one in Pisidia, not Syria—and saying the resurrection was evidence that the blessings God had promised David were being fulfilled (see Acts 13:34).

Paul: I do remember, and as well as that, I mention twice in my letters that Jesus was descended from David (see Rom 1:3; 2 Tim 2:8) for all the reasons mentioned. Although, for obvious reasons, with my being an apostle to the Gentiles, it doesn't become a major theme for me.

Chair: John, how about you?

John: Well, as for Paul, it isn't a major focus as far as I'm concerned, but I clue into it at one point when people were discussing Jesus' identity at the Feast of Tabernacles. They were questioning whether he really could be the Messiah because, they said, "Does not Scripture say that the Messiah will come from David's descendants and from Bethlehem, the town where David lived?" (Jn 7:42). Mistakenly, they thought he came from Nazareth, and so they concluded he couldn't be the Messiah. So it's there in the background.

Of course, when I'm grappling with issues of power and the triumph of God over Satan and evil in Revelation, it's different. I mention the royal connection three times: Jesus "holds the key of David" (Rev 3:7); in him we see that "the Root of David has triumphed" (Rev 5:5); and, finally, Jesus describes himself as "the Root and the Offspring of David, and the bright Morning Star" (Rev 22:16). We may differ about how, and how many times, we use the title, but we're essentially in agreement that Jesus was the expected son of David who would reestablish his glorious rule, and indeed outshine it.

Son of God

Chair: We've talked about *Son of Man* and *son of David*. How about another kind of sonship, that of *Son of God*?

Observer: This is another title with a history. Its varied background makes us ask whether the New Testament writers are using it in an ordinary sense or in a special way when they apply it to Jesus. When first used in Genesis 6:1-2, it simply meant a created human being. Luke uses it like that when he concludes his genealogy of Christ with the words, "the son of Adam, the son of God" (Lk 3:38). And perhaps that's all the angel meant when he used it of Jesus when visiting Mary (see Lk 1:35).

The term is also used, however, for Israel, who is God's son. You find it used in this way in Deuteronomy 14:1-2, and Hosea 1:10, 11:1,[11] but the idea of Israel as God's son is much wider. Matthew uses it in this sense when he relates Jesus' escape from Egypt as a young child to Hosea 11:1 (see Mt 2:14-15).

Israel's sonship also came to be personified by the king, so David and his successors are particularly designated as "sons of God" in, for example, 2 Samuel 7:14, Psalm 2:7, and elsewhere. This took on messianic overtones, as explained in the previous section.

Among the Greeks there was a concept of "the divine man," a powerful, miracle-working, exorcism-performing person. For a while some theologians thought that was the background to the title applied to Jesus, but further examination suggested that the concepts were very

---

[11]NIV (2011) has replaced *sons* with *children*.

different and that those who put forward this argument had over-estimated its significance.[12]

Then, finally, the term was used with a particular focus on a human being's religious experience—that is, his or her sense of sonship—of the close filial relationship people had with God as their Father. We can see that reflected in Exodus 4:22, John 1:12, 3:3, Romans 8:14, and Galatians 3:26, 4:5-6.

Apart from the idea of "the divine man"—a term that is never found in the New Testament—we find the other meanings applying to Jesus. And yet, as we shall see, with him the phrase also takes on a unique meaning. As the Son of God, whatever he has in common with other human beings, he is in a category of his own "because he is God and partakes of the divine nature" in a unique way.[13]

Mark: Once again, you'll find the title *Son of God* right up front in my Gospel, in the opening verse, even if not all early manuscripts included it. And if that's how I begin my Gospel, people have noted it's also how I end it! The climax of the story (that is, before I briefly report the resurrection) consists of a Roman centurion who was there at the cross declaring, "Surely this man was the [not "a"] Son of God!" (Mk 15:39). And if he's unusual as a man acknowledging who Jesus was, evil spirits, with their knowledge of the unseen world, had no such difficulty, even proclaiming him "Son of the Most High God" (Mk 5:7; cf. 3:11).

Matthew: It wasn't only evil spirits (see Mt 8:29) but also Satan himself who used the term. He used it to put the knife in during the temptations, twice saying, "If you are the Son of God . . ." (Mt 4:3, 6). This cynical line was to be taken by both the high priest (see Mt 26:63) and people at the cross, including one man condemned alongside him (see Mt 27:40, 43; Lk 23:39).

If that was the low point, there were some high points too. There were those who expressed clear faith in him as the Son of God, rather than skepticism, especially among his close disciples (see Mt 14:33; 16:16). Like Mark I note the remarkable confession of the Roman centurion and his companions

---

[12]For a discussion of "the divine man," see B. L. Blackburn, "Divine Man/*THEIOS ANĒR*," in Joel Green, Scot McKnight and I. Howard Marshall, eds., *Dictionary of Jesus and the Gospels* (Downers Grove, IL: InterVarsity Press, 1992), 189-92.

[13]Ladd, *Theology of the New Testament*, 160.

that Jesus was the Son of God, although I specifically link it to the earthquake that occurred when he died (see Mt 27:54). Whatever the details, it happened, the words were said, and the confession was made.

Luke: As you would expect, I have much in common with Mark, and even more with Matthew, in what they say about this title. However, I add an extra comment from my researches, which is that the term came up twice when the angel announced Jesus' birth to Mary (see Lk 1:32, 35).

> **THE COMMON GROUND IS SEEN**
>
> in Luke 3:38; 4:3, 9, 41; 8:28; 22:70—but note 22:48.

We shouldn't become fixated on a title, however. What we should not miss in all this is that the idea of Jesus being God's special Son is much wider than the use of certain words alone. This sense of relationship with God was evident, as we all note, at his baptism, when God said, "You are my Son, whom I love; with you I am well pleased" (Lk 3:22; Mt 3:17; Mk 1:11). That unique sonship was reaffirmed in very similar words when Jesus took on a special appearance before his close disciples on the mountain (see Lk 9:35; Mt 17:5; Mk 9:7). And Jesus was conscious throughout his ministry of this unique and intimate relationship with his Father (see Lk 10:21-22; Mt 11:25-27).

We could range wider still. The parable of the vineyard (see Lk 20:9-19; Mt 21:33-43; Mk 12:1-12) presupposes that the final messenger—a thin disguise for Jesus himself—was the owner's unique son. So, too, does the discussion that follows this parable about David's son and Lord that we've mentioned before (see Lk 20:41-44; Mt 22:41-46; Mk 12:35-37).

The use of this title reveals Jesus to be God's beloved Son.

John: I'm itching to get into this discussion because, as I reflected on the events of Jesus' life, this way of confessing Jesus became highly significant. In my prologue I say Jesus is God's unique, "one and only," Son (Jn 1:14, 18; cf. 1 Jn 4:9). Very soon after that, John the Baptist and Nathanael called Jesus "the Son of God" (Jn 1:34,[14] 49), and so did Martha later on (Jn 11:27). I use the title of Jesus (Jn 3:16, 18),[15] and he was at home using it of himself (Jn 10:36; 11:4).

---

[14]In some manuscripts only.

[15]It is unclear who is speaking at this point. I take it to be an editorial comment by John, but it may well still be Jesus himself.

Jesus' sense of being God's Son is much richer than the use of the term. So Jesus is very conscious of being sent by the Father (e.g., see Jn 3:34; 5:36-38; 7:29; 14:24; 1 Jn 4:14). He's very aware that he is in a unique relationship (see Jn 5:18). Their love is mutual: the Father loves the Son (see Jn 3:35; 5:20; 10:17; 17:24) and the Son loves the Father (see Jn 14:31). The Son is totally dependent on the Father (see Jn 5:19, 30; 7:16; 14:28, 31; 15:10). There is an absolute oneness between them (see Jn 10:30; 14:20; 17:11) because the Son knows the Father (see Jn 6:46; 10:15; 15:15), reveals the Father (see Jn 8:19; 14:8-9), and always does the Father's will, even at the cross (see Jn 8:29; 12:27-28). To honor the Son is to honor the Father (Jn 5:23).

In addition to their mutual love and knowledge, their mutuality is also seen in the theme of glory (see Jn 13:31-32; 17:1). The Father is the source of the Son's glory (see Jn 5:41, 44; 8:50, 54; 11:4; 12:28; 17:5, 22, 24), while the Son always seeks to glorify the Father (see Jn 7:18; 11:40; 14:13; 17:4). The prayer of chapter 17, which I alone record, is possibly the most sacred part of my Gospel and demonstrates the depth, intimacy, and extraordinary reciprocity of the Father-Son relationship like nothing else. And when all was done, Jesus returned home to his Father (see Jn 14:12, 28; 16:10, 28).

Oh, and remember this: although we believers are all sons or daughters of God, Jesus always placed himself in a special class as far as his sonship was concerned. It was partly because Jesus called God "his own Father" (Jn 5:18) that he was persecuted by the authorities, but the postresurrection conversation with Mary confirmed the unparalleled nature of the relationship (see Jn 20:17). So his being God's "one and only" Son is a major key to understanding who Jesus is.

That theme of Jesus as the Son of God crops up repeatedly in my first letter. I use the term just once in Revelation (Rev 2:18), but as mentioned there are plenty of other titles and descriptions there which are more appropriate to the issues I'm dealing with.

Chair: Did others take up the theme and give it the prominence that John did?

Luke: I don't recall that it surfaced

> **JESUS AS THE SON OF GOD**
>
> 1 Jn 1:3; 2:22-23; 3:23; 4:9-15; 5:5, 9-13, 20.

much in the preaching of the early apostles. Paul mentioned it only a couple of times (see Acts 9:20-22; 13:33), and one of those was a quotation.

Paul: In my teaching it becomes one of those important foundations you almost take for granted. So the gospel is "the gospel . . . regarding his Son" (Rom 1:2-3, 9), and I mention he was "appointed the Son of God in power by his resurrection from the dead" (Rom 1:4). I should explain that I didn't mean he wasn't a Son beforehand. This isn't justification for the heresy we know as adoptionism, which teaches that God was pleased with the way the man Jesus had lived and died and so he eventually adopted him as his special divine Son. It's not about him becoming something that he hadn't previously been; it is simply a way of noting the supreme significance of his resurrection, which confirmed what really needed no confirmation: that Jesus was the Son of God all along.

I refer to Jesus as the Son repeatedly. Sometimes I'm just picking up on the preaching of the gospel (see Rom 8:3; 2 Cor 1:19; Gal 1:15-16; 4:4), which, after all, is about God who rescued us "from the dominion of darkness and brought us into the kingdom of the Son he loves" (Col 1:13). By that gospel we are called into fellowship with his Son (see 1 Cor 1:9), in order that we might "be conformed to the image of his Son" (Rom 8:29), which happens as we "all reach unity . . . in the knowledge of the Son of God" (Eph 4:13). In the meantime we are waiting "for his Son from heaven" to return (1 Thess 1:10). When he does so, having won the victory over all God's enemies and having put the world into proper order, "the Son himself will be made subject to him [God the Father] . . . so that God may be all in all" (1 Cor 15:28).

Peter: We're not compelled to use precisely the same vocabulary when we write about Jesus because there are so many ways to describe this wonderful Son of God. So while I don't use the term explicitly, it's there. In 1 Peter 1:3 I speak of God as "Father of our Lord Jesus Christ," and in 2 Peter 1:17 I quote God's affirmation of Jesus as the Son he loved. That's all.

The Hebraist: I find this title a very useful way of trying to understand Jesus, so I use it on several occasions. Very much like John in the prologue to his Gospel, I describe Jesus as "The Son [who] is the radiance of God's glory and the exact representation of his being" (Heb 1:3), and I celebrate the superiority of the Son over others. For example, I describe Moses, whom we respect deeply and who played such a crucial role in Israel's formative history, as a faithful "servant" in God's house, but he stands in contrast to Jesus who "is faithful as the Son over God's house" (Heb 3:5-6). At the end of the day, however influential, servants are servants but sons are something else.

In 4:14 I declare "Jesus the Son of God" to be our great high priest. The theme continues in 5:8, where I say that although he was a Son he still "learned obedience from what he suffered." And the theme threads its way through the rest of the book, cropping up again in 6:6, 7:3, and 10:29. Each use marks Jesus out as in a supreme and intimate relationship with the Father. To honor the Son is to honor the Father. To reject the Son is to reject the Father. So "today" when we hear his voice we need to respond in faith and obedience, not with unbelief and hard hearts (Heb 3:7-19).

Lord

Chair: Let's move on. One of the most frequent designations for Jesus is *Lord*, a title frequently used of God himself. Why is it so common, and how is it used?

Luke: When we use the term *Lord* in the Gospels, we usually use it as a courtesy title until after the resurrection has occurred. Its fuller meaning is found earlier, at least in my Gospel, but only when spoken by an angel or under inspiration (see Lk 1:43, 76; 2:11). Oh, and Jesus used it of himself in a more-than-ordinary way when they were preparing for the Passover (see Lk 19:31, 34; Mt 21:3; Mk 11:3).

Matthew: Yes, it was rare to use it to mean more than "Sir," but Jesus did use it on occasions in a deeper sense. Don't forget the time he warned, "Not everyone *who says to me,* 'Lord, Lord,' will enter the kingdom of heaven, but only the one who does the will of my Father who is in heaven" (Mt 7:21; cf. Lk 6:46).

Luke: Of course. The main point, though, is that it is after the resurrection that the title comes into its own. On Easter Day, the two from Emmaus rushed back to Jerusalem after they had had their eyes opened to the resurrection to find the disciples saying, "The Lord has risen" (Lk 24:34). They weren't using it as a courtesy title then, but as a title that reached back into the ancient traditions of Israel, where there was only one Lord, and he was God.

John: I take the same view as Luke. Much of the time it's merely a respectful way of addressing Jesus, but there are times when it assumes much greater significance and points toward his divinity (see Jn 6:23; 9:38; 11:2). This comes to a climax with Thomas, who, having seen the risen Christ and his wounds, blurted out, "My Lord and my God!" (Jn 20:28). Jesus was being ascribed the title of God himself.

Luke: Yes, and that carried over into the early apostolic preaching. People have calculated that on forty-seven occasions in Acts I apply the title to Jesus, and a further eighteen times I use it of God the Father.[16] Significantly, I note how the apostles had no hesitation in applying some of the Old

Testament scriptures to Jesus when originally those scriptures had clearly applied to God himself. Peter's address at Pentecost is an example of that: he does it a couple of times (see Acts 2:20-21, 25). The basic claim of their preaching was that the crucified one had been made "both Lord and Messiah" (Acts 2:36). When speaking to Cornelius, Peter again identified the core message as "the good news of peace through Jesus Christ, who is Lord of all" (Acts 10:36). This is so much at the heart of things that they began to use a shorthand for the gospel and call it "the word of the Lord"—that is, the word about Jesus being the Lord. Since this is the good news, people are called on to turn to and believe in him as Lord (see Acts 5:14; 9:35; 11:17).

> **THE "WORD OF THE LORD"**
>
> Acts 8:25; 13:44, 49; 15:35-36; 19:20.

The resurrection was an important element in his becoming "Lord" (see Acts 2:32-36; 4:33; 10:40-42; 17:31). In rising from the dead he had defeated all the powers that death represented and that opposed God's rule. And since his victory was so secure, the apostles often ran his title and his personal name together: he was simply "the Lord Jesus" (Acts 1:21; 4:33; 7:59; 8:16; 11:17, 20; 15:26; and so on). To call Jesus "Lord" was, then, to declare him the supreme Sovereign over the earth and at the same time to give him a place in the Godhead.

Paul: Luke has identified something of utmost importance. In one of my earliest letters I refer to the confession "Jesus is Lord" (1 Cor 12:3), which was already established as a way of identifying oneself as a Christian. Much later I highlight the importance of verbally confessing as well as inwardly believing that "Jesus is Lord" (Rom 10:9). Loving and boasting about "the Lord" separated Christians out from others (1 Cor 16:22; Gal 6:14). "Jesus Christ as Lord" is what I preach and is the sum of my message (2 Cor 4:5; Col 2:6). Reaching out to all people, Gentiles as well as Jews, I want them to know that

---

[16]Ben Witherington III, *The Acts of the Apostles: A Socio-Rhetorical Commentary* (Grand Rapids: Eerdmans, 1998), 147. See further 147-53.

"Everyone who calls on the name of the Lord will be saved" (Rom 10:13). Here, and elsewhere, I'm taking what Isaiah 45:22 and Joel 2:32 said about God and applying it to Jesus.

Like others I stress the importance of his resurrection and exaltation in his unveiling as Lord (see Rom 1:4; 14:9; Phil 2:6-11). That's what shapes my thinking about Jesus' current real, though hidden, reign in heaven (see Rom 8:34; 1 Cor 15:25; Eph 1:20-23; Col 3:1). Jesus is God's viceregent over the earth. *Lord* is no mere honorific title for him; it means he will come to exercise ultimate judgment one day, since we're all accountable to him as our Lord and Master (see Col 3:22–4:1). This is what inspires me eagerly to anticipate his coming again so that he may fully and finally enter his reign (see Phil 3:20-21). That's why I encourage believers to pray the ancient prayer that goes back to the Aramaic, the language of Jesus himself: *Marana tha*, which means "Come, Lord!" (1 Cor 16:22).

Observer: James Dunn says that "the most significant way of speaking about Christ for Paul is indicated by the title *kyrios*, 'Lord.'"[17] He calculates that in the letters whose authorship by Paul is not disputed (as distinct from those where his authorship is questioned) there are two hundred uses of the term, sometimes combined with *Jesus* or *Jesus Christ*. Eighty-two times he uses the title *the Lord* without further qualification. A theme that will emerge later as of importance is the way in which he frequently speaks of being "in the Lord."

One of the recent discussions that this use of *Lord* has provoked is to what extent Paul was drawing on its Jewish background, thus identifying Jesus directly with God, and to what extent he was using it in its Gentile context, where Caesar was Lord. Some Christians, especially those influenced by the radical wing of the Reformation and others who are concerned about contemporary political power structures, often want to play up the conflict between affirming Jesus as Lord and Caesar as Lord. The claim that Jesus is Lord carries an inescapable implication that Caesar is not. The absolute claim of Jesus relativizes all claims to human power and erects a huge question mark over assertions that this or that politician is "the most powerful man or woman" on earth. Even so, the

---

[17]James D. G. Dunn, *The Theology of Paul the Apostle* (Edinburgh: T&T Clark, 1998), 244.

tension between the two can be overplayed. There is no independent evidence until after Paul's time that this was in mind.[18]

A recent collection of papers[19] that examines different parts of the New Testament on this question offers a variety of conclusions. On balance, however, it concludes that it is too easy to read anti-Roman or anti-imperialistic rhetoric into the New Testament writings. If the presence of the Roman Empire has been underplayed by previous generations of New Testament interpreters, it is important not to let the pendulum swing too far in the opposite direction. "The purpose of the kingdom of God is not to replace, so to speak, the Roman Empire; rather it is to overcome the kingdom of Satan."[20]

The Hebraist: Most of the occurrences of the word *Lord* in Hebrews are found when I am quoting the Old Testament, and therefore the words would originally have been understood as referring to God. Given that, it's all the more significant that I shift between God and Jesus as Lord with ease on a couple of occasions (see Heb 2:3; 7:14). With others, though, I also link his lordship with his resurrection. So in my closing benediction I say that God "brought back from the dead our Lord Jesus, that great Shepherd of the sheep" (Heb 13:20).

Peter: It's interesting that the Hebraist speaks of using the term *Lord* in his benediction; Paul regularly uses it in his benedictions. Not surprisingly, as Lord, Jesus is the object of our prayers and worship. I mention this because I urge Christians to "revere Christ as Lord" (1 Pet 3:15), not just in the worship service but genuinely in the whole of their lives as they are ready to speak up for him.

PAUL'S BENEDICTIONS

1 Cor 16:23; 2 Cor 13:14; Gal 6:18; Eph 6:23-24; Phil 4:23; 1 Thess 5:23; 2 Thess 3:18; 2 Tim 4:22.

Other than that, I use the term quite freely, often in combination with the name of Jesus or his work as the Christ (see 1 Pet 1:3; 2 Pet 1:2, 8, 11, 14, 16; 2:1, 20; 3:2, 18).

---

[18]Ibid., 247.
[19]Scot McKnight and Joseph B. Modica, eds., *Jesus Is Lord, Caesar Is Not: Evaluating Empire in New Testament Studies* (Downers Grove, IL: InterVarsity Press, 2013).
[20]Ibid., 213.

Jude: We all speak with one voice on this. Even in my brief letter I write of the "Lord Jesus Christ" twice (Jude 17, 21). And in ascribing "glory, majesty, power and authority" to God, in the very last verse, I say this occurs "through Jesus Christ our Lord" (Jude 25).

Servant

Chair: We may have covered the major titles you all tend to use, but there are other titles that are significant as well as these. Isaiah, for example, writes about "the servant of the LORD." In fact, he has four passages that have been acknowledged as "servant songs." They paint a remarkable picture of a divinely chosen leader whose authority is established through suffering. Those songs have been interpreted in a number of ways as pointing to an individual prophet or to the nation of Israel itself, whose role was to bring salvation to the world through its own redemptive suffering. The early Christians, however, saw the unmistakable image of Jesus Christ in them, didn't they?

> **ISAIAH'S "SERVANT SONGS"**
>
> 42:1-4; 49:1-6; 50:4-9; 52:13–53:12.

Matthew: The great song of Isaiah 53 is one that we often allude to and sometimes even link directly to Jesus' ministry. So I see Jesus' healing ministry as fulfilling Isaiah 53:4: "He took up our infirmities and bore our diseases" (Mt 8:17). Jesus' "quiet" ministry fits the servant figure of Isaiah 42:1-4 like a glove. Although much loved, Spirit filled, and passionate about justice, the servant was anything but ostentatious, not drawing attention to himself, and was gentle in dealing with people. Again and again, Isaiah's servant serves as the template for Jesus.

Mark: Probably the most significant connection is found when Jesus said, "Even the Son of Man did not come to be served, but to serve, and to give his life as a ransom for many" (Mk 10:45; Mt 20:28). He didn't actually use the title of *servant*, but virtually did so. We often found ourselves alluding to these passages in Isaiah when we were trying to explain about Jesus and his mission.[21]

Luke: Once, at the Last Supper, he directly applied Isaiah 53:12, about being "numbered with the transgressors," to himself (Lk 22:37).

---

[21]For more details, see Schreiner, *New Testament Theology*, 265-68.

John: Apart from the Baptist's comment that Jesus was "the Lamb of God, who takes away the sin of the world" (Jn 1:29)—which might be a reference to the lamb in Isaiah 53 who suffered in silence—I reach back to that chapter only once. I argue that people's lack of belief in him, in spite of the numerous signs he did, was a fulfillment of Isaiah 53:1 (see Jn 12:38).

Luke: By the time the early Christian preachers got going after the resurrection, they were unmistakably clear about the connection. They referred to Jesus as the "servant" (Acts 3:13, 26; 4:27-30). Most explicit of all, though, was the explanation Philip gave to the Ethiopian official when he was reading Isaiah 53:7-8 and asked Philip who it was talking about (see Acts 8:32-34). Philip explained that Isaiah 53 was all about Jesus.

Paul: I confess that I tend to allude to the connection rather than make it explicit, as in Romans 4:25 or 8:32-34. However, the hymn in Philippians 2:6-11 certainly echoes Isaiah 53 at a number of points.

Peter: The connection seemed so obvious to me that when I reflected on the unjust death of Jesus (see 1 Pet 2:22-25), which serves as an example to us all in how we should respond to suffering, I just had to quote it three times (Is 53:9, 5, 6)! Here was the sinless, silent, suffering substitute who bore our sins on the cross.

John: In Revelation I don't fit Jesus exactly into the framework of Isaiah's servant, but the picture of Jesus as "a Lamb, looking as if it had been slain" (Rev 5:6) draws from a common tradition to which Isaiah has contributed.

Logos: Word and Wisdom

John: I have a couple of distinctive ways of writing about Jesus that are worth bringing to the discussion. I introduce him in my Gospel as "the Word" (*logos*), using the word (sorry about that!) three times in the opening verse and picking it up again in verse 14. Since it is unusual, I know my use of it has given rise to all sorts of speculation as to what it means and where it came from. *Word* obviously refers to "speech" or "message." The Greek world developed that, and many think that I was adopting (and adapting) their idea of the word as the organizing principle of the world, which was reason or the communication of reason.

Observer: This meaning entered Jewish thinking through a scholar called Philo (ca. 20 BC–AD 50). So I'm sure his ideas were understood in Jesus' day.

John: Actually, though, you don't have to look in that direction to understand it, since the Old Testament itself is full of references to God's "word." The creation took place when God spoke, and light and life came into being by his word (see Gen 1:3-26; Ps 33:6, 9). His words carry authority and are always effective in accomplishing his aims (see Ps 147:15-18; Is 55:10-11). They also reveal his nature and his will, as when the prophets spoke "the word of the LORD" (e.g., Jer 20:9; Ezek 33:7; Mic 1:1; Zeph 1:1; Hag 1:1). To understand Jesus as the ultimate Word of God seemed a very natural thing to do, especially since he could be described as "life" and "light," the two elements that were very evident in the creation story (Jn 1:3-10).

I might also mention that some connect this idea of the *logos* with the idea of wisdom that occurs in Proverbs 8:12-36. Wisdom is personified in that poem, exists prior to the creation, and is "constantly at [God's] side," "rejoicing always in his presence," as creation unfolds. That gives wisdom the authority to be a wise instructor and to demand that people listen to her. There are certainly echoes of Proverbs 8 not only in my prologue but throughout my Gospel. And yet Jesus somehow surpasses the description given of wisdom there.

Even if somewhat puzzling, then, describing Jesus as "the Word" is a wonderfully deep metaphor that is capable of revealing a multitude of riches. I return to it once more in Revelation 19:13, where it is affirmed that Jesus is "the Word of God."

Observer: It was a Christian leader in the next century called Justin Martyr (AD 100–165), a great apologist for the faith, who is credited with being the principal voice of "Logos Christology." He was steeped in Greek philosophical teaching and sought to interpret the Christian faith for that audience. He saw Jesus as the rational force in the universe and argued that human reasoning partook of the divine reason. Justin was not, however, uncritical of Greek philosophy and put Jesus in a class of his own, rather than lumping him with other Greek philosophers. He was eventually martyred for his commitment to Christ, which is why his name is Justin "Martyr."

"I Am"

Chair: Thank you, John. There is another way you speak of Jesus Christ, which is, I think it's fair to say, a little more obvious, but no less striking. Tell us about the way you use the verb form "I am."

John: What needs to be understood, of course, is that "I am" is the sacred name for God, as revealed to Moses at the burning bush (Ex 3:14). I use it repeatedly of Jesus, but in two different ways.

First, I tell of how he made various claims about himself by using various metaphors. I have shaped my Gospel partly around the number seven, a number that symbolizes fullness or completeness to us Jews. So I record seven of his key sayings: "I am the bread of life" (Jn 6:35); "the light of the world" (Jn 8:12); "the gate for the sheep" (Jn 10:7); "the good shepherd" (Jn 10:11, 14); "the resurrection and the life" (Jn 11:25); "the way and the truth and the life" (Jn 14:6); and, finally, "the true vine" (Jn 15:1). People should note that these claims are connected to the "signs" (miracles) he did and sometimes to a wider theme as well. Often the saying occurs in the midst of the sign. So he claims to be the bread of life after having just fed five thousand people (see Jn 6:1-15). He claims to be "the resurrection and the life" in the lead-up to raising his friend Lazarus from the dead. Sometimes the theme's a bit longer-running. So I speak of him as "light" in 1:5, a claim he endorses at 8:12, and then illustrates as he banishes the darkness from a blind man, illuminating his eyes, in 9:1-34.

It wasn't the use of "I am" on its own that made us think he was claiming to be God. After all, we all have to use the verb "I am" in an ordinary sense about ourselves and we're not claiming to be God when we do so! No, we thought he was using it in the more-than-ordinary sense because of what followed his "I am." We believed God was the bread of life, the light, the good shepherd, the way, and so on. So when he said he was, and we didn't think of him as mad for making the claim, we were implicitly acknowledging he was equal with God.

That's where the second use of the "I am" phrase comes in. Another seven times I quote some unqualified or absolute uses of "I am." Here they don't lead to a metaphor or a claim; they're complete in themselves. They occur at 4:26; 6:20; 8:24, 28, 58; 13:19; and 18:5 (repeated for rhetorical purposes in vv. 6 and 8). If the first way the phrase is used stops short of completely establishing his identification with God, this second way doesn't. It's a pretty clear claim to deity.

Observer: Richard Bauckham, in *Jesus and the God of Israel*, insightfully links these seven references in John to seven Old Testament texts—namely, Deuteronomy 32:39 and Isaiah 41:4; 43:10, 13; 46:4; 48:12; 52:6. As a result he concludes, "The series of sayings thus comprehensively identifies Jesus with the God of Israel who sums up his identity in the declaration, 'I am he.' More than that, they identify Jesus as the eschatological revelation of the unique identity of God, predicted by Deutero-Isaiah."[22]

John: Let me add two footnotes. The first is that these sayings are closely related to his work of salvation on the cross. The claim to be "I am" was to be vindicated when he was "lifted up" on the cross, through which he would also save people from dying in their sins (Jn 8:24, 28).

The second footnote is to say that a variation on this language is found in Revelation. There Jesus says, "I am the First and the Last" (Rev 1:17; 2:8). More fully he says of himself, "I am the Alpha and the Omega, the First and the Last, the Beginning and the End" (Rev 22:13), which repeats the very words applied to God himself earlier (Rev 1:8; 21:6). So it is a pretty clear indication that "the Word was God" (Jn 1:1).

Savior

Chair: Israel constantly celebrated God as their Savior. Does that title cross over to the New Testament, and, if so, how?

Luke: When Mary learned she was pregnant, her immediate response was to rejoice "in God my Savior" (Lk 1:47). When Jesus was born, the angels used the same word, announcing to the shepherds, "in the town of David a Savior has been born to you; he is the Messiah, the Lord" (Lk 2:11). Having said that, the apostles spoke of "the Savior Jesus" rarely (Acts 13:23; cf. 5:31).

Peter: Well, Luke, that's what you may record in your history of the early church, but I used the title *Savior* quite a bit in my second letter, often saying that Jesus is "our Lord and Savior" (2 Pet 1:1, 11; 2:20; 3:2, 18). In fact, it's my favorite way of talking about him.

Paul: I admit it's not to be found too frequently in my writings (see Eph 5:23; Phil 3:20; 2 Tim 2:10; Tit 1:4;

GOD OUR SAVIOR

1 Tim 1:1; 2:3; 4:10; Tit 2:10; 3:4.

---

[22]Richard Bauckham, *Jesus and the God of Israel* (Milton Keynes: Paternoster, 2008), 40n5.

2:13; 3:6) in comparison with other titles. But I'll point out a significant thing to you: I talk about both Jesus and God as Savior almost indiscriminately. I had no reservation in applying the traditional title for God to Jesus because both were vitally involved in our salvation, and also because Jesus was none other than God himself incarnate among us.

John: On the couple of occasions I refer to Jesus in this way, I give it a universal spin. He is none other than "the Savior of the world" (Jn 4:42; 1 Jn 4:14).

Matthew: It's curious we make more use of other titles. I don't call him "Savior" at all, but, of course, his very name means he is the Savior (see Mt 1:21).

> **Observer:** It's often suggested that the New Testament did not call Jesus "Savior" for two reasons. On the one hand, the term had been devalued and was used frequently to refer to Greek gods whom people looked to for modest protection in this world. The salvation Jesus offered was far more profound and related to salvation not only in this age but for the age to come as well. On the other hand, people hailed Roman emperors as "Savior," and Caesar Augustus claimed to be "the Savior of the world." Therefore, to use the title for Jesus would be a direct challenge to the claims Roman rulers made. It is doubtful that the apostles would have been too nervous about this since the same was equally true of the title *Lord* and so much else they preached and wrote. The claim that Jesus was the ultimate "Lord and Savior" certainly relativized Rome's power in a way it would not have welcomed.

Chair: That's been a tour de force, though I'm aware we haven't exhausted the issue. We might have examined why Jesus was sometimes called a prophet, although that seems quickly to have been displaced by other descriptions because it wasn't sufficient. Then, too, we might have examined him as priest, a role much loved in the letter to the Hebrews. We might profitably have examined in more detail some of the purple passages about Christ's identity—by which I mean John 1:1-18, Philippians 2:6-11, Colossians 1:15-20, and Hebrews 1:1-3. We could also have searched through the book of Revelation, where a wonderful thesaurus of creative titles is awarded to Christ. Perhaps, though, it's time to focus on another topic. Let's look more closely at the relationship between Jesus and God.

JESUS AND GOD

Having said all we've said about his titles, we can't affirm too strongly that the clearest picture, or fullest revelation, of God takes place through Jesus. If we truly want to know what God is like, we must look at Jesus (see Jn 14:7-9).

Jesus as God

John: The remarkable thing was that when we encountered Jesus we saw God in him to such an extent that we were nudged toward the conclusion he actually was God. We came to this conclusion when we looked at what he did. Chapter 6 in my Gospel gives a couple of examples, even if I don't make the parallels explicit. Jesus fed five thousand in the wilderness, just as God had done earlier in the time of Moses. Jesus himself made the connection and went on to explain how he was the bread of life (see Jn 6:32-59; Ex 16:1-36). Then that same evening he walked across the water to his disciples' boat in the middle of the lake (see Jn 6:16-21). As Jews we believed that it was God who walked like this on water (see Ps 77:19; Job 9:8).

Jesus certainly claimed complete identification with the Father, as when he claimed that the Father "has entrusted all judgment to the Son, that all may honor the Son just as they honor the Father" (Jn 5:22-23). So we weren't altogether surprised when, as mentioned earlier, Jesus somewhat wearily said to Philip, "Don't you know me, Philip, even after I have been among you such a long time? Anyone who has seen me has seen the Father. . . . Don't you believe that I am in the Father, and that the Father is in me?" (Jn 14:9-10).

Mark: That's a picture of Jesus I agree with and would supplement. His critics were right to ask, "Who can forgive sins but God alone?" He, however, not only claimed the right to do so but authenticated his claim by performing an incredible miracle (Mk 2:1-12). When he calmed the storm on the Sea of Galilee (see Mk 4:35-41) he reminded us of God himself who, we believed, alone had the power to tame the chaos of the sea (see Gen 1:2, 6-7; Ps 74:12-14; 107:27-30). We didn't even find his claim to be "Lord even of the Sabbath" (Mk 2:28) laughable, although that was a prerogative that belonged to God. We certainly would have disbelieved anyone else who made such a claim.

Chair: There is another element to this as well, which we've briefly mentioned before: the way statements about God in the Old Testament get applied, without hesitation, to Jesus.

The Hebraist: Agreed. I do that a couple of times just in my opening chapter. I cite both Psalms 45:6-7 and 102:25-27, words that originally applied to God, and state unapologetically, in verses 8 and 10-12, that they were really about Jesus.

Paul: I take the same approach when, for example, I'm quoting some very significant passages about God, such as Deuteronomy 6:4 in 1 Corinthians 8:5-6 or Isaiah 45:23 in Philippians 2:9-11. Both are highly significant, the former especially so because it takes the Hebrew *shema*, the most fundamental statement and prayer of Judaism, and extends the idea of the oneness of God to incorporate Jesus within it. I do this in a discussion about Christians eating meat offered to idols, and so it has two important implications. First, it relates to the doctrine of the living God: he (with the Lord Jesus Christ) uniquely and really exists, as opposed to the so-called gods that are idols; and, second, it relates to worship. The *shema* is a prayer regularly used in the synagogue about God. It has now been revised to become a prayer about Jesus also, who is at the heart of our worship.

Only one is worthy of worship: God himself.[23] Yet I often speak of Jesus as the subject of doxology (see Rom 9:5; 2 Tim 4:18), address prayers to him (see 1 Cor 16:22), and pronounce blessing in his name (see 1 Thess 3:11-12; 2 Thess 3:5-6). Although people query the obvious reading of my words because they're unusual, both Romans 9:5, "the Messiah, who is God over all," and Titus 2:13, "the appearing of the glory of our great God and Savior, Jesus Christ," are pretty explicit indications that I truly believe Jesus is God.

John: I couldn't agree more. Need I remind you of the introduction to my Gospel, where I begin, "the Word was with God, and the Word was God" (1:1-18)? And in Revelation I recall that praise is ascribed to him (1:5-6); that the singing of a new song is addressed to him, analogous to praise addressed to God (5:8-14); that blessing comes from him (1:4-5); and that prayer is addressed to him (22:20). I stress "that Christ shares the names, the throne, the work and the worship of God."[24] That's a pretty close relationship!

Luke: Addressing prayer to Jesus is something we'd only do if we considered him the object of worship—that is to say, that he was divine. It

---

[23]On the importance of the worship of Jesus for our understanding of his divinity, see Larry Hurtado, *Lord Jesus Christ: Devotion to Jesus in Earliest Christianity* (Grand Rapids: Eerdmans, 2003).

[24]Ben Witherington III, *Revelation,* New Cambridge Bible Commentary (Cambridge: Cambridge University Press, 2003), 30.

reminds me of the way Stephen petitioned the "Lord Jesus" even as he was being executed (Acts 7:59-60).

Peter: I don't want to miss out on this because, as our Savior, Jesus is worthy of all the praise we can muster as human beings. I begin 2 Peter by speaking about "the righteousness of our God and Savior Jesus Christ" (2 Pet 1:1). I know some have understood this to refer to God and Jesus as two separate beings (God and Jesus), whereas it might more correctly be read to mean that our Savior Jesus Christ is also our God. If that's where I start, I come full circle and end with the words, "To him [our Lord and Savior Jesus Christ] be glory both now and forever! Amen" (2 Pet 3:18).

Observer: How could rigorous monotheists like the Jews have come to believe that Jesus was God? Would that not have undermined their monotheism and suggested there were two Gods?

As suggested above, the starting point was probably that they saw Jesus functioning as only God could do. So they drew the straight line between them. However, this is not the whole story, because they were claiming more than that Jesus did what God does; they were claiming he was God. That's about his being, not just his doing! They thought this from the earliest days, as we see from the fact that the New Testament documents assume it and don't set out to prove it. So it wasn't, as some assert, that Jesus started as a remarkable spiritual person who, as time went by, was boosted higher and higher in the church's opinion until they declared him God. That's where they started. But how so?

The Old Testament prepared the path in various ways. It had always had a place for "wisdom" and "the Word" as intrinsically participating in God's creative work and sovereign rule. Some see intimations and hints of the Trinity scattered here and there from Genesis 1:2, which speaks of the Spirit or wind of God (the word *ruach* could mean either), onward. The angels or messengers of God seem somewhat ambiguous figures as far as human, spirit, or divine identity was concerned. Abraham's three visitors are alternately spoken of as "three men" and "the Lord" (Gen 18:1-33).

By the time of the Second Temple (that is, post-exile), as Richard Bauckham explains, the "Jewish understanding of the divine uniqueness does not define it as unitariness and does not make distinctions within the divine identity inconceivable."[25] So there was no "obstacle to the inclusion of Jesus in the unique divine identity,"[26] as Creator of all things, sovereign ruler over all, exalted to the heavenly throne, and bearer of the divine name.[27] That is how they could reformulate their understanding of God to incorporate Jesus and use a "breathtaking renewed *Shema*"[28] as they do in 1 Corinthians 8:6.

It's been summed up by the acronym HANDS: indications of the deity of Jesus are found in the way he shares God's *H*onor, *A*ttributes, *N*ames, *D*eeds, and has a *S*eat next to God's throne.[29]

Jesus' Relation to the Father

Chair: We have already mentioned that Jesus never put his own filial relation to the Father in the same category as that of his disciples. As Son he seems to have been in a seamless relationship with the Father in a way we mere humans can never have in this life. John, you dwell on this quite a bit in your Gospel. Can you help us here?

John: There were certainly some memorable moments that revealed just how close the Father and Son were. Let me highlight a couple by way of illustration and reminder. First, there was the controversy that arose when Jesus healed the despairing old man at the pool of Bethesda, which took place on the sabbath (see Jn 5:1-15). When the Jewish leaders challenged Jesus about his "working" a miracle on the sabbath he replied, "My Father is always at his work to this very day, and I too am working" (Jn 5:17). Talk about pouring oil on a fire! By replying like this they thought he was "calling God his own Father [and] making himself equal with God," so they wanted to kill him (Jn 5:18). The conversation that followed revealed what deep harmony there was between what the Father and Son do (see Jn 5:19), what love the Father had for his Son (see Jn 5:20; cf. 3:35), and what complete openness there was between them as a result of this love. Furthermore, Jesus revealed some amazing parallels between the Father and the Son.

---

[25]Bauckham, *Jesus and the God of Israel*, 17.
[26]Ibid., 19.
[27]Ibid., 16-31.
[28]N. T. Wright, *Paul and the Faithfulness of God* (London: SPCK, 2013), 1516.
[29]Robert M. Bowman and J. Ed Komoszewski, *Putting Jesus in His Place: The Case for the Deity of Christ* (Grand Rapids: Kregel, 2007), 23, cited by Bird, *Evangelical Theology*, 470-72.

Both give life to people (see Jn 5:21). God, the Judge, had "entrusted all judgment to the Son" (Jn 5:22). The Son was to be honored as much as the Father (see Jn 5:23). As the Father was eternally self-existent, so the Son also had "life in himself" (Jn 5:26). And yet, for all their equality and intimacy, the Son lived in complete dependence on and obedience to his Father (see Jn 5:30; cf. 14:28).

As a second illustration, we could linger on sacred ground and eavesdrop on Jesus' prayer to his Father in the garden of Gethsemane (see Jn 17:1-26). It was a deep prayer, but let me draw out a few things that show the quality of their relationship. They were mutually engaged in glorifying each other— that is, in mutually displaying their "bright splendor."[30] Together they were the means of eternal life (see Jn 17:3). The disciples belonged both to the Father and to the Son (see Jn 17:6-19), and they had confidence that Jesus "came from you [the Father], and they believed that you sent me" (Jn 17:8). Most remarkable of all, Jesus' prayer for the disciples' unity caught them up in a sort of triangular relationship. He prayed that "the world will know that you sent me and have loved them even as you have loved me" (Jn 17:23). Jesus' claim to "know" the Father in a way "the world does not" and to have made him known to the disciples was a claim of great intimacy that arose out of the Father's love for the Son (Jn 17:25-26).

There's surely no way to express a closer intimacy between Father and Son than we find here, so much so that Jesus' claim "I and the Father are one" (Jn 10:30) didn't shock us.

Jesus' Relation to the Spirit

Chair: What about his relationship with the Holy Spirit, who came to be known as the third member of the Trinity?

Luke: When it comes to the life of Jesus, I'm the one who draws particular attention to the work of the Spirit in his ministry, with my fellow Synoptic Gospel writers overlapping to varying degrees. So I note the conception of Jesus as an act of the Spirit (see Lk 1:35) and the recognition of his special role both by "Aunt" Elizabeth and the aged Simeon as

> ## THE HOLY SPIRIT AND JESUS
>
> Mt 1:18, 20; 3:16; 4:1; Mk 1:10, 12.

---

[30]Eugene Peterson, *The Message* (Colorado Springs: NavPress, 2002).

inspired by the Spirit (see Lk 1:41; 2:25-27). In fact, the Spirit gets mentioned three times in connection with Simeon's brief appearance on the stage. At Jesus' baptism, "the Holy Spirit descended on him" (Lk 3:22) and afterward promptly led him into the wilderness for a showdown with Satan (see Lk 4:1), which must have been a bit of an anticlimax but was necessary if Jesus was to triumph over Satan and be a genuine Savior. When he came out of the wilderness he "returned to Galilee in the power of the Spirit" (Lk 4:14), where he announced, "The Spirit of the Lord is on me" (Lk 4:18), applying the synagogue reading of Isaiah 61:1 to himself. Once when he prayed he was "full of joy through the Holy Spirit" (Lk 10:21).

Matthew: Jesus quoted Isaiah several times, and I once used Isaiah 42:1, one of the "servant songs," to explain to a large crowd who had just witnessed many healings that it was because God's Spirit was on him (see Mt 12:18). In the controversy that followed, Jesus didn't back down but again said that he drove out demons "by the Spirit of God" (Mt 12:28).

John: My way of saying some of that is to cite Jesus' own comment that "the one whom God has sent speaks the words of God, for God gives the Spirit without limit" (Jn 3:34). His was a life in which the Spirit was not partially present, nor intermittently present, nor subject to ebb and flow, but was constantly full to overflowing.

We learned more about the relationship between the two of them from the teaching he gave to his disciples in that last week of his life when they were together in the "upper room." The Spirit, he taught, was his alter ego. Having declared himself to be "the way and the truth and the life" (Jn 14:6), he assured his disciples that when he had departed he would send "another advocate" (Jn 14:16)—the word *another* here meant another of the same kind rather than another of a different kind—known as the "Spirit of truth" (Jn 14:17), whom he then identified as "the Holy Spirit" (Jn 14:26). And in case we didn't get how close their relationship is, Jesus slipped from talking about sending the Spirit to saying, "I will come to you" in the same breath (Jn 14:18). The Spirit would be sent, he said, "in my name" and would remind them "of everything I have said to you" (Jn 14:26).

He revisited the topic a little later, trying to convince his disciples that it was even "for your good that I am going away. [For] unless I go away, the Advocate will not come to you" (Jn 16:7). The word *Advocate* in Greek is *paraklētos*; it is difficult to translate in English, but it means something like "an active defender." Well, after his departure, the Advocate would guide their understanding of the truth needed for their mission. Like Jesus, he wouldn't invent his message but would "speak only what he hears" (Jn 16:13; cf. 3:34; 7:17; 8:28). And just as Jesus passed on what he'd received from the Father, so the Spirit would pass on what he had received from Jesus (see Jn 16:15). They are inseparable.

Luke: That's exactly what happened with the early church—but let's take one step back before I explain that. There is one comment John the Baptizer made about Jesus that was so significant that all four of us Gospel writers record it. In my version John said, "I baptize you with water. But one who is more powerful than I will come, the

> ### JOHN THE BAPTIZER ON JESUS
>
> Mt 3:11; Mk 1:7-8; Jn 1:33-34.

straps of whose sandals I am not worthy to untie. He will baptize you with the Holy Spirit and fire" (Lk 3:16). Jesus wasn't only the bearer of the Holy Spirit but also the dispenser of the Holy Spirit.[31] I took this to be a reference to what happened at Pentecost (although some have thought it applied to individuals).[32] My second volume reports the dynamic power of the Holy Spirit at work, so much that some call it "the Acts of the Holy Spirit"; but I conceived it from beginning to end as a record of "all that Jesus began to do and to teach" (Acts 1:1). His mission continued to the final chapter "with all boldness and without hindrance!" (Acts 28:31). The Spirit really was the one who pointed to Jesus and magnified him.

Paul: There's much more to say about the Spirit, and I'm sure we'll return to looking at him in his own right later. For the moment our focus is on Jesus and the Spirit, so let me just add that I have no doubts that, even if in some respects we can distinguish them, they're so closely identified with each other as to be inseparable. I'm more than happy to assert that, "if anyone does not have the Spirit of Christ, they do not belong to Christ" (Rom 8:9). You simply can't have one without the other. Once I even described him as "the Spirit of Jesus Christ" (Phil 1:19).

---

[31] Adapted from Bird, *Evangelical Theology*, 344.
[32] See further chap. 7, 163-66.

Implicit Trinitarianism

Chair: Does all this amount to a doctrine of the Trinity?

Observer: It is hard to avoid the conclusion that this is the clear direction in which the New Testament authors are pointing, even if the doctrine of the Trinity was not formulated properly until the Athanasian Creed around the fifth century.

> ### TRINITARIAN PASSAGES
>
> 1 Cor 12:3-7; 2 Cor 1:21-22; Eph 1:3-14; 2 Thess 2:13-14; Tit 3:4-7; 1 Pet 1:2; 1 Jn 4:2-3; Rev 1:4-5.

Already in the New Testament we see the three persons of the Godhead involved at the baptism of Jesus (see Mt 3:16-17) and we are instructed to baptize new disciples "in the name of the Father and of the Son and of the Holy Spirit" (Mt 28:19). The threefold-but-one nature of God is implicit in so many of the writings, perhaps even unconsciously, as when Paul writes in Romans 1:1-4 about "the gospel of God . . . regarding his Son . . . through the Spirit," or in 1 Corinthians 2:1-4 where he writes about "the testimony about God . . . [knowing] nothing while I was with you except Jesus Christ . . . with a demonstration of the Spirit's power." Some argue, without convincing evidence, that the trinitarian benediction of 2 Corinthians 13:14 is a later addition. Even if that were true, the trinitarian structure of several passages penned by some writers is so obvious that the doctrine cannot be marginalized.

The Athanasian Creed, which spoke of God as one substance yet three persons, was building on the earlier work of Athanasius (ca. 296–373) and Augustine (354–430), and was also building on solid New Testament foundations. Its poetic style means it is often used in liturgy. It includes the words:

That we worship one God in Trinity, and Trinity in Unity;

Neither confounding the Persons: nor dividing the Substance.

For there is one Person of the Father, another of the Son, and another of the Holy Ghost.

But the Godhead of the Father, of the Son, and of the Holy Ghost, is all one:

The Glory equal, the Majesty co-eternal.

Chair: Time to turn to our next topic. Having discussed who Jesus was, it's time to ask what Jesus did. Exactly how was he good news?

6

How Was Jesus Good News?

Chair: We've established that in the eyes of the early Christians Jesus was the unique Son of God, Messiah and Lord, and, indeed, God himself living on earth in human form. However, while that itself is good news, it is not really sufficient in itself. We surely need to ask more about what he did while here on earth, about his life, mission, teaching, and especially about his manner of leaving the earth, if we're to get our heads around how he was good news for us.

THE KINGDOM OF GOD

Chair: Let's start with the great theme around which everything in his life revolved: the kingdom of God.

Mark: That's a great place to start. His first public pronouncement said the good news was about exactly that. "'The time has come,' he said. 'The kingdom of God has come near. Repent and believe the good news!'" (Mk 1:15; cf. Mt 4:17; 9:35). To be honest, his sayings about the kingdom of God could be enigmatic and multifaceted, so we didn't always understand them at first—but some things were clear from that first sermon. He announced that God was taking over

> **MARK'S REFERENCES TO THE KINGDOM OF GOD**
>
> 1:15; 4:11, 26, 30; 9:1, 47; 10:14-15, 23-25; 11:10; 12:34; 14:25; 15:43.

his world again. The revolution had begun. God was taking back control from Satan who, through deception, had usurped his legitimate authority. What's more, this kingdom "has come near." The words *come near (engiken)* probably should be understood as "a declaration of arrival"[1] rather than merely "It's on its way." The arrival of this kingdom coincided with the arrival of Jesus, and it became increasingly clear that this was no mere coincidence. He not only *brought* good news; he *was* the good news. He would inaugurate God's kingdom and bring it to its consummation. So he threw out the challenge for people to repent, which meant to throw off their allegiance to Satan and take their stand behind Jesus and believe the message he was bringing.

Background to the Kingdom

Observer: "The kingdom of God" is the central message of the Gospels and occurs (depending on how you count them) ninety times on the lips of Jesus and 122 times in all in the New Testament. Mark's comment that "Joseph of Arimathea, a prominent member of the [Jewish] Council . . . was himself waiting for the kingdom of God" (Mk 15:43) suggests the idea was widely known in Jesus' day. However, since the phrase "kingdom of God" is never actually used in the Old Testament, where did the idea come from?

The phrase may not be found in the Old Testament, but the idea is there in several ways. First, Israel recognized God as their only King, at least to start with (see 1 Sam 12:12). "The LORD," to quote Psalm 95:3, "is the great God, the great King above all gods." Such quotations could be multiplied. Israel worshiped the God who reigns (see Ps 5:2; 97:1; 99:1). As his chosen people, Israel were in a covenant relationship with him. Weak peoples entered into covenants with stronger powers so that they would be protected and provided for. The covenant always required the weaker party to submit to the stronger party's rule. So, as stressed in Deuteronomy, which sets out the covenant, Israel could only depend on God's blessing providing they exclusively worshiped and wholeheartedly obeyed his commands (see Deut 28:1-2; 30:17-18). So God was their Sovereign and King. David ruled Israel on his behalf as his viceregent and at the best led them to experience the blessings of the covenant.

---

[1] R. T. France, *Divine Governance: God's Kingship in the Gospel of Mark* (London: SPCK, 1990), 24.

However, as the nations increasingly persecuted Israel and Judah, the consciousness that God's kingdom was in conflict with the "kingdoms of the earth" became more prominent in their thinking. This reached its peak in Daniel's writing, which gave voice to the conviction that God's "dominion is an eternal dominion; his kingdom endures from generation to generation" (Dan 4:34). As hopes continued to disappoint, Israel didn't jettison their belief in God's covenant or his reign, but looked forward to a new covenant (Jer 31; Ezek 34) and to the future day when "The LORD will be king over the whole earth" (Zech 14:9; cf. Is 9:6-7; 45:23).

The concept had become so firmly established that the closing prayer (the *Kaddish*) in the synagogue contained the words: "Exalted and hallowed be his great name in the world which he created according to his will. May he let his kingdom rule in your lifetime and in your days and in the lifetime of the whole house of Israel, speedily and soon."[2]

So there were plenty of sources that flowed into the concept of the kingdom of God, which would have been a common, if ill-understood, idea by the time of Jesus.

The Kingdom Has Arrived

Matthew: Mark rightly identifies the kingdom of God as a key theme of Jesus' life and teaching, and both Luke and I borrow from him and build on the sayings he quotes. I use the phrase "kingdom of heaven" rather than "of God" out of respect for the Jewish way of avoiding mentioning the sacred name,[3] but it means the same thing.

There are lots of different strands to it. Perhaps the overwhelming impression was that, with the coming of Jesus, God really was reasserting his authority again. We saw that in the miracles he did and the exorcisms he conducted as people were released from Satan's bondage. When John the Baptizer expressed some doubts about Jesus from his prison cell, Jesus told

---

[2]Jeremias's translation. Joachim Jeremias, *New Testament Theology*, trans. John Bowden, vol. 1 (London: SCM Press, 1971), 243.

[3]Joel Green points out that this may not be the reason Matthew uses *kingdom of heaven* rather than *kingdom of God*, since Matthew does not avoid using the divine name elsewhere. He suggests Matthew does so because he is influenced by Dan 2–7 where God, as heavenly King, is in contrast to earthly kings. Joel B. Green, *Why Salvation?* (Nashville: Abingdon Press, 2013), 99.

the messengers to report what they had heard and seen: "the blind receive sight, the lame walk, those who have leprosy are cleansed, the deaf hear, the dead are raised, and the good news is proclaimed to the poor" (Mt 11:2-6). This was exactly what Isaiah 35:5-6 led us to believe would characterize the coming of God to the earth again. It was as if Jesus had entered a strong man's house, subdued him, and carried off his possessions (see Mt 12:29). This was all a thinly disguised reference to Satan holding people captive. His releasing people from Satan's tyranny meant, as Jesus said, that "the kingdom of God [had] come upon [them]" (Mt 12:28). The kingdom of God really had arrived.

As far as his teaching goes, he would often speak of "entering the kingdom" (Mt 5:20; 7:21; 18:3; 19:23-24; 21:31; 23:13; with 18:8-9 being a variation on the same theme), by which he meant coming under God's rule. He made it clear that entering his kingdom was no easy thing to do since it required most people to change radically the direction of their lives, to become humble (see Mt 19:13-14), poor (see Mt 19:16-30), and totally commit themselves to it (see Mt 13:44-46). It would result in keeping company with those "unruly" people society avoided (see Mt 9:10-13; 18:1-5; 20:16). It might even result in being subject to violence (see Mt 11:12).[4] Yet it would all be worth it, for entering his kingdom was like going to a party (see Mt 9:9-13; 11:16-19) or finding a treasure of great value (see Mt 13:44-46).

His Sermon on the Mount sets out the lifestyle of those who are citizens of God's kingdom (see Mt 5–7).[5] From the start, this sermon turned everything we'd learned on its head. It was the poor, not the rich; the mournful, not the happy-go-lucky; the meek, not those who threw their weight around; the merciful, not the hard-nosed realists; and so on, who were blessed by God. The standards God required weren't measured by external acts but by inner attitudes. We were supposed to love enemies, give generously, pray privately, trust unwaveringly, and judge ourselves rather than others. Being a true disciple, or citizen of this kingdom, meant persisting on a narrow, unpopular path; but when the storms of God's judgment blew, we'd know we had built on the right foundations.

Both his actions and his teaching led people to believe that the kingdom of David, for which they had longed, was about to be restored. So, very near

---

[4]This is a difficult verse to translate, but the NIV rendering, on which this comment rests, is to be preferred.
[5]See further chap. 9, 216-18.

the end of his life, as he went into Jerusalem on a donkey—the only time he did anything other than walk, except when he was in a boat—they greeted him like a celebrity, or more than a celebrity: as royalty, as David's Son, who came in the Lord's name (see Mt 21:1-11) to restore the kingdom to Israel. Little did they understand that his kingdom was not the nationalistic kingdom they had in mind but rather was to be a community of disciples from many nations who would come to obey his teaching (see Mt 28:19-20).

Chair: Luke, have you anything to add to what Matthew has said so far?

Luke: Assuming that Matthew will mention later that Jesus also spoke about the kingdom as if it was yet to arrive, I've little to add. My picture of Jesus is encapsulated by what happened when the crowds followed him one day, and "he welcomed them and spoke to them about the kingdom of God, and healed those who needed healing" (Lk 9:11). The kingdom was something he delighted to share, and he looked forward to sharing it more completely with his disciples (see Lk 12:32; 22:29-30). Oh, and as you can imagine by now, I'm not shy in talking about the undesirable status, as judged by normal, "respectable" standards, of those who will be found in the kingdom—like those who are excluded from temple worship because they are "the poor, the crippled, the lame and the blind" (Lk 14:15-24). God's kingdom does turn everything upside down.

John: Before we go any further, let me clear up a possible misunderstanding. I don't mention the kingdom of God in my Gospel except on three occasions (Jn 3:3, 5; 18:36), but that is simply because I use the term *eternal life* (of which more later), which isn't identical but overlaps significantly.

Observer: We should note that Jesus' teaching that the kingdom was already present was a radical modification of the traditional Jewish view. To paraphrase George Eldon Ladd, the Jewish view, both in the Old Testament and in the Judaism of Jesus' day, "looked forward to a single day" that would occur at the end of the age when God's reign would begin. They called it the Day of the Lord.[6] Jesus, however, taught (and demonstrated) that that day had already arrived, even if not yet fully. So the future had been brought forward, and people now live in the overlap of two ages.

---

[6]G. E. Ladd, *A Theology of the New Testament*, ed. D. A. Hagner, 2nd ed. (Grand Rapids: Eerdmans, 1974), 66.

The Kingdom Has Not Yet Fully Arrived

Matthew: There is this other dimension to Jesus' teaching of the kingdom. So far, we've concentrated on the way Jesus taught it was already present among us. That could sometimes encourage unwise speculation as to how soon a political revolution was going to be triggered. So he also taught us that we wouldn't experience the full realization of the kingdom immediately. That's why he taught us to pray, "Your kingdom come," in the model prayer he gave his disciples (Mt 6:9-13; cf. Lk 11:2-4). He wouldn't have taught us that if it had completely arrived already.

Much of his teaching on this took the form of parables. I collected several of them together in chapter 13 of my Gospel. The parable of the weeds points to a future harvest "at the end of the age" (Mt 13:24-30, 36-43); those of the mustard seed and the yeast point to future growth, with the yeast working "all through the dough," signaling God's kingdom permeating the whole world (Mt 13:31-35); and the parable of the net refers to the separation again "at the end of the age" (Mt 13:47-50).

Several other parables are found in chapter 25. They have an edge to them, warning us to be ready for his return. There's the parable of the ten virgins, only some of whom were prepared for the bridegroom's arrival (see Mt 25:1-13). That's followed by the parable about a slave owner who went away and then returned "after a long time" and required his slaves to account for how they'd used the resources he had given them before he left on his journey (Mt 25:14-30; cf. Luke 19:11-27). Then there's the parable about the separation of sheep and goats, a parable in fact about God's justice being put into effect "when the Son of Man comes in his glory" (Mt 25:31-46). Luke records that same point in his parable of the persistent widow, where God promises that his chosen ones will receive justice, which he immediately connects with "when the Son of Man comes" (Lk 18:1-8). Jesus taught that his coming again to consummate his kingdom work would be like the arrival of a burglar. His return will occur suddenly at an unexpected, unknown hour (see Mt 24:36-51)—more on that later.

Kingdom Secrecy

Mark: There was something a little mysterious about Jesus' teaching about the kingdom. I'm not thinking of the way he often instructed demons and the people he'd healed not to say anything about it (see Mk 1:34, 43-45; 5:43; 7:36; 8:26); that was understandable. He was trying to keep the lid on things so people wouldn't jump to the wrong conclusions about the kind of Messiah or King he was going to be and prematurely force his hand.

No, the sort of enigma I have in mind is the way he'd tell parables and then ask if we understood them. They were good stories, and of course we understood them at one level. Their deeper meaning, though, often mystified even his disciples, despite him saying, "The secret of the kingdom of God has been given to you. But to those on the outside everything is said in parables" (Mk 4:11). He supported this comment with a quotation from Isaiah 6:9-10 about people seeing but not perceiving, hearing but not understanding, "otherwise they might turn and be forgiven" (Mk 4:12). Well, traditionally, a parable means a riddle or enigma, which is what his were![7]

Kingdom parables were a mystery in the sense of being hidden to those who lacked faith. The truth is that they weren't hidden at all from those who believed. They were revealed to them. They weren't like a mystery religion when only a select few insiders can solve the puzzle; their mystery was proclaimed to all. It wasn't hard to grasp, nor really incomprehensible. The key to understanding them was to have faith. They were privileged information for his disciples—but anyone could become a disciple.[8]

What Happened to the Kingdom?

Chair: While the kingdom of God was the central message of Jesus, it wasn't that prominent in the preaching and writing of his followers subsequently, was it?

Luke: That's a bit of an overstatement, Chair. If you read the Acts, you'll see it still gets a fair mention. Philip "proclaimed the good news of the kingdom of God" in Samaria (Acts 8:12). Paul talked about it in Syrian Antioch (see Acts 14:22) and spoke of it continuously for three months in Ephesus (see Acts 19:8). In Thessalonica he was speaking kingdom language when he preached that "there is another king" (Acts 17:7). When he reached Rome he took all day "explaining about the kingdom of God" (Acts 28:23). My final glimpse of him has him still "proclaim[ing] the kingdom of God" (Acts 28:31). And that's only a few select reports—the tip of the iceberg, if you like. They were very sure that Jesus was the King who was putting in place God's ultimate rule. So perhaps one reason why

---

[7]G. R. Beasley-Murray, *Jesus and the Kingdom of God* (Grand Rapids: Eerdmans, 1986), 105.
[8]See further, R. T. France, *The Gospel of Mark*, New International Greek Testament Commentary (Grand Rapids: Eerdmans, 2002), 196.

the idea of "the kingdom of God" occurs less is that they talked more about the King than about the kingdom. A second reason, perhaps, is that the idea of the kingdom made more sense to those who had a Jewish background than to the Gentiles. So the same message tended to get translated into another language.

Paul: Good for Luke. It is possible to get things out of proportion. I may introduce a number of other key perspectives on the gospel, some of which are closely associated with my name, but I still use "kingdom of God" language. I refer to it ten times in my letters, just as the Gospels do: either as something we are experiencing now (see Rom 14:17; 1 Cor 4:20; Col 4:11; 1 Thess 2:12), or as something to be inherited in the future (see 1 Cor 6:9-10; 15:24, 50; Gal 5:21; Eph 5:5; 2 Thess 1:5).

I, as much as anyone, have a vision of the future when God will reign completely and unopposed. This "end will come, when [Christ] hands over the kingdom to God the Father after he has destroyed all dominion, authority and power." Christ himself reigns in the interim, "until he has put all his enemies under his feet. The last enemy to be destroyed is death" (1 Cor 15:24-26). Make no mistake: although I may not always use the phrase or even the code word, the same idea is often found—as, for example, in Philippians 2:5-22 and Colossians 1:15-20. God is establishing his kingdom, albeit "in a totally new and unexpected way,"[9] through Jesus and his Spirit.

Chair: Do any of the rest of you make anything of it?

James: Sometimes the true significance of an idea is not measured by *how often* it's used but by *how* it's used. In line with the Gospels, I mention that "God [has] chosen those who are poor in the eyes of the world to be rich in faith and to inherit the kingdom he promised those who love him" (Jas 2:5). That just goes to show how much ideas about the kingdom had sunk into our consciousnesses.

The Hebraist: I use *kingdom* only once (Heb 1:8), when I'm quoting Psalm 45:6, but God's sovereign rule permeates my book. I transpose the talk about the kingdom into talk about the "throne." A throne, after all, is the focal point of a kingdom. The idea of the throne conjures up a vision of majesty, but the description I like most is that it is a "throne of grace" (Heb 4:16).

---

[9]N. T. Wright, *Paul and the Faithfulness of God* (London: SPCK, 2013), 733.

John: Well, you'll know just how often I mention the kingdom and the throne. Sometimes, as James has just said, I just slip it in because it's a given for believers. So I describe myself to my readers as "your brother and companion in the suffering *and kingdom* and patient endurance that are ours in Jesus" (Rev 1:9). My readers are people who've been made "a kingdom and priests" (Rev 1:6; 5:10; cf. 1 Pet 2:9). Usually, of course, I portray the theme on a much larger and more stunning canvas than that. So, in chapters 4 and 5, the scene is set in God's throne room in heaven where he and the Lamb, who is also "at the center of the throne," are worshiped both by the redeemed and by the whole of creation. Then the climax is reached: "I heard a loud voice in heaven say: 'Now have come the salvation and the power and the kingdom of our God, and the authority of his Messiah. For the accuser of our brothers and sisters, who accuses them before our God day and night, has been hurled down'" (Rev 12:10). This is one of a couple of battle scenes in my apocalypse that celebrate the triumph of God and the final defeat of evil in all its forms. The battle for sovereignty over creation, which began in Eden, will finally be over, and God's invincible rule will be established for ever and ever. But then, in all honesty, Satan's was always a lost cause. So I have the privilege of bringing the "kingdom of God" theme to its final resolution.

Kingdom Ethics

Chair: Awesome. It makes you want to join in the choirs of heaven already, but we must pursue our task here on earth for the moment. I'm aware that quite a bit of Jesus' teaching about God's kingdom contained instructions as to how its citizens should live. Jesus taught them, for example, to "seek first his kingdom and his righteousness" (Mt 6:33). I'm going to suggest, though, that we leave the matter of how God's subjects are to behave—what is sometimes called "kingdom ethics"—until later.[10]

Instead, I want us to examine the life of Jesus more fully.

THE LIFE AND MINISTRY OF JESUS

Chair: Sometimes people speak as if the life of Jesus was merely a preface to the cross, where the real business of salvation was done; but it must have greater significance than that. The documents show no interest in his

---

[10]See chap. 9, 216-18.

physical appearance. We know something of his family, who apparently didn't share his convictions during his lifetime (see Mk 3:31-32; 6:1-2), that he owned no home of his own (see Mt 8:20), and that he was constantly on the road, relying on the hospitality of friends (see Mt 26:6; Mk 14:3; Lk 10:38-42). What more can we say about his life?

His Sense of Sonship

Luke: Let me take the lead and speak for the other Synoptic Gospel writers. One of the most immediate impressions people gained of Jesus was his close and intimate relationship with God his Father. Right at the start of his public ministry his cousin John baptized him in the River Jordan. "As he was praying, heaven was opened. . . . And a voice came from heaven: 'You are my Son, whom I love; with you I am well pleased'" (Lk 3:21-22; cf. Mt 3:16-17; Mk 1:11). That was an unprecedented endorsement of his relationship with God, and it colored all his ministry from then on.

He taught his disciples to pray to God as "Father" (Lk 11:2; Mt 6:9), which was a pretty unusual thing for Jews to do at the time. Mark recalls how in the garden of Gethsemane Jesus even used the word *Abba* when addressing God (Mk 14:36). That was a much more intimate, though respectful, Aramaic term than the usual word for "father." I didn't come across that when I was researching for my Gospel, but I did learn of the way Jesus addressed God twice from the cross using the normal term, *Pater*. First, he asked his "Father" to forgive those who were crucifying him (Lk 23:34), and, second, he prayed, "Father, into your hands I commit my spirit" (Lk 23:46). Both of these showed him to be a trusting Son who had faith in his Father to the last.

Matthew: Interesting. I don't quote those sayings from the cross, but I agree with what Luke has just said. I recall his praying one day and saying, "All things have been committed to me by my Father. No one knows the Son except the Father, and no one knows the Father except the Son and those to whom the Son chooses to reveal him" (Mt 11:27; cf. Lk 10:22). That sounds like something John would record in his Gospel, but I record it because it spoke of the uniquely intimate relationship Jesus had with God.

John: That does indeed sound like an extract from my Gospel, Matthew, but it isn't. I've a lot of similar sayings and claims, but I've already had a few good innings and won't add to what I said earlier.[11]

---

[11]See chap. 5, 82.

> **Observer:** A later writer summed it up like this: "In short, we can say with some confidence that Jesus experienced an intimate relation of sonship in prayer: he found God characteristically to be 'Father' and this sense of God was so real, so loving, so compelling, that whenever he turned to God it was the cry 'Abba' that came to his lips."[12]

His Teaching

Chair: From what we might call his religious experience, let's turn to his teaching. We have already explored his teaching about the kingdom of God, although there is more to say about the ethics of kingdom living; but not all his teaching is neatly packaged under the heading of "kingdom," so what else might we say about it?

Luke: Before we get too far into what he taught, let me comment on how he taught. Don't be misled by the word *teaching* into thinking that he sat his disciples down in a classroom and stood at the front unloading previously prepared lesson plans on them. On occasions he taught them as they gathered around him in groups, but much of his teaching was on the road. It arose as they were walking and seemed almost a spontaneous response to what they encountered, even though he clearly wasn't making it up on the spot. His parable about a good Samaritan (see Lk 10:25-37) and his teaching on a narrow door (see Lk 13:22-28), lost possessions, including a lost son (see Lk 15:1-32), a widow's offering (see Lk 21:1-4), and the destruction of the temple (see Lk 21:5-38) all illustrate this.

Matthew: Agreed, but I'm much more anxious to get to the content of that teaching, which I arrange, as any decent teacher would, into organized sections so that it's not haphazard or piecemeal. It's found in chapters 5–7; 10; 13; 18; and 23–25.

The heart of his teaching lay in the command to love.[13] He said that the greatest commandments were, first, to "love the Lord your God with all your heart and with all your soul and with all your mind"; and, second, to "love your neighbor as yourself" (Mt 22:37-40; Mk 12:29-31; Lk 10:27). Much of his instruction was determined by this dual command. The former was to do with worship, prayer, giving, inner purity, and honoring God by one's

---

[12]James D. G. Dunn, *Jesus and the Spirit*, New Testament Library (London: SCM Press, 1975), 26.
[13]See further chap. 9, 213-16.

lifestyle. Much of that lifestyle was demonstrated in how we loved the real people we shared our lives and journeys with. So, if we truly loved as Christ taught, we wouldn't retaliate (see Mt 5:38-42), would forgive those who offended us (see Mt 6:14-15), and would love even our enemies, providing hospitality not just to those who'd invite us back but also to those who weren't in a position to do so (see Mt 5:43-48).

It was all quite revolutionary. That last bit, for example, completely undermined the values everyone had been taught, which was that you were to judge carefully what relationships you entered into to ensure they were to your advantage. We lived in a reciprocal culture, one where you only gave when you were going to receive some benefit in return—not the sort of generous and uncalculating giving Jesus advocated. It would have been thought absurd by most people to live like that. In teaching this, however, Jesus claimed not to be overriding the law but rather capturing its real meaning, one that had been forgotten over the years since it had been buried beneath a load of rabbinic interpretations (see Mt 5:17-20). It was all summed up by the golden rule: "do to others what you would have them do to you" (Mt 7:12; Lk 6:31). It made perfect sense when you thought about it, but it was different from the way we'd been accustomed to living.

John: The teaching of Jesus that really concerns me is about his identity. I record some lengthy dialogues he had on that topic especially with Jewish leaders, such as in 5:16-47; 6:25-59; 8:12-58—but I equally stress his teaching on love. Just after Jesus had predicted his betrayal by Judas and denial by Peter, just before that final Passover, he said to his disciples, "A new command I give you: love one another. As I have loved you, so you must love one another. By this everyone will know that you are my disciples, if you love one another" (Jn 13:34-35).

Luke: I want to explore further the radical nature of his teaching that Matthew highlighted a moment ago. As he mentioned, Jesus was constantly turning conventional thinking on its head. He does it in the Beatitudes (see Lk 6:20-26; cf. Mt 5:1-12) when he teaches that those who are poor, hungry, mournful, and persecuted, rather than the rich, well fed, happy, and free, are the ones who are truly blessed. His parables are riddled with it, as when he talks about a master waiting on his servants (see Lk 12:37); or a rich man going to Hades while Lazarus, a beggar, is enjoying bliss at Abraham's side (see Lk 16:19-31); or a tax collector being "justified" by God rather than the religiously respectable Pharisee (Lk 18:9-14). Who'd ever heard of such a thing? In challenging conventional purity rules, as he often did, or saying that God revealed himself to "little children" rather than to "the wise and learned" (Lk 10:21), he taught that God worked in a "topsy-turvy way."[14] It was all captured in his astonishing saying: "Indeed there are those who are last who will be first, and first who will be last" (Lk 13:30).

Chair: After the Gospels there is very little reference to what Jesus actually said: Luke records Paul quoting him only once, when saying goodbye to the elders in Ephesus (see Acts 20:35). Let's establish first how much he's actually cited and then ask ourselves why so little.

Paul: You'll find I quote what the Lord told me on three occasions in my letters (1 Cor 7:10; 9:14; 11:23-26), with the last of these about the Lord's Supper also quoting a few words from the Gospels (Mt 26:26-27; Mk 14:22-24). People have quite rightly found some very clear echoes of Jesus' teaching elsewhere in my writings—namely, in Romans 12:14, 17; 13:7; 14:13-14; 1 Corinthians 13:2; and 1 Thessalonians 5:2, 13, 15. The links are obvious even if I didn't put the words in quotation marks (but then we didn't use quotation marks in my day!). The Gospel writers had told us what the Messiah said and did. I was more concerned about what it meant.

Chair: James, as the Lord's brother writing about the practice of Christian living, we might have expected you to quote Jesus, but you don't do so even once.

James: No, I don't—but my letter is clearly immersed in his teaching nonetheless. The point is that, writing in the wisdom tradition, it wasn't our custom to quote our teachers. Instead, we imbibed their teaching, reflected on it deeply, and then creatively and freely reexpressed it to apply to the new situations we were facing, rather than slavishly repeating it.[15] So you can't drive a wedge between what I wrote and what my half brother, Jesus, taught.

Chair: Others of you don't quote Jesus even where it's clear you are following his teaching. So where does that leave us?

---

[14]Joel Green, *The Gospel of Luke*, New International Commentary on the New Testament (Grand Rapids: Eerdmans, 1997), 423.
[15]See further, Richard Bauckham, *James*, New Testament Readings (New York: Routledge, 1999), 30.

Observer: Perhaps this is a place where a little distance is needed. Some have tried to argue that there are two versions of Christianity: one pre-Pentecost, focused on Jesus and his simple ethical teaching, and one post-Pentecost, which develops a dehistoricized, theological Christ. Such a solution is, however, unnecessary and flies in the face of the close connection evident between the pre- and post-Pentecost presentation of the gospel of Jesus.[16]

There is a simple answer to this contention. N. T. Wright expresses it well when he refers to there being "a twofold pattern: first the Messiah's work; second, the apostolic ministry through which that work is put into operation." There is, he says, a "to-and-fro between the unique *achievement* of the Messiah and its *implementation* in the work of the gospel." He illustrates it from 2 Corinthians 5:15, which speaks first of what Christ did—"he died for all"—and then of what this meant—"that those who live should no longer live for themselves but for him who died for them and was raised again."[17]

There is no gospel without history. What happened in the life, death, and resurrection of Jesus matters (see 1 Cor 15:1-8). However, merely repeating history is not gospel either. The events through which God revealed himself in Christ need interpreting, applying, and, above all, appropriating by faith. So the Synoptic Gospel writers essentially tell us what happened, with some implicit theology under the surface. The apostles tell us why it happened, what difference it makes, and what we should do about it. With them the actual events and sayings of Jesus become largely implicit and just under the surface.

His Demonstration of the Kingdom

Chair: To some extent we have already covered Jesus' demonstration of the kingdom, but it's worth revisiting.

Mark: I'm certainly anxious to do so. My Gospel doesn't ignore Jesus' teaching, as some wrongly suggest it does, but it's true the others say more about that while I bring his actions center stage. Having said that the good

---

[16]For those who want to explore this further, see David Wenham, *Paul: Follower of Jesus or Founder of Christianity?* (Grand Rapids: Eerdmans, 1995).

[17]Wright, *Paul and the Faithfulness of God*, 880.

news is about the in-breaking of the kingdom of God, I give plenty of evidence to show that God was reestablishing his reign. So the first miracle I mention is when he visited the synagogue at Capernaum one sabbath and cast out a demon from a man who was present (see Mk 1:21-28). The spirit didn't leave quietly! From then on Jesus "drove out many demons" and "healed many who had

> ## MARK'S REFERENCES TO THE KINGDOM OF GOD
>
> 1:15; 4:11, 26, 30; 9:1, 47; 10:14-15, 23-25; 11:10; 12:34; 14:25; 15:43.

various diseases" (Mk 1:34). There were other types of miracles too, besides healing—such as when he calmed the storm (see Mk 4:37-41); fed the five thousand (see Mk 6:35-44); walked on water (see Mk 6:47-51); fed four thousand (see Mk 8:1-9); and cursed a fig tree (see Mk 11:12-14, 20-25). That's quite a tally for no more than a couple of years of public ministry, especially because Matthew and Luke record some other miracles as well.

The significance of these miraculous acts, in addition to the value they had for the people involved, was, first, that they showed us a glimpse of his true identity,[18] and, second, that they gave us a glimpse of what the world would be like if God ruled it without opposition. People would be free and at peace rather than falling apart because of inner demons,

> ## OTHER MIRACLES IN MARK
>
> Exorcisms: 1:39; 3:7-12; 5:1-20; 7:24-30; 9:14-29.
> Healings: 1:29-34, 40-42; 2:3-12; 3:1-5; 5:22-43; 6:56; 7:24-30, 31-37; 8:22-26; 10:46-52.

bodies would be whole, resources like food would be ample for all, and nature would be under control rather than potentially destructive.

John: As we've said, I don't use the language of the kingdom much, but I do record my own favorite miracles, such as his changing water into wine at Cana (see Jn 2:1-11) and raising Lazarus (see Jn 11:1-44; see also 4:46-54; 5:1-9; 21:1-14). The thing I want to say, though, is that I deliberately call

---

[18]G. R. Beasley-Murray explains the way the miracles variously "bear witness to the nature of the lordship of Jesus" as Savior of the world, master of evil powers, prince of creation, revealer of God, and bestower of life. *Preaching the Gospel from the Gospels* (Peabody, MA: Hendrickson, 1996), 67-105.

miracles "signs." So, commenting on Cana, I say that this "was the first of the signs through which he revealed his glory" (Jn 2:11). Signs point to something else, and, in this case, they pointed to his glory, to eternal life—or, if you like, to God's coming kingdom. The signs were a foretaste of the reality we'll one day experience fully when God's universal reign triumphs.

His Active Obedience

Chair: Earlier we mentioned that Jesus Christ was sinless, but that needs probing further. First, it comes at Jesus' life negatively, defining him in terms of what he did not do. Can we come at it positively, defining him as actively not only doing good to people, as Acts 10:38 says, but also being good in God's eyes? We can all perhaps avoid trouble, but that doesn't mean we're good. Second, can we explore whether he merely went along with God's will passively, even to the extent of being crucified, or whether we can say that he willingly and actively did God's will throughout his life?

The Hebraist: That's an important issue to me. God's preference, according to Psalm 40:6-8,[19] which I quote and unpack in 10:5-10, is not to receive endless animal sacrifices and offerings but for people to offer him obedient lives. Sacrifices should be resorted to only when they have failed to do that. It was essential that Jesus offered his Father the whole of his life in perfect obedience, including ultimately his body on the cross. It's because he is our substitute that "we have been made holy"—that is, set apart acceptably to God. If he had sinned, he would not have been qualified to achieve that, but would have had to offer sacrifice for his own sin. If he'd lived conforming to God's will only at surface level, outwardly conforming but inwardly resentful, he would've been just like the dumb animals that had no choice when they were put on the altar of sacrifice. It was necessary for him to offer genuinely free and willing obedience. As willful, sentient human beings who choose to sin, we need an equally willful, sentient human being who chooses to do right to be our substitute if we are to find atonement. His life was marked by obedience and perfection (see Heb 5:8-9).

John: There's a paradox in all this. No one has ever lived as freely as Jesus Christ did, liberated from conventions, people's opinions, or social restraints, and yet no one has ever been more dependent on God or more obedient to him than Jesus. He lived out exactly what he said: "I have come down from

---

[19]Cf. 1 Sam 15:22.

heaven not to do my will but to do the will of him who sent me" (Jn 6:38). Voluntary obedience was the hallmark of his life and of his death (see Jn 10:17-18).

Mark: Matthew, Luke, and I don't speak much about Jesus obeying God or doing his will. We were instead more impressed by the way evil spirits obeyed him and fled from his presence when he commanded them to. Even so, we make the point in different ways. We comment, for example, on his prayer life (see Mk 1:35; 6:46), when he "often withdrew to lonely places and prayed" (Lk 5:16), clearly communicating with his Father. The most outstanding example of this was in the garden of Gethsemane when, having asked *Abba* Father to remove the cup of suffering from him, he went on to pray, "Yet not what I will, but what you will" (Mk 14:36; cf. Mt 26:39; Lk 22:42). There can be no greater proof of his willing, active obedience than his praying this at such a moment.

Paul: I recognize with the others the crucial importance of his active obedience. Adam chose to disobey God, and the only way to reverse the dreadful consequences of that act was to find another man—a second Adam—who would choose to obey God from the heart (see Rom 5:19). He lived obediently even to the point of facing death (see Phil 2:7-8). So, yes, the way he lived, as well as the way he died, was crucial for our salvation.

Observer: Later writers came to develop this further. Irenaeus (130–200) spoke in terms of "recapitulation." The incarnate Christ was all that Adam failed to be. By living the perfect and truly faithful human life from cradle to grave, he was able to restore humanity to communion with God and reverse Adam's disobedience.

John Calvin endorsed the idea, saying that it was a requirement of salvation that Adam's disobedience was countered by another man's obedience, to "satisfy the justice of God and pay the penalty for sin."[20] A little later, Calvin wrote that Christ accomplished the removal of "the enmity between God and us" "by the whole course of his life." His life was much more than a preface to his death, even though we acknowledge that salvation is "ascribed more peculiarly and specially to the death of Christ." "From the moment when he assumed the form of

---

[20]John Calvin, *Institutes of the Christian Religion* 2.12.3.

a servant," Calvin wrote, "he began, in order to redeem us, to pay the price of deliverance."[21]

A later writer, John Murray, argues that "the concept of obedience supplies us with an inclusive category in terms of which the atoning work of Christ may be viewed, and which established at the outset the active agency of Christ in the accomplishment of redemption."[22]

The whole life of Christ, including the manner of his death, exhibits an active obedience that resulted in our salvation. He was no passive victim, compelled to live in a way that had been imposed on him by God and then condemned to endure a brutal death. He was the one perfect human being because he was the one willingly obedient human being who in living and dying as he did accomplished our reconciliation with God.

His Fulfillment of Israel's Vocation

Chair: Some have seen another dimension to the life of Christ in that he personifies and fulfills all that Israel was called to be. What do you make of this?

The Hebraist: At its simplest, this is what I pointed out just now. As a covenant people, Israel was meant to live in complete obedience to God. But whereas they failed in that vocation, he fulfilled it to perfection (see Heb 10:5-10). He also brought to completion Israel's sabbath rest (see Heb 4:1-13), priesthood (see Heb 4:14–5:10; 7:1–8:5), final covenant (see Heb 8:6-13), temple (see Heb 9:1-28), and sacrificial system (see Heb 10:1-18).

Matthew: That's a good starting point and just the sort of thing I noted in Jesus. I see him as the fulfillment of Old Testament prophecies and say so on numerous occasions, quoting the prophecies he fulfilled. Indeed, some argue this is the central theme of my Gospel, and I wouldn't disagree.[23]

> **MATTHEW'S FULFILLMENT PASSAGES**
>
> 1:22-23; 2:5-6, 15, 17-18, 23; 4:14-16; 8:17; 12:17-21; 13:14, 35; 21:4-5; 26:54, 56; 27:9-10.

---

[21]Ibid., 2.16.5.

[22]John Murray, *Redemption: Accomplished and Applied* (Edinburgh: Banner of Truth, 1961), 24.

[23]R. T. France, *Matthew: Evangelist and Teacher* (Exeter: Paternoster, 1989), 166-205.

Take just one passage in my Gospel as an example, one that doesn't use the word *fulfill* to begin with, but that demonstrates the theme in glorious color. I'm thinking of 12:1-21, where several of the central concerns of Israel's faith are mentioned. There's the sabbath, King David, the law, the temple, sacrifices, and then, when I eventually do use my favorite fulfillment formula, the servant.

Jesus showed himself to be "Lord of the Sabbath" (Mt 12:8). The sabbath, originally intended to be a life-enhancing facility, had become an instrument of oppression. He showed himself Lord of it when he allowed his disciples to pick grain and healed a man's shriveled hand on the sabbath. King David is mentioned as a precedent here, and his reign was to become a much more important paradigm for the Messiah's work as the gospel unfolded.

The law was one of the prize assets of Israel, yet they didn't always understand its intent. Here, and frequently elsewhere, Jesus demonstrated through his actions not only his true understanding of it but also his ability to put it perfectly into effect. The temple is spoken of in passing but later becomes much more prominent, as I'm sure we'll discuss later. As for sacrifices, again, their true meaning is exposed while at the same time we see that Jesus alone perfectly put that meaning into practice. The servant song I quote here (see Mt 12:18-21) is from Isaiah 42:1-4 and speaks of the gentle character of the servant God has anointed. Others, as mentioned before, emphasize the redemptive suffering of the servant. Many took this to be a reference to Israel, but it became clear that it was most exactly personified in the suffering of Jesus himself.

So Jesus touched here on several of the distinguishing marks of the Jewish faith—sabbath, law, temple, David, sacrifices and servant—and showed how they all came into focus in him and were all carried through and brought to completion in him. It's important to realize that Jesus wasn't starting something new but enacting a new and unimagined chapter of something old. He stood in continuity with the faith of Israel, while liberating it from the failures and misinterpretations that had plagued it for so long.

John: Matthew referred briefly to the temple, and I want to jump in and comment on that. It was a key symbol of the Jewish nation. We all mention the so-called cleansing of the temple (see Jn 2:13-21; Mt 21:12-17; Mk 11:15-19; Lk 19:45-48). Briefly put, the temple authorities had seized on a gap in the market to sell worshipers the sacrifices they needed—at a profitable, marked-up price, of course. The problem was, they'd set up their stalls in the Court of the Gentiles, the closest place non-Jews could get to the temple building itself. It had been designed as a place where the nations could draw near to God, but their actions had pushed the nations further away from God and were in effect telling them that God wasn't interested in them.

I bring that incident right up front in my Gospel because the temple was so important to the Jews (see Jn 11:45-50). Jesus had said, "Destroy this temple, and I will raise it again in three days." They thought him mad, since to date it had taken forty-six years to build the temple and it still wasn't finished. The point was, though, that they misunderstood him completely. The temple he was talking about was the temple of his body that was to be destroyed on a cross and rebuilt through the resurrection (Jn 2:19-22). Malachi had predicted that "suddenly the Lord you are seeking will come to his temple" (Mal 3:1), and that was actually happening before their eyes; but they were too blinded by their own religious prejudices to see it.

Let me give you other ways in which Jesus fulfills the vocation of Israel. Israel was to be a light to the Gentiles (see Is 42:6; 49:6), but it was a dim light at best. Then Jesus boasted, "I am the light of the world.

ISRAEL AS A VINE

Ps 80:8-16; Is 5:1-7; 27:2-6; Jer 2:21; 12:10-13; Ezek 15:1-8; 17:1-21; Hos 10:1-2.

Whoever follows me will never walk in darkness, but will have the light of life" (Jn 8:12)—a direct claim to be what Israel was called to be, and one that made sense to people who knew him. The same was true of his claim to be the "true vine." Israel saw itself as God's vine, carefully tended by him. Sadly, however, it had only produced "bad fruit" and the vineyard had become a wasteland. Now Jesus was fulfilling the true calling of Israel.

Mark: Let me briefly comment that we Synoptic writers say quite a bit about the temple besides its cleansing. We record Jesus talking of its destruction (see Mk 13:1-4; Mt 24:1-3; Lk 21:5-6) but also mention the hugely significant symbolism of the temple curtain being ripped in two at the moment of his death (see Mk 15:38; Mt 27:51; Lk 23:45). From now on, all people could have access to God's throne through his death.

I suppose I also should enter one qualification, though. Jesus does fulfill Israel's vocation and reengineers the major symbols of their faith, but sometimes that reengineering seems to be so radical as to appear contradictory. I'm thinking of the food laws here and the concern that developed with ritual washing before eating. Jesus turns these laws, as understood in his time, on their head, declaring that "nothing outside a person can defile them by going into them. Rather, it is what comes out of a person that defiles them" (Mk 7:1-23). He told them straight that all their petty rules, which they thought were ways of protecting the law, were actually ways by which they cleverly avoided it.

Paul: Let's not get too sidetracked. I agree the theme needs to be nuanced, but so often that has meant it has ended up being obscured, as if Jesus wasn't a Jewish man, working within the context of the calling of Israel. So let's return to the theme of Jesus fulfilling Israel's vocation, which seems to me to permeate everything, and, as such, deserves a whole book in its own right.

Briefly, God called Israel to a particular vocation in the world as his elect people, and that purpose was actually achieved through Jesus, the Messiah. I know I use very different language than we've been using about this topic up to now, but the meaning is the same. In Romans, for example, I develop the big themes that are central to Israel's faith—those of David's royal house, the privilege of election, circumcision, God's faithfulness, promise, the faith of Abraham, the problem of sin and our being children of Adam, inheritance, the claims and fulfillment of the law, the future of Israel, how to achieve the covenant blessings, and so on. Above all, it is about the triumph of the righteousness or justice of God. The references are too numerous to mention; you'll need to read my letter, which isn't nearly as daunting as its reputation suggests! Each of these themes comes to a point of—so far unknown—completion in Christ.

And the miracle is that he not only accomplished all these things in his own life, but also did so in a way that benefits both Jews and Gentiles. By being incorporated into Christ—I speak a lot of being "in Christ," so more on that later[24]—whatever their ethnic background, people may live through faith the life of the Spirit that God intended.[25]

So the language and even thought forms may appear to be different, but the meaning is the same. Jesus, the Messiah, personally and perfectly embodies the

---

[24]See chap. 7, 134-38.
[25]For an accessible introduction to this theme, see N. T. Wright, *Paul: Fresh Perspectives* (London: SPCK, 2005).

vocation of Israel and their key symbols, such as the law, and in doing so makes Israel's blessings available to any who unite themselves to him by trusting their lives to him.

The Death of Jesus

Chair: There's so much more we could say about the life of Jesus, but let's turn to his death. Even those who are barely acquainted with Jesus know there was something extraordinary about it. You, Paul, sum up your message at one point with the simple claim, "We preach Christ crucified" (1 Cor 1:23), and later in the same letter, you talk of his dying "for our sins according to the Scriptures" as "of first importance" (1 Cor 15:3). So what is so special about his death? Let's begin by looking at the facts before turning our attention to the interpretation, if such a distinction is possible.

Mark: Separating facts from interpretation is actually impossible, since the very facts you choose to report carry an implicit interpretation with them. Nonetheless, there is a relative difference between our reporting the event of the crucifixion in the Gospels and the spelling out of the meaning of that event later in the New Testament.

The Gospels are not ordinary biographies, since they spend a disproportionate amount of space dealing with the death of Jesus. No normal biography devotes such space to its subject's death. What is more, his death is mentioned long before Jesus was betrayed, arrested, tried, tortured, and executed. In my short Gospel I refer to three standout occasions when he predicted he would die (Mk 8:31; 9:31; 10:32-34).

> **PARALLEL PREDICTIONS**
>
> Mt 16:21; 17:22-23; 20:17-19; Lk 9:22, 44; 18:31-34.

The general reaction was one of incomprehension, and Peter once even rebuked him for such a prediction. The disciples were building up hopes that Jesus was the Messiah, the Son of David, and, to put it mildly, his being crucified didn't fit with that. In fact, it was in flat contradiction to the path they thought the Messiah would follow. But Jesus, of course, was right all along, and he did end up getting crucified.

We all have our own way of reporting it. I tell it as sparingly as I can. I make a brief and embarrassing cameo appearance in Gethsemane myself (see Mk 14:51-52), but since I'm recording Peter's memories, I say quite a bit about the mockery of a trial Jesus endured at the high priest's house and

Peter's betraying him there (see Mk 14:53-72). The Jewish authorities had no legal right to execute anyone, so they then sent Jesus on to Pilate, the Roman governor, and transposed the charges from religious ones concerning blasphemy into political ones concerning treason. Pilate was a weak ruler and a people-pleaser, so he gave way to the mob and sentenced Jesus to death (see Mk 15:1-15). There was a well-worn ritual of execution for condemned nobodies in the Roman Empire that now kicked in: the condemned were flogged, mocked, marched to the execution site, stripped, strung up on a crossbeam in the air, and left to the taunts of the crowd until life expired. That's what happened to Jesus.

There were a couple of things I particularly draw attention to (see Mk 15:23-41). There was the irony that the notice of his crime simply read, "THE KING OF THE JEWS" (Mk 15:26), but others note that too. What was particularly striking was the bleakness of the scene. At noon the whole land went dark, and a couple of hours later he cried out, "My God, my God, why have you forsaken me?" (Mk 15:34). Oh, and "the curtain of the temple was torn in two from top to bottom" (Mk 15:38). Each of these could be said to carry messages about the significance of his death implicitly.

Matthew: Although I include extra information around the crucifixion, such as about what happened to Judas (see Mt 27:1-10), my account of the actual crucifixion follows Mark's very closely (see Mt 27:32-52). I add just one more detail that fits with the amazing things that were going on in Jerusalem at the time of the crucifixion. I mention the darkness and the temple curtain being torn in two, but add that "at that moment" "the earth shook, the rocks split and the tombs broke open. The bodies of many holy people who had died were raised to life" (Mt 27:51-52). I don't explain it; I just report it. Surely, though, these events signaled the huge significance of his death for the passing of the old creation and the coming of the new.

Luke: Following my research, I pick up on a couple of different aspects of the crucifixion as people reported them to me. The impression people left me with was how selfless Jesus was to the last. In Gethsemane there was a bit of a skirmish, and one of the ears of the high priest's servant was injured. Jesus instantly calmed the situation and healed the servant's ear (see Lk 22:50-51). When on his death march, he spoke directly to the women of Jerusalem who were weeping for him (see Lk 23:27-32). When crucified, he asked God to forgive those executing him (see Lk 23:33-34), and he showed compassion to one of the terrorists crucified with him (see Lk 23:39-43). Amazingly, it wasn't the bleakness of the scene I picked up on but the trust Jesus showed in God to the last. Just before he expired he said in "a loud voice, 'Father, into your hands I commit my spirit'" (Lk 23:46). That sense of sonship we've mentioned before was real, right to the very last moment of his life.

John: While my account of the actual crucifixion is substantially the same as the others, writing a little later and with a view to providing more theological reflection I approach the matter a little differently. I don't include the explicit predictions of his death that the others do, although I report Jesus talking of the need to eat the flesh and drink the blood of the Son of Man (see Jn 6:53-59) and also his comments about the good shepherd laying down his life for the sheep (see Jn 10:14-18), which they omit. I don't record much of a trial before the high priest, because I report that he'd made up his mind about things earlier on (see Jn 11:50). And the actual account of the crucifixion is a little different too, so as to bring out its meaning in two particular ways.

First, you may have noticed that my Gospel is framed with the motif of the "Lamb of God." I mention it first in 1:29, 36, and my account of the crucifixion subtly takes it up again. I record Jesus being sentenced to be crucified a little earlier than the other Gospels, at noon on "the day of Preparation of the Passover" (Jn 19:14). That was the very moment the Passover lambs would have been slaughtered.[26] At the crucifixion itself I refer to the hyssop plant and to none of his bones being broken (see Jn 19:28-34). Both these details recall the Passover meal (see Ex 12:22, 46). The flow of blood and water from his side (see Jn 19:34) was reminiscent of the blood sacrifices of Israel in general.

Second, Jesus seems to have been in charge throughout the final events. It was the "hour" in which he was to be "glorified" (e.g., see Jn 12:23; 13:1; 17:1). When faced with his personal charisma in Gethsemane, people "drew back and fell to the ground" (Jn 18:6). Things happened because he orchestrated them. I focus on the trial before Pilate with its discussion about the nature of kingship (see Jn 18:28-40). And it was as a king that he died: Pilate

---

[26]John's chronology is often a little different from that of the Synoptic Gospels because, some say, he is governed by literary purposes; others see the timings as reconcilable.

presented him to the crowd with the words, "Here is your king," before re-
luctantly handing him over for execution (Jn 19:14-16). He refused to tone
down the indictment displayed on the cross from "The King of the Jews" to
"this man claimed to be king of the Jews," as the religious leaders wanted (Jn
19:21). Jesus died undefeated, a strong man who "[carried] his own cross" (Jn
19:17) to the site of execution, and his final words were those of victory: "It
is finished" (Jn 19:30).

In Revelation I speak of Jesus as "the Lion of the tribe of Judah" and the
"Lamb" who was slain (Rev 5:5-6). Those twin images were implicit in my
account of the crucifixion.

Observer: It's often said that, according to Acts, the apostles made
little of the cross in their preaching. It's true that with one possible exception, where Paul implies the cross as a redemption payment (see Acts
20:28), their references to the crucifixion are essentially simple reports
of the event. As Leon Morris wrote, Luke "rarely addresses himself to
such questions" as those of meaning or interpretation.[27] Yet Luke is not devoid of a theology of the cross; it's embedded in the titles *servant*

REFERENCES TO CHRIST'S DEATH ON THE CROSS

Acts 2:23, 36; 3:13, 15; 4:10; 5:28,
30; 10:39; 13:28-29; 20:28.

(Acts 3:13, 26; 4:27, 30) and *the Righteous One* (Acts 3:14; 7:52; 22:14) that
he gives to Jesus. Even so, the fuller explanation of the significance of
the cross is drawn out in the letters of the New Testament.

Paul: Where to begin? The cross really is the most decisive event in our
salvation. Perhaps I express it at its simplest when I say in Galatians 2:20,
"the Son of God . . . loved me and gave himself for me"; but those simple
words mask great depths of theology.

For Jewish people, atonement for sin had always come through the offering of blood sacrifices. Dependence on the law (which was in itself good)
for salvation was never going to work. The law was toxic when mixed with
human lives since people were never able to keep it, so it always ended up

---

[27]Leon Morris, *New Testament Theology* (Grand Rapids: Zondervan, 1996), 187.

condemning them, not saving them. So sacrifices repaired the rupture of relationships between God and human beings that occurred because of sin. Those sacrifices were pointing forward to a greater sacrifice that became a reality in Jesus' death. Therefore I write, "But now apart from the law the righteousness [justice] of God has been made known, to which the Law and the Prophets testify. . . . God presented Christ as a sacrifice of atonement, through the shedding of his blood—to be received by faith" (Rom 3:21, 25; cf. 5:9). Just as the blood of animal sacrifices was believed to make atonement in Jewish ritual, so now the blood of Christ atones for our sin, if we put our faith in him.

Of course, the very idea seemed absurd to people in my world. Jewish people looked for a sign of strength or power as the means by which God would rescue the world, not the nonsensical weakness of a crucifixion. Greek people looked for dignified gods who would apply strategic wisdom to resolving the problems of the world, not this absurd and undignified act of folly. Yet Christ was "the power of God and the wisdom of God," and his cross demonstrated that God's weakness and folly were stronger and wiser than the world could ever conceive (1 Cor 1:20-25).

One reason why Jewish people didn't find this obvious was their long-held belief that anyone hung on a tree was cursed by God (see Gal 3:13; Deut 21:23). So how could God save the world through his Son becoming cursed? What they missed was that the curse wasn't his but ours. He was bearing it as our substitute, which is why the little phrase "gave himself for me" is so important. The word *for* is the Greek word *hyper*, which means he gave himself on my behalf, as my substitute. I explain the same thing to the Romans in terms of Jesus paying the wages of our sin (see Rom 6:23). To the Corinthians I put it like this: "God made him who had no sin to be sin for us, so that in him we might become the righteousness of God" (2 Cor 5:21). Perhaps I'm only saying what Mark did when he reported the darkness and godforsakeness of the cross. Be that as it may, the cross becomes not something to be quiet or embarrassed about, but something to shout and boast about (see Gal 6:14).

The achievement of the cross was far greater than the saving of individuals from God's wrath, important though that is. The cross is the means by which people who are historically hostile to one another, Jews and Gentiles, are reconciled and become one body (see Eph 2:16).

Moreover, it is the way in which God is going to reconcile all things to himself and establish peace in his creation (see Col 1:20). On that cross he "disarmed the powers and authorities" that are opposed to God, and destructive for us, and "made a public spectacle of them, triumphing over them" (Col 2:15). I believe the Hebraist says something very similar in Hebrews 2:14-15 when he mentions the death of Christ spelling the defeat of the devil.

The Hebraist: I do.

Chair: I'm sure we'll explore the benefits of the cross more in our next discussion.

The Hebraist: When Paul refers to Christ's death as a "sacrifice of atonement," he mentions something close to my heart. For those with a Jewish background I think the best way of explaining Jesus' death is in terms of the great sacrifice offered on the Day of Atonement (see Lev 16:1-34). That annual ritual was designed to remove all the wickedness, uncleanness, and rebellion of Israel and to make atonement for "whatever their sins have been" (Lev 16:16). Christ's sacrifice did that in a far superior way, as I explain in 10:1-18. As a human being, he was an altogether more satisfactory sacrifice than any animal could ever be. The earlier sacrifices had to be repeatedly offered because the truth was that they "can never take away sins." Jesus, however, had to offer himself only "once for all" and the job was done. Moreover, that one sacrifice not only removed the consequences of past sin but also made those who put their confidence in it "holy" or "perfect." His sacrifice outclassed any previous sacrifice, bar none.

John: I want to chime in because I thoroughly endorse the idea that Christ's death was "an atoning sacrifice." People can easily misunderstand

> ## THE NEW TESTAMENT USES VARIOUS WORDS TO TALK ABOUT THE DEATH OF CHRIST
>
> "The cross": 1 Cor 1:17-18; Gal 5:11; 6:12, 14; Eph 2:16; Phil 2:8; 3:18; Col 1:20; 2:14-15; Heb 12:2. "Crucifixion": Rom 6:6; 1 Cor 1:23; 2:2, 8; 2 Cor 13:4; Gal 2:20; 3:1. "The blood" of Christ: Rom 3:25; 5:9; Eph 1:7; Heb 9:12; 10:19; 12:22-24; 1 Pet 1:19; 1 Jn 1:7; Rev 1:5; 5:9; 7:14. The "death" of Christ: Rom 4:25; 5:10; 1 Cor 11:26; Phil 2:8; Heb 2:9, 14; 1 Pet 3:18.

the emphasis in my first letter that "God is love" (1 Jn 4:8), as if the cross were simply an expression of affection or an appeal for us to love God in return. His love, though, is a costly love, not a sentimental one; it is a love that overcomes the obstacle that gets in its way—namely, sin. For God is not only love but also light (see 1 Jn 1:5), and if he is to love us, he has to deal with the darkness there is in our lives. He has done so by sending his Son "as an atoning sacrifice for our sins"—a phrase I use twice in this short letter, at 2:2 and 4:10. Love and atonement belong together. The heart of our gospel is that we know God loves us because "Jesus Christ laid down his life for us" (1 Jn 3:16).

Peter: We're of one mind on this. I don't use the word *atonement*, or even *sacrifice*, but, using related words, it's all there. The importance of Christ's death runs through my first letter. First, I speak of my readers as those who are set apart "to be obedient to Jesus Christ and sprinkled with his blood" (1 Pet 1:2). That's the language of covenant and sacrifice. Second, I speak of our being "redeemed from [an] empty way of life" "with the precious blood of Christ, a lamb without blemish or defect" (1 Pet 1:18-19). That's a pretty obvious reference to sacrifice. Third, I use Isaiah 53 to describe his unjust but uncomplaining suffering, saying, "'He himself bore our sins' in his body on the cross, so that we might die to sins and live for righteousness; 'by his wounds you have been healed'" (1 Pet 2:24). That speaks of his death as a substitute as well as of the suffering servant. Fourth, I say that he "suffered once for sins, the righteous for the unrighteous, to bring you to God. He was put to death in the body but made alive in the Spirit" (1 Pet 3:18); and I go on to celebrate the triumph of his death as the completed act that Hebrews expresses so well.

John: Peter's mention of the "lamb" prompts me to repeat myself a little. In Revelation I record the vision of the worship of heaven, at the center of which was the throne of "the Lion of the tribe of Judah," mentioned just now, who had triumphed over God's enemies and was worthy of unlocking the rest of history that would result in God's ultimate victory over all evil. However, when I looked for the Lion I actually saw "a Lamb, looking as if it had been slain" (Rev 5:4-6). *The Lamb* then becomes my favorite term for Jesus Christ in the rest of my apocalypse. He may have been battered and abused, but everything about him—his posture, his location, his actions, and even his eyes—showed him to be unbeaten and undefeated. So I began my Gospel with "Look, the Lamb of God, who takes away the sin of the world!" (Jn 1:29), and I end my writings, and indeed the whole New Testament, with "the throne of God and of the Lamb" (Rev 22:1, 3). Through death, the Lamb has conquered all.

Chair: None of this gives a cause-and-effect explanation of why Christ's death on behalf of sinful human beings deals with the problem—although the writings are full of suggestive models and images, especially from Israel's own story, which the original readers would have readily understood as explaining why it made sense for God to bring about salvation and atonement in this way.

If we try to summarize this, with a few texts by way of support, we might say:

- His death penalty was caused by our sin (see Rom 6:23; Gal 3:13; 1 Pet 2:24).

- His death was as a substitute (see Mk 10:45; 2 Cor 5:21; Gal 2:20; 3:13).

- His death was seen as an atoning sacrifice (see Rom 3:25; Heb 10:12; 1 Jn 2:2; 4:10).

- His death was a victory over God's enemies, and ours (see Col 2:13-15; Heb 2:14-15).

- His death was "once for all" (Heb 10:11-14).

- His death also serves as a continuing pattern of Christian living (see Gal 5:24; Phil 2:5-11; 3:10-11; 1 Pet 2:21-25).

THE RESURRECTION AND EXALTATION OF JESUS

The Centrality and Significance of the Resurrection

Chair: Though distinguishable from it, the death of Jesus is inseparable from his resurrection. They are two sides of the same coin of God's salvation act. Introducing the discussion on the death of Jesus, I quoted Paul as saying that it was "of first importance"; but to quote him more fully, what is "of first importance" is that "Christ died for our sins according to the Scriptures, that he was buried, that he was raised on the third day according to the Scriptures, and that he appeared" (1 Cor 15:3-5). Why is the resurrection so important?

Luke: Well, if ever there was good news, this was it. The resurrection showed that the Messiah "was not abandoned to the realm of the dead, nor did his body see decay," but rather that "God has raised this Jesus to life" (Acts 2:31-32). The apostles repeatedly claimed the resurrection as an act of God. By it, death has been defeated,

THE RESURRECTION IN ACTS

2:24, 31-32; 3:15; 4:2, 10, 33; 5:30; 10:40; 13:30, 34, 37; 17:3, 18, 31-32; 23:6; 24:15, 21; 26:23.

Jesus' sacrifice on the cross has been accepted, and his right to reign has been established beyond question. True, it was hard to understand, and sometimes, as when Paul was preaching in Athens, people went along with what he said until he mentioned the resurrection (see Acts 17:22-32). That was so far outside their normal frame of reference that they just sneered at him.

> **Observer:** In the apostles' preaching recorded in the book of Acts, for every ten times the resurrection is mentioned, the cross is mentioned just short of nine times, Jesus as Lord is mentioned six times, forgiveness six times and repentance five. In other words, resurrection is mentioned twice as often as repentance.[28]

Matthew: It was hard to imagine that Jesus had come back to life, which is why I sandwich my brief account of the resurrection (see Mt 28:1-10) between two other little but important episodes. Leading up to the resurrection I report that the tomb was heavily guarded and secured so as to ensure that no one could steal the body and pretend he had risen (see Mt 27:62-66). After the resurrection, I report how the senior religious leaders bribed the guards, who'd been scared to death by the earthquake that accompanied his resurrection (see Mt 28:2-4), to tell a lie and make up the story that his body had been stolen (see Mt 28:11-15). But his resurrection really happened, and we have the eyewitness accounts to prove it (see Mt 28:1-10).

Mark: My first account of the resurrection is also concise and centers on the women who encountered the risen Christ when visiting the tomb (see Mk 16:1-8). However briefly I record it, I pick up on a couple of distinct

---

[28]Ross Clifford and Philip Johnson, *The Cross Is Not Enough: Living as Witnesses to the Resurrection* (Grand Rapids: Baker Books, 2012), 20.

things about it. First, the women were told to go and "tell his disciples *and Peter*" that he was alive again and would meet them in Galilee. Since Peter had denied knowing Jesus three times at the high priest's house (see Mk 14:66-72), it meant a lot to him that Jesus mentioned him by name. Then I honestly admit that the women who conveyed the message were "trembling and bewildered" by what they'd witnessed and were somewhat afraid as well (Mk 16:8). Well, it wasn't every day you saw a man whom you knew for sure was dead, alive again!

I mentioned my "first account" because in the longer ending of my Gospel[29] I add a little more, but I still emphasize how hard it was for people to believe it had happened (see Mk 16:9-14). Oh, and you'll know that my Gospel is always in a hurry, so I truncate the end somewhat and write that Jesus commissioned his disciples to preach the good news "to all creation" as he made one of his appearances to the Eleven shortly after his resurrection.

Chair: Luke, do you have anything distinctive to add?

Luke: Yes, I do. I provide the longest account, partly because I wanted to remind people that Jesus had predicted that after his crucifixion he would "on the third day be raised again" (Lk 24:7). I record him prophesying this twice (Lk 9:22; 18:33). Mark records he said it on three occasions (Mk 8:31; 9:31; 10:34).

Another reason for the length of my report is that I have an exclusive! I include an account of a journey and conversation Jesus had with a couple of his disciples on the evening of resurrection day, when the truth eventually dawned on their befuddled minds (see Lk 24:13-35). As a result, they returned to Jerusalem, only to discover that the Eleven had come to the same conclusion. They were greeted with the words, "It is true! The Lord has risen" (Lk 24:34). Just then, Jesus appeared to them all again and explained what had happened, using the Scriptures to give them understanding. Somewhat unusually, it's me, not Matthew, who's concerned to point out that the resurrection fulfilled ancient prophecy!

Chair: John, is there anything left to add to the reports of these events?

John: Plenty, I assure you. I actually devote two chapters to the resurrection and the postresurrection appearances Jesus made. I tell the story in a little more detail, describing what Mary Magdalene was faced with at the

---

[29]The longer ending doesn't appear in the earliest manuscripts.

tomb (see Jn 20:1-2), what Peter and I saw in the tomb (see Jn 20:3-10), how Jesus appeared to Mary outside the tomb (see Jn 20:11-18), then how he appeared to all his disciples, *except* Thomas (see Jn 20:19-23), and then to them all with Thomas present when he had an unforgettable conversation with that skeptic (see Jn 20:24-29). It was in one of those meetings that Jesus was able to dispense the Spirit whom he had said would come after he'd been taken out of the world (see Jn 20:19-22; cf. 16:7). So the next stage of God's plan of salvation was about to begin.

Later on I report his meeting up with his disciples in Galilee, where they'd gone back to their old jobs as fishermen, and how he worked yet another miracle there (see Jn 21:1-14). Most precious of all was the conversation he had after breakfast with Peter. Using Peter's old name, Jesus asked him three times, "Simon son of John, do you love me?" perhaps to match Peter's threefold denial. When Peter assured Jesus his love was authentic, he was restored to his role as the leading apostle (Jn 21:15-23).

Actually, if I may say so, my account is carefully crafted. If you look deeply at the wording, you'll find that so many of the themes that I introduce at the beginning of my Gospel and that thread their way through it are tied up in this account.[30]

Chair: So that deals essentially with the accounts of the resurrection, even if they give a hint here and there about its significance. How does the rest of the New Testament draw out its significance?

Paul: Its significance is absolutely fundamental. Let me mention six things that result from his resurrection. I mention them in the major chapter I wrote on the topic in 1 Corinthians 15. First, "if Christ has not been raised . . . you are still in your sins" (1 Cor 15:17). I say something similar in Romans 4:25: "He was delivered over to death for our sins and was raised to life for our justification" (cf. Rom 5:10). The death and resurrection of Jesus work in concert in terms of dealing with our sins. If his death secured our acquittal from sin, his resurrection not only showed us that God had accepted his sacrifice, but also released us to live a new life in the power of his Spirit. If his death was all we had, it might have been no more than the death of a martyr. His resurrection, however, shows us God, the life-giver, was doing something altogether new.

---

[30]Derek Tidball, "Completing the Circle: The Resurrection According to John," *Evangelical Review of Theology* 30, no. 2 (2006): 169-83.

Second, because of his resurrection, we who have been united with him may already "live a new life" (Rom 6:4; cf. 1 Cor 15:22; Eph 2:5-7; Col 2:12; 3:1-2). The life we now live is the life of the Spirit, "who raised Jesus from the dead" and now lives in us "[giving] life to [our] mortal bodies" (Rom 8:11). The resurrection is the paradigm for the life Christians live.

Third, the resurrection establishes Christ's victory over all that would oppose God and demonstrates once and for all that he is the most powerful ruler in the universe (see 1 Cor 15:24-28). He was the first to rise from the dead because he has the preeminence in all things (Col 1:18).

Fourth, the resurrection provides us with hope for the future and a realistic expectation of a new age to come (see 1 Cor 15:12-22, 28). Without it, we would literally be a hopeless people and our belief in Christ would be "futile."

Fifth, his resurrection provides us with the model for our own, when, eventually, we will rise with transformed bodies that will prove imperishable and immortal (see 1 Cor 15:20, 35-57; cf. 6:14; 2 Cor 4:14; Phil 3:10-12).

Sixth, his resurrection proves to us that our final enemy, death, which in part, at least, is a penalty for sin, has been overcome (see 1 Cor 15:54-57).

We could say more. His resurrection was a step on the path toward his exaltation and the ultimate destination of his return. We "wait for [God's] Son from heaven, whom he raised from the dead—Jesus, who rescues us from the coming wrath" (1 Thess 1:10; cf. Phil 3:12).

Peter: I only say a little about the resurrection, but I particularly identify with what Paul has just said about hope. Christians have been born "into a living hope through the resurrection of Jesus Christ from the dead, and into an inheritance that can never perish, spoil or fade" (1 Pet 1:3-4). It's the resurrection that gives us hope in God (see 1 Pet 1:21).

The Hebraist: Like Peter, I don't exactly say much about it. My real concern is with Jesus' present ministry as our great high priest, and that makes no sense unless the resurrection had taken place. So I say little about it but assume it a lot. The one place I explicitly mention it is in my benediction, where I claim it plays a vital role in confirming Jesus as "that great Shepherd of the sheep" who continues to equip us for the challenges we face (Heb 13:20-21).

John: It's something of a surprise to many that I don't actually mention the resurrection in my letters. The surprise is compounded by the fact that "life" is one of the running themes of my first letter (see 1 Jn 1:2; 2:25; 3:14;

4:9; 5:11-13, 16, 20). And that, of course, is also the reason why it's not mentioned explicitly. Jesus Christ was quite simply "the life," which appeared among us (1 Jn 1:2) and which proved irrepressible and undefeatable even when he "laid down his life for us" (1 Jn 3:16).

It is mentioned twice at the start of Revelation, when I speak of Jesus as "the firstborn from the dead" (Rev 1:5) and when Jesus introduces himself as "the Living One; I was dead, and now look, I am alive for ever and ever!" (Rev 1:18). After that it becomes pretty obvious not only that he's alive but also that he reigns, and is actively working out God's plan finally and fully to abolish evil and restore good to his creation.

James: Well, that's an exciting theme to hear expounded! I confess that neither Jude nor I mention it, but you can't mention everything in short letters, and the resurrection was not so germane to our purposes as were other things.

The Physicality of the Resurrection

Observer: Let me fill in some of the background here that helps to make sense of the insistence that Jesus did not rise again as a "spirit" or as a "soul," but as a real, if different, material body.

With the exception of the Sadducees, who did not believe in resurrection, Jewish belief anticipated a general resurrection at the last day. Paul takes that for granted (and the judgment that is involved) in his speech to Felix in Acts 24:15. But no one at the time expected to witness someone rising from the dead until then, nor was it a major concern. Yet "something happened to Jesus that had happened to nobody else."[31] It was unprecedented. His resurrection was a resurrection to a new embodied life, a difficult-to-describe transphysical life, but definitely not a resurrection to some form of eternal soul existence or spirit life.[32] Jesus might be able to appear through locked doors and solid walls, but he also walked many miles to Emmaus, ate fish in the upper room, invited Thomas to examine his body, and cooked breakfast on the Galilean lakeshore. Yet that transphysical body was incapable of dying, of decaying, or of corruption (see Acts 13:34; 1 Cor 15:15-56). So it was the

---

[31]N. T. Wright, *The Resurrection of the Son of God* (London: SPCK, 2003), 83.
[32]Ibid., 477.

same but different; there was continuity and discontinuity with the pre-crucified Jesus.

Although the concept of resurrection was used in Judaism metaphorically to refer to the restoration of Israel (e.g., see Ezek 37), it was never an abstract idea used in the sense of disembodied bliss or resurrection of the spirit to heaven without the body. When the early Christians moved resurrection from "circumference to center,"[33] it meant bodily resurrection. That was denied by pagans but affirmed, in reference to the general resurrection, by a large and influential part of Judaism.

Furthermore, there was no way in which the early Christians could have made it any clearer in their writings or preaching that Jesus died physically and equally rose physically from the dead. That's what the words they used meant.[34] There were plenty of other ways they could have expressed it if all they meant was the idea that somehow Jesus continued with us, or lived on, or had not been defeated after his crucifixion. The unprecedented nature of his resurrection is possibly why the Gospel writers and Paul are concerned to emphasize the details of it, give prominence to the eyewitness accounts of it, and even counter some of the arguments that would detract from it.

The physicality of the resurrection is important. We can have no certainty that death has been defeated or that we have any hope of a transformed body unless Jesus physically rose from the dead. In Jesus the resurrection has been divided into two moments: a historical one in which Jesus has risen from the dead, and a future one in which humankind will rise at the end of the age.[35] So in Christ the future has powerfully interrupted the present. Consequently, we live in the in-between times of the already and the not yet.

The Ascension and Exaltation of Jesus

Chair: After the resurrection came the ascension. What do you all make of it?

---

[33]C. F. Evans, cited by Wright, *Resurrection*, 210.
[34]Wright, *Resurrection*, 330.
[35]Ibid., 372-73.

Matthew: I don't speak of it as such, ending my Gospel with what's become known as "the great commission" rather than an account of his departure. However, in doing so I do draw attention to the all-embracing authority he claimed at that time (see Mt 28:18).

Mark: In my longer ending I simply say that Jesus "was taken up into heaven and he sat at the right hand of God" (Mk 16:19). It's a lean statement and yet includes not only a record of the event ("taken up") but also the significance of it ("sat at the right hand of God"), which begins to show why it was important. Others develop that.

John: I also admit that I make nothing of the event itself, but I was very aware it would happen to Jesus sometime (see Jn 3:13; 6:62; 20:17).

Luke: I'm the one who mentions it big time. To begin with, I tell the story of his ascension twice. The first time I recall him blessing the disciples, after which "he left them and was taken up into heaven" (Lk 24:51). The second time I say more and record the instructions he gave to his disciples about waiting for the Holy Spirit to visit them, after which they were to be his "witnesses in Jerusalem, and in all Judea and Samaria, and to the ends of the earth" (Acts 1:1-11). The perceptive may have noticed that this becomes the framework for the book of Acts. Understandably, the disciples who were present were so mesmerized by the experience that messengers from heaven had to tell them to get going and start putting his instructions into action.

The meaning of what happened to Jesus on that occasion became a major focus of their preaching. The apostles spoke of it as if Jesus was a king, returning victorious from a battle, ascending to his throne. Referring to it they said things like, "God has made this Jesus, whom you crucified, both Lord and Messiah" (Acts 2:36). They didn't mean by that that Jesus was promoted to be something he wasn't before. Rather, he was being reinvested with his legitimate exalted status, which had been temporarily laid aside, and the greatness of his achievements was being recognized by God.[36] Peter used Psalm 110:1, a royal psalm that celebrates one of David's victories, to explain Jesus' greater victory and that what they were witnessing was like his enthronement. Jesus had previously applied this psalm to himself (see Mt 22:44; Mk 12:36; Lk 20:42-43).

---

[36]Adapted from George Caird, *New Testament Theology*, ed. L. D. Hurst (Oxford: Oxford University Press, 1994), 170.

The Hebraist: Excuse my interrupting, but I use exactly that same psalm twice in my opening chapter (see Heb 1:3, 13) to make the same point.

Luke: That's OK. Yes, it was commonly believed and by no means unique to me. I was just going to add that Stephen in his dying vision saw Jesus "standing at the right hand of God"—that is, in the place of real authority in the cosmos (Acts 7:56).

The Hebraist: I'm very much in tune with that. Four times I mention that following the ascension Jesus "sat down at the right hand of God" (Heb 10:12; cf. 1:3; 8:1; 12:2). It's an evocative image that suggests that his work on earth was completed, that all that he did and taught was vindicated, and that now he's right at the heart of our universe, sharing God's rule over it.

Paul: There are several elements here that it may be good to unravel. I refer to them all at different times. There's the element of the vindication of his finished work, which I allude to when I speak of Jesus being "taken up in glory" (1 Tim 3:16). There's the element of celebration, just as you'd get at any coronation. You'll find it in Ephesians 4:7-13, and even more clearly in the hymn we sing, found in Philippians 2, where following his death on the cross we proclaim, "Therefore God exalted him to the highest place and gave him the name that is above every name" (Phil 2:9). Then there's also the element of his reigning now, which I especially stress. He is indeed "at the right hand of God" (Rom 8:34; Col 3:1), but he's not just sitting idly on the throne. He's actively "interceding for us" (Rom 8:34). He is reigning now and will continue to do so "until he has put all his enemies under his feet" and he hands the kingdom over to his Father (1 Cor 15:25). So he may have been vindicated and his achievements recognized, but he is not inactive.

The Hebraist: Sorry to jump in again, but I get excited by these thoughts. Jesus is indeed not on a vacation in heaven. I picture him as the great high priest who, because he was once human, is able "to empathize with our weaknesses" and gives us confidence to approach God's throne, where we "may receive mercy and find grace to help us in our time of need" (Heb 4:15-16). Then, because he rose from the dead, never to die again, I point out that "he is able to save completely those who come to God through him"—and here's the point of our present discussion—"because he always lives to intercede for them" (Heb 7:25).

Peter: Let me just interject here. Like the others I speak of the resurrected Jesus as having "gone into heaven and [being] at God's right hand—with angels, authorities and powers in submission to him" (1 Pet 3:22). In those few words you'll find an assertion of his permanent victory and of him currently exercising sovereign power.

Chair: John, we've mentioned your Gospel, but you must have a lot to say about these themes in your other writings.

John: Well, I mention his present ministry once in my letters, saying that when anyone sins "we have an advocate with the Father—Jesus Christ, the Righteous One" (1 Jn 2:1). So he's certainly using his irresistible influence with God on our behalf, right now.

It's in Revelation, though, that the theme of his exaltation becomes prominent. Sometimes it's very obvious, as when I have the vision of "someone like a son of man" (Rev 1:12-16), a vision that picks up elements of Ezekiel 1 and Daniel 7:13-14 and clearly portrays one who reigns supreme. It's obvious too in the vision of worship offered to the Lamb in chapter 5. Then there are the titles that are given to him, clearly communicating his triumph and reign; among them are "the ruler of the kings of the earth" (Rev 1:5), "the Amen" (Rev 3:14), and "Lord of lords and King of kings" (Rev 17:14; 19:16).

There are some more subtle details, however, that also show Jesus not only as vindicated but as reigning and interceding. I'm thinking of the way he walks among "seven golden lampstands" and holds the "seven stars," symbols of the churches, in his right hand. He's actively overseeing their lives. The twenty-four elders who are worshiping the Lamb "were holding golden bowls full of incense" before him, which we're told are "the prayers of God's people" (Rev 5:8). The concerns of earth are presented to him in heaven as he is at God's right hand. However much the church may be suffering, the risen Christ is not indifferent to it, but reigns actively in the midst of it.

Chair: Perhaps we can conclude from all this that the resurrection and ascension are not a convenient, if imaginative, way of bringing the earthly life of Jesus to a conclusion, but vital components of the story if we human beings, and the larger creation, are to enter into God's salvation. They are an essential step on the road toward the completion of God's plan. Jesus reigns now, but the day is coming when, to quote that hymn again, "at the name of Jesus every knee [shall] bow, in heaven and on earth and under the earth, and every tongue acknowledge that Jesus Christ is Lord, to the glory of God the Father" (Phil 2:10-11).

WHAT DOES JESUS
OFFER NOW?

The Good News Today

Chair: In this next discussion we want to explore how all that we've been saying about Jesus applies to us today. Up to now we've been mainly concerned about what is called Christology—that is, the person and work of Christ. The balance of our attention has tipped toward the Gospels. Here we turn to the implications of all that for believers in Christ and discuss more fully the doctrines of salvation and atonement. That's sometimes called "soteriology" in the trade. In doing so our focus will shift to the letters, where it was all spelled out to different audiences.

The topic is immense, and we'll have to break it down into several areas. Let's begin with something that occupies substantial sections of Paul's writings, but not by any means all of them: the question of the law.

A NEW LIBERTY: FREEDOM FROM THE LAW

Chair: At a popular level, we often correctly understand sin as a breaking of God's law—but, Paul, you do tend to write in a somewhat complex way about it. Can you explain?

Paul: My defense is that it is complex and we shouldn't reduce "the whole will of God" (Acts 20:27) to simple slogans or sound bites. I write about it a lot because it was an issue that greatly concerned the Jewish people who proudly saw themselves as custodians of the law. Even if they didn't actually believe they were saved by it, they did believe that obeying it would ensure they stayed within the covenant and so would receive God's favor. As will become apparent, the law was not of concern to Gentiles, and with them we approach the whole question somewhat differently. I suppose the confusion you refer to arises from the fact that, on the one hand, I believe the law to be "holy, righteous and good," even "spiritual" (Rom 7:12, 14); yet, on the other hand, I argue it only succeeds in magnifying people's offenses and compounding their sin, so is unable to effect salvation and ends up condemning people (see Rom 7:1–8:13; 2 Cor 3:7-11).

Let me try to explain. To start with, we use the word *law* in different ways. One meaning of *law* is the revelation of God's good character. Obedience to this law would benefit everyone and has global significance, as is obvious if you think about the Ten Commandments alone. Another meaning of *law* is "the law of Moses," which includes instructions about circumcision, sacrifices, and diet. This law was essentially binding on Israel as God's elect people with whom he'd made a particular covenant. The niceties of that law were never imposed on Gentiles (see Rom 2:17-29; 3:27-31). It was a way of marking them out as distinct from other people. So when we read about the law we always need to ask which meaning of *law* is meant.

If we refer to the law in the sense of "the law of Moses," the covenant law of Israel, we can detect a threefold movement in my writings.[1]

The Law Is Repudiated

In the first movement we note those texts where the law is repudiated,[2] and I explain that the law is now a thing of the past. Believers, Jewish or otherwise, are no longer "under the law" (Rom 6:14; Gal 5:18), and "circumcision is nothing and uncircumcision is nothing" (1 Cor 7:19). It may have been our "guardian until Christ came . . . [but] we are no longer under a guardian" (Gal 3:24-25; see vv. 21-25). It has been "set aside" by Christ's coming (Eph 2:15), when he "canceled the charge of our legal indebtedness, which stood against us and condemned us" (Col 2:14).

The reason for this is twofold. First, the basis on which God related to his people was always that of promise. You have only to read Abraham's story

---

[1] I owe the following analysis to Brian Rosner, *Paul and the Law: Keeping the Commandments of God*, New Studies in Biblical Theology (Downers Grove, IL: InterVarsity Press, 2013), which I closely follow here.

[2] The terms *repudiated*, *replaced*, and *re-appropriated* are Rosner's.

to see that (see Rom 4:1-25; Gal 3:15-22). The law of Moses, which concerned circumcision, diet, and sabbath observance, had a proper place for a time, but since Christ came it may be said to have been "pensioned off." It has served its purpose, which chiefly was to reveal how truly desperate our situation was and drive us to Christ.

That, however, leads me to the second reason why it is now defunct: it was never really able to achieve its ultimate purpose in the first place. There was nothing wrong with it, but when it came into contact with human beings they were completely unable to live up to it, so it simply compounded their difficulties. It could never set people free and was powerless to do so "because it was weakened by the flesh" (Rom 8:3).

Just in case someone asks, I might say that in 1 Corinthians 9:20 I speak of becoming "like one under the law . . . so as to win those under the law"; but I make it clear that, while I may adopt the lifestyle of the law for evangelistic purposes, I don't place my trust in it for salvation, and therefore I include the words "though I myself am not under the law." I of all people measured up quite well when judged by the law, but I rejected that whole approach to things and put my faith in Christ instead (see Phil 3:1-11). I've repudiated trust in the law and now live in the new age of grace and of the life-giving Spirit.

The Law Is Replaced

The second movement demonstrates how the law has been replaced. The law of Moses is replaced by "the law of Christ," a term I use in 1 Corinthians 9:21 and Galatians 6:2 with variations of it in Romans 3:27 ("the law that requires faith") and 8:1-2 ("the law of the Spirit"). Our hope is in Christ, who fulfills the law for us. That, however, doesn't mean we are a lawless people. No, we don't repudiate the law of Moses so we can live however we like, in a sort of moral vacuum (see Rom 6:15). Instead, as I make clear in a multitude of places, we use our freedom to "serve one another humbly in love" (Gal 5:13). We act "in line with the truth of the gospel" (Gal 2:14), as we are "led by the Spirit" (Gal 5:18). We now live lives that are worthy of the gospel and conform to its teaching (see Eph 4:1; 1 Tim 1:8-11).

The Law Is Re-appropriated

The third movement explains how the law is re-appropriated. Briefly put, there are two lenses that bring the Old Testament Torah (the Pentateuch, which contains the law of Moses) into focus in particular ways. The first is *the lens of prophecy*, which looks forward to the future. We have plenty of examples of that in my letters, such as when I relate the stories of Abraham (see Rom 4:1-3), Adam (see Rom 5:12-21; 1 Cor 15:45), Sarah and Hagar (see Gal 4:21-31), or the festivals (see Col 2:8-23) to believers in Jesus. I also show how passages like Deuteronomy 30:6, 11-14 work out in the new age in Romans 10:5-10. The second lens is *the lens of wisdom*, which looks to life in the present. The law is about how to live wisely. When we have faith in Christ, the Spirit enables us to do so (see Rom 8:4). Echoes of the Torah as wisdom are found in Romans 12:19-20; 1 Corinthians 9:9; 10:11; 2 Corinthians 8:15; 13:1; Ephesians 6:1-3; Colossians 3:9-10; and 2 Timothy 3:16-17. Galatians 5:14, which cites the law of Leviticus 19:18, sums it up: "the entire law is fulfilled in keeping this one command: 'Love your neighbor as yourself.'"

So the law does not, indeed cannot, save us. We're no longer slaves to it and need not fear being judged or condemned by it once we have faith in Christ. Instead we live a new kind of life, that of the Spirit, under a new kind of law, which is taught and modeled by Christ. In this way we "uphold the law" (Rom 3:31).

Chair: What do the rest of you make of that?

Matthew: Well, in some respects I share Paul's agenda but come at it very differently, perhaps much less abstractly. Within my general aim of telling the story of Jesus, I'm trying to answer a particular set of questions. How does the gospel of Jesus relate to Israel's scriptures? How was it that the mission of Jesus that was confined to the people of Israel (see Mt 15:24; cf. 10:6) now embraces people of "all nations"? And how are relations between Jewish and Gentile converts to be worked out in "the church" (Mt 16:18; 18:15-17)? This naturally throws up the question of the place of the law for this ethnically mixed community of believers in Jesus. The most important thing I say is that Jesus fulfilled the law in his own person (see Mt 5:17-20), which at the very least means he lived by it faultlessly. He certainly wasn't about abolishing it, but he knew it had achieved its fulfillment, as the prophets had also reached theirs, with his coming (see Mt 11:13).

The idea of fulfillment wasn't a simple one. By it Jesus meant giving a truer interpretation of it, as when he took the superficial teachings of contemporary religious leaders and drilled them deeper. Truly understood, he taught, the law forbade not only murder, but hatred; not only adultery, but lust—and so on (see Mt 5:21-42). Jesus not only reinforced the command to love one's neighbor, which Paul mentioned, but also challenged people to love their enemies too (see Mt 5:43-48). The law was meant to aid the achievement of a righteous life, but Jesus advocated righteous living that went far beyond anything people thought the law demanded (see Mt 5:21). He repeatedly taught that a true understanding of the law resulted not in observing superficial rituals but in a genuinely pure inner nature (see Mt 15:1-20).

So the place of the law may have been misunderstood in the common Jewish religion of his day, but, properly understood, it still had a continuing role, not in salvation, but in training believers for the "perfect" life (Mt 5:48).

John: Some have read me as presenting Jesus as a "new Moses," on the basis of my statement (and other allusions) that "the law was given through Moses; grace and truth came through Jesus Christ" (Jn 1:17). That wasn't intended as a contrast so much a statement that the proper intent of the law was "grace and truth," and these were revealed and released through Jesus.

Of course there is some discontinuity between law and grace, but don't read my words through the spectacles of Paul, who contrasts them in a major way. Like Matthew, I reflect Jesus' same ambivalence toward the law as popularly understood. Jesus was happy to assert its authority since, he said, "Scripture cannot be set aside" (Jn 10:35). Yet he showed himself to be master of it and used it to his own advantage (see Jn 8:17; 10:34-39). He ran into trouble more than once because he didn't abide by the petty interpretations of the Pharisees, especially about the sabbath (see Jn 5:1-18; 9:13-41). To use Mark's phrase, he was "Lord even of the Sabbath" (Mk 2:28). I also have my own way of emphasizing the importance of the love command, which took on a whole new complexion in him (see Jn 13:34). That simply highlights that the key point is to keep the true purpose of the law central and refuse to let it drift into some narrow legalism.

Chair: James, I'd love to hear you on this because your background and writing are steeped in a Jewish heritage. So presumably the law is something you deal with a lot.

James: Well, I don't give a sustained exposition of the law as Paul does, but I make a couple of significant references to it, in ways that resonate perfectly with what others are saying. I take the law "found in Scripture" (Jas 2:8) very seriously. In the main section where I speak of the law (see Jas 2:8-13), you'll find I am building on Leviticus 19:15, 18; Exodus 20; and Deuteronomy 5—all of which are major statements of the law. I refer to it as "the royal law" since it is decreed by God himself. The law focuses on love, and, properly understood, should lead to mercy. It was never designed to be debilitating, nagging, or paralyzing. Rather, its purpose was to release us to live a healthy life together. That's why I twice call it "the law that gives freedom" (Jas 2:12; 1:25) and why my description of it not only as "royal" but also as "perfect" is justified. I mention Jesus Christ only once in my letter (Jas 1:1), but, in effect, the law I'm talking about is what Paul calls "the law of Christ."

ATONEMENT FROM SIN: VARIOUS MODELS

Chair: The constant affirmation of the New Testament, variously expressed, is that "Christ . . . loved me and gave himself for me" (Gal 2:20). We already discussed some of the significance of this when we were looking at the death of Jesus Christ,[3] but we admitted then that the writers never exactly explain how his death atones for us in any causal way, except that they see it in sacrificial and forensic terms. Leviticus 17:11, which says, "the life of a creature is in the blood, and I have given it to you to make atonement for yourselves . . . it is the blood that makes atonement for one's life," hovers in the background here. It would seem that sin robs us of life, puts a price on our heads that can be paid only by blood, and, as seen elsewhere in Leviticus, contaminates us, requiring cleansing by blood. It's the offering of a substitute in a blood sacrifice that restores our relationship with God.

Down the centuries, theologians have tried to make up for the absence of any explicit causal explanation of the atonement and have often done so in ways heavily influenced by the culture of their day. They have usually constructed models by piecing together a variety of texts and observing a common pattern in them.

---

[3]See chap. 6, 109-16.

Observer: There are four main groups of atonement models.

Satisfaction models. These models essentially argue that God's honor has been slighted by sin and he requires satisfaction. They made great sense in the context of medieval feudalism but do not enjoy great currency in the contemporary world. Anselm of Canterbury (1033–1109) was one exponent of the idea who, in his book *Cur Deus Homo?*, said the only way of repaying the debt was for a person of "infinite greatness" to repay it on our behalf. Satisfaction here is about restitution of honor. It's not penal substitution, which is about accepting punishment on behalf of the guilty.

A particular version of this approach, developed under Hugo Grotius (1583–1645), is known as the "governmental theory." He argued that Christ's death was a deserved punishment in which he substituted himself for us, but it was not a punishment that exactly corresponded to our sin. The crucifixion was more an exemplary punishment than an exact retribution. Having demonstrated the seriousness of sin and having satisfied honor at this point, God can forgive (pass over) other sins where there is repentance. It's not about retributive justice but rather about God publicly upholding his regal authority.

Penal substitutionary models. This has been the principal evangelical view that, although biblical in its origins, was articulated most clearly by the Reformers and their heirs. Proponents of this view argue that it is the most fundamental theory as it (a) relates to God's law and his holiness; (b) builds on the sacrificial system of the Old Testament; (c) makes most sense of Isaiah 53, which is used frequently in the New Testament; and (d) alone truly makes sense of ideas such as ransom (see below) or "the blood of the covenant" language. It plumbs the depths of godforsakenness at the cross (see Mk 15:34) as well as being explicitly taught in the idea of the sin offering referred to in Romans 3:25 (*hilastērion*: atonement); 8:3; Galatians 3:13 (cf. Deut 21:23); and Hebrews 10:6-12; 13:11. N. T. Wright says of Romans 8:3, "No clearer statement is found in Paul . . . of the early Christian belief that what happened on the cross was the judicial punishment of sin."[4] Schreiner

---

[4]N. T. Wright, "Romans," in *The New Interpreter's Bible*, vol. 10, ed. Leander E. Keck (Nashville: Abingdon Press, 2002), 574-75.

describes it as "the anchor and heart of the atonement."[5]

However, several criticisms are mounted against this view today. Is it an explanation that makes sense in the contemporary world, where restitution rather than retributive justice is more valued? Does *hilastērion* refer to the mercy seat on the ark of the covenant, or to expiation (the removal of sin), or, alternatively, to propitiation (the removal of wrath)?[6] Does it overplay penal substitution in the face of New Testament preaching on the resurrection, especially in Acts, and other perspectives on the cross? Do we read *substitution* where *representation* is meant? Is it as central as its proponents make out? The model can be too easy to caricature as a holy father punishing an unwilling son, thus dividing the Trinity. Some say it leads to easy salvation, and to salvation as a legal fiction rather than anything authentic. Then, how does it relate to other doctrines, such as creation, being in Christ, and so on? Credible theologians have satisfactorily answered each of these questions in recent days.[7]

Christus Victor *models.* Michael Bird sees this approach as "the crucial integrative hub of the atonement."[8] Some claim (in reality, overclaim) that this was *the* classic apostolic model of atonement that has been revived recently through Gustaf Aulén's *Christus Victor*, published in 1931. This model views the cross as the means by which God overcomes evil by love. More precisely, Christ embraced nonviolence and nonretaliation on his cross and in doing so defeated God's enemies and released humanity from their captivity. Key texts that support it are found in Colossians 2:15 and Hebrews 2:14-15, as well as in those verses that emphasize the victory of Christ over death and the world (see Jn 12:31-32; 16:11, 33; 2 Tim 1:10; 1 Jn 2:14). It fits well with the overall narrative

---

[5]Thomas R. Schreiner, "The Penal Substitution View," in J. Beilby and P. R. Eddy, eds., *The Nature of the Atonement: Four Views* (Downers Grove, IL: InterVarsity Press, 2006), 93.

[6]A brief overview of these questions is found in Derek Tidball, *The Message of the Cross*, The Bible Speaks Today (Nottingham, UK: Inter-Varsity Press, 2001), 194-96.

[7]Excellent recent expositions of this view are found in John Stott, *The Cross of Christ* (Leicester: Inter-Varsity Press, 1986); I. Howard Marshall, *Aspects of Atonement* (London: Paternoster, 2007); and Donald Macleod, *Christ Crucified: Understanding the Atonement* (Nottingham: Inter-Varsity Press, 2014).

[8]Michael F. Bird, *Evangelical Theology: A Biblical and Systematic Introduction* (Grand Rapids: Zondervan, 2013), 414.

and plan of God toward the re-creation of the world, which is the story of salvation unfolded from Genesis 3:15 to Revelation 12 or 20. It also integrates well with the idea of the kingdom of God.

None can argue that such a view does not arise from the New Testament; it does. The debate revolves around whether it is the most fundamental view or not. It's a popular one today since it resonates with the anti- or nonviolence themes of our culture and emphasizes that the cross does not perpetuate violence but absorbs it.[9]

Subjective models, such as moral influence models. These models take various forms, including the ideas that the cross illuminates people's minds (Clement of Alexandria, 150–215) or sets a moral example (Socinius, 1539–1604) to which humanity responds. Its chief historical exponent was Peter Abelard (1079–1142), who taught that when God demonstrated his love for us on the cross it evoked in us a response of love in return. It is based on verses such as Luke 7:47, Romans 5:5, and 1 John 4:7-12.

These models are termed "subjective models" because they start with us responding to God's appeal of love. In this understanding, nothing actually is altered by or is achieved on the cross. If it did, the models would be objective, with God as the subject and ourselves as the beneficiaries. The models ignore issues of the justice and holiness of God and have no answer to human guilt or divine wrath. Furthermore, while in part intended to lessen the horror of a penal view of the cross, they do not provide a more satisfactory alternative explanation for the pain, shame, and horror of the crucifixion.[10]

A NEW RELATIONSHIP: UNION WITH CHRIST AND BEING "IN CHRIST"

Chair: Reading your letters, Paul, there would seem to be two concepts that are given greater weight than others in your exposition of salvation. They are the idea of "union with Christ" or our being "in Christ," on the one hand,

---

[9]See further, Gregory Boyd, "Christus Victor View," in Beilby and Eddy, *Nature of the Atonement*, 23-49.

[10]One recent sophisticated exposition of this model is found in Paul Fiddes, *Past Event, Present Salvation* (London: Darton, Longman & Todd, 1989).

and "justification by faith," on the other. They're not unrelated. Help us understand them, starting with what it means to be "in Christ."

Paul: Being "in Christ" really is fundamental to my theology. I use the phrase, or closely related phrases like "in the Lord" or "with Christ," frequently throughout all my letters. It's not confined to any one period of my writing or to addressing any one particular issue in the church. To be a Christian is more than being a disciple of Jesus who retains his or her own individual identity; it is about being incorporated into him. Take Romans 6:1-11 as expressing the core of it, even though the actual phrase "in Christ" isn't used here. Instead I use synonymous phrases like "into Christ" and "with him." Answering those who say, "If the more we sin, the more God's grace is at work, so let's keep on sinning," I show that this is deeply to misunderstand the nature of Christian commitment and experience. I explain that "all of us who were baptized into Christ Jesus were baptized into his death," and we've been joined to him in the closest possible way, experiencing his death, burial, and resurrection in our own lives. "For if we have been united with him in a death like his, we will certainly also be united with him in a resurrection like his." So we can't possibly go on living our old sin-filled lives. It means the pattern of our lives must be defined by the pattern of his life, central to which were his death, burial, and resurrection.

Observer: It's worth saying that Paul uses "in Christ" or "in Christ Jesus" eighty-three times in his writings and "in the Lord" or "in the Lord Jesus" a further forty-seven times. His use of it is spread throughout his letters. There are a host of closely related phrases as well, such as "in him," "into Christ," "through Christ," and "with Christ." Verbs that begin with the prefix *with* (*syn*) are common and are used twenty-one times about believers' dying, rising, reigning, and suffering with Christ as well as being conformed to him. The use of *with* highlights that the believer's personal relationship is not the full story. To be "with him" inevitably brings us into relationship with others who are also "with him." Being incorporated into Christ is to be incorporated into his body, the church.[11]

---

[11]For further details, see James D. G. Dunn, *The Theology of Paul the Apostle* (Edinburgh: T&T Clark, 1998), 390-412.

Paul: To be "in Christ" is a wonderfully adaptable idea. Sometimes it emphasizes our union with him through our having faith in him. Sometimes it is about our participation in his story, as mentioned above—that is, our mirroring his story in our own lives. Sometimes it is about our identification with him, especially when it comes to understanding that he is risen, reigning, and victorious. Sometimes it is about joining him and so being incorporated into his collective body. Being "in Christ" stands in strong contrast to being "in Adam," as we've mentioned before.

The idea has both an objective and a subjective meaning. Objectively, those who are "in Christ" are justified and have received redemption: "there is now no condemnation for those who are in Christ Jesus" (Rom 8:1). This aspect deals with the facts of our faith, with what was accomplished by Christ, the grace received from God through Christ, and the result of our joining with Christ (see Rom 3:24; 6:23; 8:39; 1 Cor 1:4; 15:22; 2 Cor 3:14; Gal 5:6).

The subjective side of being "in Christ" speaks of our experience of being "in him": we are "made . . . alive with Christ" (Eph 2:5). Truly, "if anyone is in Christ, the new creation has come" (2 Cor 5:17). This new life impacts so many different dimensions of our experience (see Rom 6:11; 1 Cor 1:30; Gal 3:28; Eph 6:10), especially the area of our ethical behavior (see Rom 14:14; 1 Cor 7:22; 15:58; Eph 6:1; Phil 3:1; 4:1-2; Col 2:6; 2:9-23).

As you can see, this subjective element is not about some form of mysticism whereby we have some out-of-the-body type experience of close and intimate fellowship with Christ. Such things do happen, and I myself have experienced them (see 2 Cor 12:1-5). It's obvious, though, isn't it? that when I'm speaking about the experience of being "in Christ" I'm talking about how we live in our present material world and in our real flesh-and-blood relationships. So don't misunderstand a phrase like the one I use in Ephesians 1:3, where I offer praise to God "who has blessed us in the heavenly realms with every spiritual blessing in Christ." As the rest of the letter shows, those blessings, conceived and delivered from and secure in heaven, are very much to do with life on earth.

Let me say a couple more things briefly. I'm aware that this extraordinarily rich idea can be used merely as a synonym for being a Christian, but such a superficial use would miss out on its depths. Being "in Christ" denotes a transfer of lordship to Christ and an existential participation in his life. It is about a departure from the way of life that was once dominated by sin but is now dead, into a new form of life controlled by Christ who now "lives in me" (Gal 2:19-20; cf. Rom 5:12–6:14). In Christ we can legitimately say in that sense, "I no longer live." It is a sign of the new creation that is dawning (see 2 Cor 5:17). So it's pretty radical.

On occasions I speak of the need to "clothe yourselves with the Lord Jesus Christ" (Rom 13:14; Gal 3:27). It isn't meant to suggest we can put him on and take him off, as we do a coat; it is another way of talking about being "in Christ." I also sometimes reverse the relationship, and instead of talking about us being in Christ, I talk about him being in us (see Rom 8:10; 2 Cor 13:5; Gal 2:19-20; Eph 3:17; Col 1:27). It amounts to the same thing and merely highlights the close reciprocal relationship between believers and their Lord.[12]

A final point, if I may: the chair commented that my other big idea is that of justification. The relationship between them is really quite simple. Justification is the verdict passed on those who are "in Christ" (see Rom 3:24; Gal 2:17; Phil 3:8-9). The basis for people being declared in the right, or righteous, is that they are found in the Messiah. So it's two different perspectives on one spiritual reality.[13]

> **Observer:** In a thorough recent study of Paul's teaching about union with Christ, Constantine Campbell has concluded that it is not the center of Paul's theology, since a center "is the one element that controls the others and creates coherence between them all." The center is God; but this teaching is the key which, like any key that unlocks a door, gives access to all that is within Paul's theology without controlling or reducing those other aspects to itself.[14]
>
> Campbell sums up the significance of Paul's teaching on union with Christ by saying,
>
>> virtually every element of Christ's work that is of interest to Paul is connected in some way to union with Christ. Salvation, redemption, reconciliation, creation, election, predestination, adoption, sanctification, headship, provision, his death, resurrection, ascension, glorification, self-giving, the gifts of grace, peace, eternal life, the Spirit, spiritual riches and blessings, freedom, and the fulfillment of God's promises are all related to union with Christ.[15]

---

[12]As an analogy, someone once commented that if you immerse a bucket in the ocean, you can legitimately say both that the water is in the bucket and that the bucket is in the water!

[13]See further, N. T. Wright, *Paul and the Faithfulness of God* (London: SPCK, 2013), 950, 858.

[14]Constantine R. Campbell, *Paul and Union with Christ: An Exegetical and Theological Study* (Grand Rapids: Zondervan, 2012), 439.

[15]Ibid., 331-32.

Peter: Before we leave this, I want to point out that I also speak of being "in Christ," though obviously not as much as Paul does—but then I didn't write as much as he did! My use of the phrase also demonstrates something of the varied uses to which it can be put. First, I write of it in an ethical sense about my readers' "good behavior in Christ" (1 Pet 3:16). Second, I use it to assure them of their future: they are a people who after suffering are "called ... to [God's] eternal glory in Christ" (1 Pet 5:10). Third, I use it to pray for God's peace to be experienced by "all of you who are in Christ"—that is, all who are Christians (1 Pet 5:14).

John: I want to go further and say that I share Paul's emphasis and frequently refer to it. I may not use the phrase "in Christ" because in my Gospel at least I'm recording Christ's words in the first person. So Jesus said, "Whoever eats my flesh and drinks my blood remains in me, and I in them" (Jn 6:56). What else is that but the union with Christ that Paul expounds? Jesus spoke to the disciples of the Spirit as one who "lives with you and will be in you" (Jn 14:17). Since it is plain that he is never anything other than the Spirit of Jesus, that pretty much amounts to Paul's idea of "Christ in you." When Jesus used the image of the vine and the branches, he told his disciples we would bear fruit only "if you remain *in me* and I in you" (Jn 15:5; see also 15:2, 4, 6, 7). Similarly, in Gethsemane Jesus prayed that his disciples might be one, "Father, just as you are in me and I am in you. May they also be in us so that the world may believe that you have sent me" (Jn 17:21). I mention this mutual indwelling in 14:20, 23 and 17:23 as well.

The phrase "in him," or similar, also weaves its way through my first letter (1 Jn 2:5-6, 24, 27-28; 3:6, 24; 4:12-13, 15-16; 5:20). That's an awful lot of references for a short letter. You might even say that the need to "continue in him" is the major theme of the letter. And while it doesn't crop up nearly as often in Revelation, where I'm obviously dealing with different issues, it's not altogether absent there either. I use it mostly in a modified form there since I sometimes speak of being "in the Spirit" (Rev 1:10; 4:2; 14:13; 17:3; 21:10).

Chair: Okay. So Paul has made the phrase "in Christ" peculiarly his own, but he certainly has no monopoly on the idea and others use it in their own way. The frequency with which it's mentioned points to its importance. Its meaning is simultaneously transparent, comprehensive, and profound.

Let's leave that there, however, and take a look at Paul's other great concept—that of justification.

A New Standing Before God: Justification by Faith

Chair: Paul, please would you explain where the concept of justification came from and what it means? Apart from one passing reference in the parable of the Pharisee and the tax collector (see Lk 18:9-14), where we read that the tax collector went home "justified," you are the only person to speak about justification.

Paul: Well, for me it is a major way of viewing what God was doing in and through Jesus Christ, and so it's an idea I develop in some detail. My headline is that we are "justified freely by his grace through the redemption that came by Christ Jesus" (Rom 3:24). The term belongs to the world of the law courts, where a person who has been accused of something is judged to be in the right and acquitted. For us it means being brought to a position of right standing before God, and furthermore being brought into a right relationship with God. So we might say the idea is both legal (*forensic* is the term sometimes used) and relational. It is profoundly relational, much more relational than the later state-controlled legal system became.

How can we be justified, since we are obviously guilty of sin? It happens because "while we were still sinners" God demonstrated "his own love for us" (Rom 5:8) and gave the gift of his Son, whose obedience (see Rom 5:19), death (see Rom 4:25; 5:8), blood (see Rom 5:9), and resurrection (see Rom 4:25) as our substitute lead to our being declared "righteous"—that is, "in the right" before God.

You'll find that when I speak of being justified I often speak at the same time about believing or having faith in Jesus Christ. His life and work become effective for us when we trust our lives and salvation to him. Negatively, this means we don't trust in keeping the law to save us, as I said when preaching in Pisidian Antioch (see Acts 13:39) and as I wrote and explained to the Galatians (see Gal 2:15-21). The "works of the law" I mention are those particular rituals and customs that mark the Jewish people as distinct from others, such as circumcision, sabbath keeping, and food regulations. The key point here is that faith in Christ is open to all, regardless of their ethnic background, and no one is required to adopt Jewish customs in order to experience God's grace. More widely, however, we dare not trust in any part of the law to save us, since we're unable to keep it. All it does is condemn us, rather than "justify" us, as mentioned before.[16]

---

[16]See chap. 7, 127-28.

None of this comes out of the blue. Israel has long seen God as the Judge and been concerned about the justice of God. Israel has also always believed that being in a right standing with God is about believing his promise rather than living a perfect life, as the life of Abraham illustrates (see Rom 4:1-25). As I say twice, "Abraham believed God, and it was credited to him as righteousness" (Rom 4:3, 22). Abraham did not have righteousness credited to his account because of what he did but because of the one whom he trusted. And that claim goes all the way back to Genesis 15:6. So God has not changed the basis on which he relates to sinful humanity. It was always about their believing his promise.

The prophets taught the same thing. Twice I cite Habakkuk 2:4 as saying "The righteous will live by faith." You'll find it in Romans 1:17 and Galatians 3:11, and, because it's so fundamental, I'm glad to see it crops up again in Hebrews 10:38. The straightforward meaning of this, as you'll see from Ephesians 2:8-9, is that those who exercise (or live by) faith in the Messiah are the ones who are declared righteous.

> **Observer:** Let's just take time out from Paul for a moment because what he has just said about the meaning of the statement, "The righteous [or just] shall live by faith," has been subject to much discussion recently. To start with, the word *faith* could equally be translated "faithfulness." That certainly stresses that faith is not a one-off commitment but an ongoing way of life. I guess no one would want to question the need for ongoing faith in practice, would they? Becoming a Christian is not about a once-in-a-lifetime "decision" that has no bearing on the rest of one's life.
>
> The more contentious part of the discussion raises the question as to whose faith, or faithfulness, is referred to here. Does it refer to our faith, and mean that it is our trust in Christ that enables our justification? Or does it refer to the faithfulness of God or the Son of God? After all, Romans puts quite a premium on Christ's undeviating faithfulness even to the point of being crucified (see Rom 5:12-20). And God certainly is faithful—to his word and to showing mercy to the people he created. Our salvation does depend on God proving reliable. So it could well mean that it is the faithfulness of God himself, or of his Son, that leads to people being justified. However, Ephesians 2:8-9 ("For it is by grace

you have been saved, through faith—and this is not from yourselves, it is the gift of God—not by works, so that no one can boast") and Galatians 2:20 ("The life I now live in the body, I live by faith in the Son of God") read more naturally if taken in the traditional way: it is by exercising faith in Christ that people are justified. That should influence how we read other references—namely, as "our faith in Christ" rather than as "the faithfulness of Christ."

Paul: In my mind, justification assumes some priority over other insights into the gospel, but it should never be divorced from the other aspects I mention. It would be all too easy for people to misunderstand it, as some have done, and think that if they are justified simply by believing in Christ, they don't need to change their behavior, but can go on sinning. That would make justification to be nothing more than a legal transaction, or even what might more appropriately be called a legal "fiction." That's a distortion of my teaching. I confronted this very attitude in Romans 6:1-14, where my reply to it is that justification and being "in Christ" go hand in hand. You can't have the one without the other. In altering our standing before God, justification inevitably alters our ongoing relationship with him.

A New Life: Concepts of Salvation

Chair: "Justification" is one way of describing what Jude 3 calls "the salvation we share"; but it is such a wonderfully rich salvation that no single concept can do justice (forgive the pun!) to it. As I read the New Testament documents, I find that the images, models, metaphors, or concepts, call them what you will, that illustrate and explain the New Testament seem almost to tumble over one another. So let's spend some time reviewing what the major concepts of salvation are.

Observer: A bit of background may be helpful here.

First, the language of salvation is an obvious way of describing the work of Christ because it draws on a rich Old Testament heritage.[17] To be saved is to be rescued or delivered, as Israel were from slavery in Egypt. That rescue colored all their subsequent experiences and understanding

---

[17]See also chap. 3, 21.

of God. They constantly referred back to it. The New Testament portrays Christ's work of salvation in those terms, only much greater still. The Hebrew word for it (*yaša*) means to be brought out of confinement into a spacious place. That's a wonderful image of salvation. As George Caird commented, it is the same in the New Testament, for "through all the varieties of emphasis [about salvation] there runs the one dominant theme of life: rich, full, abundant, and free, a pulsating and irrepressible vitality."[18]

Second, we need to say that all the concepts we'll mention here are built on one crucial foundation: that salvation has its origin in the grace of God. This should already be obvious from what we've said about justification, but grace lies behind every concept of salvation. People are delivered from sin, the present evil age, the law, Satan, and the wrath of God, not because they deserve it or have earned it, but purely because God chooses to pour out his undeserved love on us. Salvation is sheer grace, as everyone agrees.

> ### SELECT LIST OF TEXTS ABOUT GRACE
>
> Jn 1:16-17; Acts 11:23; 14:3; 15:11; 20:24; Rom 3:24; 4:16; 5:2, 15-17; 11:5-6; 2 Cor 8:9; Gal 1:6; 2:21; Eph 1:6-7; 2:5-8; Phil 1:7; Col 1:6; 2 Tim 1:9; Tit 2:11; 3:7; 1 Pet 5:10.

Third, we might comment that, while people use different words for it, we have chosen to speak of *concepts* of salvation. *Concepts* embraces all the other words used, such as *images*, *metaphors*, and *models*. Images are often flimsy and insubstantial.[19] Metaphors define one thing by another and are imaginative, if illuminating constructions that we don't expect to be real. (For example, we do not literally think that God is a rock.) Models are often scaled-down versions of the real thing. Concepts will help us to focus on the reality of salvation.

---

[18]George Caird, *New Testament Theology*, ed. L. D. Hurst (Oxford: Oxford University Press, 1994), 179.

[19]One of the best recent introductions to these concepts is Brenda B. Colijn, *Images of Salvation in the New Testament* (Downers Grove, IL: IVP Academic, 2010). Her use of *images* does not mean she regards them as insubstantial, superficial, or flimsy.

Chair: Now, the way we're going to approach this is by organizing the different concepts into a number of categories. It'll become obvious as we go along. Let's begin.

From the Family: New Birth and Adoption

Chair: There are a couple of ideas that relate to the joy of having a newborn in the family or of adopting a child into a family.

John: The concept of being "born again" is one way I talk about salvation. In the introduction to my Gospel I distinguish between natural birth and those who are "born of God" (Jn 1:13). Jesus used a similar idea when he told Nicodemus first, as a matter of general principle, that "no one can see the kingdom of God unless they are born again" (Jn 3:3) and then, quite personally, "You must be born again" (Jn 3:7).

In fact, the word *again* could also mean "from above" (cf. Jn 3:31; 8:23), meaning from God. Jesus explained we need to be "born of water and the Spirit" (Jn 3:5), which some have taken to mean "naturally and spiritually." Others have read a reference to baptism into his words, but that almost certainly wasn't in his mind. Rather, his words pick up on passages like Ezekiel 36:25–37:14, which speaks about the restoration of Israel through, first, its cleansing and, second, God's breathing new life into it. The concept indicates how there are two very distinct ways of living and that all human beings, even teachers in Israel like Nicodemus, need a second birth—"an infusion of supernatural, eschatological life"[20]— in addition to their natural birth and to know the Spirit's regenerating power within them.

In my first letter I assume this concept and speak six times of being "born of God" (1 Jn 2:29; 3:9; 4:7; 5:1, 4, 18), mainly to point out that those who are "born again" do not continue to sin.

Peter: I use the idea just once, but link it to the resurrection rather than to the Holy Spirit when I praise God that "in his great mercy he has given us new birth into a living hope through the resurrection of Jesus Christ from the dead" (1 Pet 1:3). I assume it when addressing my readers as "newborn babies" and encouraging them to "crave pure spiritual milk, so that by it [they] may grow up in [their] salvation" (1 Pet 2:2).

---

[20]Paul A. Rainbow, *Johannine Theology: The Gospel, the Epistles and the Apocalypse* (Downers Grove, IL: InterVarsity Press, 2014), 278.

Paul: On one occasion I too use an almost identical term and speak of "the washing of rebirth" (Tit 3:5). Some assume any reference to washing or water must be a reference to baptism, and sometimes it is; but, as John has explained, here the washing is primarily a reference to cleansing.

It's the other family image I use more—that of adoption, partly because it made more sense in the Gentile world where it was well defined and frequently practiced. I use the idea to contrast the experience of being a slave in a family with that of being a son. So I remind Roman Christians that the Spirit "brought about your adoption to sonship" (Rom 8:15) and say something very similar to the Galatians (see Gal 4:5). I mention it again in Ephesians 1:5. Each time it highlights the privileges of security and intimacy we enjoy as those chosen by God to be members of his family. Of course it involves responsibilities as well, but let's not undervalue the advantage and honor we have of being his children. We were used to thinking of Israel as enjoying the privileges of adoption (see Rom 9:4-5), so we're only reworking and extending an old idea.

Chair: Another concept that could fit here is that of reconciliation, since reconciliation is often something that takes place within the family—but we'll leave that for later.

From Creation: New Creation, Regeneration, and Illumination

Chair: I know there are a cluster of concepts that loosely coalesce around the idea of creation. Who would like to tell us about those?

Paul: I imagine I provide the most frequently quoted sound bite here in 2 Corinthians 5:17. Most people think I wrote, "If anyone is in Christ, he or she is a new creation." Of course that's true—but it's not what I wrote, or not the key point I was making. I didn't say, "*He or she is* a new creation"; I wrote, "If anyone is in Christ, the new creation has come: the old has gone, the new is here!" The point wasn't about individuals starting life again when they are "in Christ," but that they are evidence of the new age having dawned, of the new world Christ is restoring having come into existence. What happens on an individual level is "a small window on the new, large eschatological reality. God is renewing the world," and people who are "in Christ" "are agents of that renewal."[21]

My new-creation language always concerns more than the individual. The new creation has ethnic and religious significance. Christ fundamentally

---

[21]The quotation is from Wright, *Paul and the Faithfulness of God*, 1072.

reconstructs the things in those spheres that belonged to the old order (see Gal 6:15; Eph 2:14-18, esp. v. 15).

Peter: Yes, when I think of a new creation I think primarily in terms of future cosmic renewal (see 2 Pet 3:10-13), although even that has massive implications for how we live now (see 2 Pet 3:11, 14, 18).

John: No one needs to convince me that we look forward in hope to a future cosmic renewal. You only have to read Revelation 19–22 to see that.

Going back, though, to the use of creation themes to describe our present salvation, I'd point to my speaking about eternal life. My starting point is to present Jesus in terms of the first creation. Jesus, the Word, "was life, and that life was the light of all mankind." Genesis 1:3 reverberates in John 1:4 (cf. Jn 5:26). Darkness is hostile to life. It tried to overwhelm Jesus' light but couldn't do so. Jesus liberates people from darkness so that "they may have life, and have it to the full" (Jn 10:10).

Using different metaphors, Jesus described himself as "the bread of life" (Jn 6:35, 48, 51) and "the resurrection and the life" (Jn 11:25). Bread is the staple diet that keeps us alive, while resurrection points to a life not snuffed out by death. Without Christ there is no life. He is simply "the way and the truth and *the life*" (Jn 14:6).

In order that people might grasp the true significance of the life Jesus came to give, I use the term *eternal life*. The life Jesus offers isn't mere existence or more of the same, but a different quality of life altogether. The word *eternal* (*aiōnios*) refers not to the everlasting length of the new life, but to it being the life of the age to come, which we already begin to experience now. So it's about the new creation having broken in and taking hold of people's lives. If you look up how I use the phrase, you'll see that time and again I explain that this life isn't experienced

> ### "ETERNAL LIFE" IN JOHN
>
> 3:15-16, 36; 4:14, 36; 5:24, 39; 6:27, 40, 47, 54, 68; 10:28; 12:25, 50; 17:2-3. Also 1 Jn 1:2; 2:25; 3:15; 5:11, 13, 20.

by everyone, but only by those who believe in Christ. It's my theme tune, if you like. So in 1 John 1:2 I sum it up in saying, "The life appeared; we have seen it and testify to it, and we proclaim to you the eternal life."

No other New Testament writer speaks of "eternal life," but even so there is connection between my use of it and other approaches. To gain eternal life one has to be "born again" (Jn 3:1-15). Another word for that would be *regenerated*. And that is something others clue into.

Paul: Ah, I see the connection. While my vision of regeneration is often about the regeneration of creation itself, I also use the idea for an individual being given new life. I praise God that he "made us alive with Christ even when we were dead in transgressions" (Eph 2:5) and remind the Colossians that "God made you alive with Christ" (Col 2:13). I'm not sure whether that's regeneration or resurrection, to be honest, but such precision doesn't matter. They're shorthand statements for my lengthy exposition in Romans 6–8, where I show how this new life in Christ becomes a reality through the Holy Spirit.

John: Let's explore a bit more the theme of light, which both Paul and I use, because it is relevant. God's first recorded spoken word at creation, as we've noted, was "Let there be light," and light came into being (Gen 1:3). I've already acknowledged the link between light and life, but we need to add that Jesus proclaimed himself to be "the light of the world" (Jn 8:12). His "I am" claims were usually backed up by a sign, and this one was backed up by his giving sight to a blind man (see Jn 9:1-11). The darkness this man had experienced since birth was dispelled by the healing power of Jesus and replaced by light. To be a Christian can be seen as being illuminated or enlightened.

Paul: John's right to say I use the idea of light, but I muse on it in very different ways from him. My experience of light on the Damascus Road (see Acts 9:3) attracts me to the image. Once I relate it directly to the creation story: the God who turned on the lights then has "made his light shine in our hearts to give us the light of the knowledge of God's glory displayed in the face of Christ" (2 Cor 4:6). You can't fail to see echoes of my Damascus Road experience in that! When the light is switched on, we see Jesus for who he really is, not as a crucified troublemaker but as a glorious Lord and the very image of God himself (see 2 Cor 4:4-5; cf. 5:16).

I play with that image in different ways. Christians are "children of the light" (1 Thess 5:5; Eph 5:8-9) called to "shine . . . like stars in the sky as [they] hold firmly to the word of life" (Phil 2:15-16; cf. Dan 12:3).

Matthew: Taking up that point, I would remind people that Jesus told his disciples that they were "the light of the world" (Mt 5:14), presumably taking their light from him and fulfilling the mission which was originally given to Israel (see Is 49:6).

The Hebraist: I guess the image of light was fairly common among us, since in a passing comment I ask my readers to remember their early days as Christians "after you had received the light" (Heb 10:32).

Peter: I think it was indeed common. I speak of it actively rather than passively, as you do, when I say our task is to "declare the praises of him who called you out of darkness into his wonderful light" (1 Pet 2:9). This is not a theoretical theological statement but a cause of wonder and worship.

From History: Ransom and Redemption

Chair: We could say more, but let's turn to a different area, that of ransom and redemption. These concepts could fit under a number of headings, but they are so ingrained in Israel's history that our consideration of them can at least start there. Let's begin with *ransom*, the less frequently mentioned of the two.

Mark: In a very memorable saying, Jesus said his purpose in coming was "not . . . to be served, but to serve, and to give his life as a ransom for many" (Mk 10:45).

Paul: Makes you think, doesn't it? Since Jesus made such a clear statement about being a ransom, why do I use *ransom* only once (1 Tim 2:6)? I think it must be because it is subsumed under the wider concept of redemption.

The Hebraist: Agreed. I mention it just once as well, although in a highly significant way. The importance of something, remember, doesn't always go hand in hand with how often we mention it. In talking of Jesus as "the mediator of a new covenant," I say that "he has died as a ransom to set them free from the sins committed under the first covenant" (Heb 9:15). However, just a few verses earlier I'd talked of "eternal redemption" (Heb 9:12), which, as Paul says, is the more common word in this area.

Observer: Ransom theology certainly has roots in the Old Testament (e.g., see Ex 30:12; Lev 19:20; Ps 49:8; Is 43:3) as a payment to secure life or freedom. However, in the New Testament it is somewhat redundant in the face of the language of redemption. Ransom is mostly used as a noun and simply means the price paid for redemption.

After the New Testament period the idea of a ransom sometimes raised unhelpful questions, chiefly when people pushed the simple metaphor too far and tried to turn it into a complete analogy. So, Origen (ca. 185–254) and other early exponents of the idea suggested that God paid the ransom of Christ's life to the evil one, who on receipt of the payment released sinners from his control. Gregory of Nyssa (330–395) went further, saying the devil was "a hungry fish who swallowed the bait of Christ's humanity but got caught on the hook of his deity."[22]

If this explanation is legitimate, doesn't that make Satan greater than God, since he is able to make demands that God feels obliged to meet? And doesn't Gregory's comment imply that God could gain our freedom only by deception? These views give too much credence to a thoroughly corrupted devil.

Chair: Before seeing how you all use it, let me give some background to the more frequent language of "redemption." Israel's DNA was essentially that of having been redeemed from Egypt. To "redeem" is to secure freedom, or to release people or things to fulfill their true purpose, by the payment of a redemption price. It was the "mighty arm" of the Lord and the blood of the Passover lamb (see Ex 6:6; 15:13; Neh. 1:10) that redeemed Israel from Egypt.

Redemption language is, however, also embedded in other aspects of Old Testament experience and worship. The firstborn in Israel—animals and sons—were the Lord's and had to be redeemed by the payment of a redemption price if people were to use them or let them enjoy their freedom (see Ex 13:13, 15). Under certain circumstances slaves, animals, and property could all be redeemed (e.g., see Ex 21:8, 30; Lev 27). Ruth was released from her nonstatus as a foreign widow by the kinsman-redeemer. The language of redemption was readily applied later to the return from exile: "I, the LORD, am your Savior, your Redeemer, the Mighty One of Jacob" (Is 49:26; cf. 43:1). And in the Psalms God's redemption is the regular cause of prayer and praise: "They remembered that God was their Rock, that God Most High was their Redeemer" (Ps 78:35).

Luke: In Jesus' day, the Jewish nation longed to be free from Roman oppression, just as they'd once been set free from Egyptian bondage. Their past experience gave them hope that God would do it again! So at his birth there was much talk about the redemption of Israel. It cropped up in Zechariah's song (see Lk 1:68) and Anna's thanksgiving (see Lk 2:38), and was scarcely

---

[22]Cited in Bird, *Evangelical Theology*, 391.

below the surface of Mary's song as well (see Lk 1:46-55). Toward the end of his earthly life they were still looking forward to redemption (see Lk 21:28; 24:21). Redemption was obviously not from a political occupying power, as they'd hoped, but from the much greater evil of sin.

Paul: Given that history, redemption is a wonderful way of describing the salvation we have in Jesus, "who has become for us . . . our . . . redemption" (1 Cor 1:30). The gospel can be summed up by saying, "In him we have redemption through his blood, the forgiveness of sins, in accordance with the riches of God's grace" (Eph 1:7). As a description of our salvation, redemption doesn't need any qualifying words (see Rom 3:24; Col 1:14). However, redemption usually means being set free from something that would imprison us, and in our case that might be "the curse of the law" (Gal 3:13), "wickedness" (Tit 2:14) or even our decaying bodies (see Rom 8:23). Positively, we are redeemed for the purpose of receiving the blessing God gave through Abraham (see Gal 3:14). We experience redemption now, but, as Luke indicated, it's true that there is more to come on what I termed "the day of redemption" (Eph 1:14; 4:30). Then we'll enter fully into our inheritance.

The Hebraist: When talking about *ransom* just now I mentioned that I speak about the "eternal redemption" (Heb 9:12) that Christ's blood has secured for us.

Peter: That's exactly the point I make when I speak of redemption: "you know that it was not with perishable things such as silver or gold [cf. Acts 3:6] that you were redeemed from the empty way of life handed down to you from your ancestors, but with the precious blood of Christ, a lamb without blemish or defect" (1 Pet 1:18-19).

John: *Redemption* is a great word, with a great insight into the meaning of salvation. If I hadn't developed my own way of looking at that salvation, I might well have used it more; as it is, I mention it only once in a slightly different way, of the "144,000 who had been redeemed from [persecution on] the earth" (Rev 14:3).

Chair: Well, that's a good overview of the word *redemption*. It's a word, of course, that not only made sense because of Israel's story but also had an obvious attraction in the world of the Roman Empire, where so many slaves were working toward gaining their freedom through the payment of a redemption price.

From the Hospital: Healing

Chair: If we turn to the area of healing, I suspect we will encounter some complexity rather than a superficial image. One of the reasons why it's complex is because the language of healing often overlaps with the language of salvation; another is because salvation is spoken of in several tenses.

Mark: Those are good points. The essence of salvation is deliverance or rescue, and it is used in our Gospels to describe physical healing—that is, deliverance from sickness (see Mk 3:2; 5:28, 34; 6:56; 10:52; cf. Mt 9:22; Lk 8:48; 17:19; 18:42); rescue from natural disaster—that is, deliverance from trouble (see Mt 8:25; 14:36); exorcisms—that is, deliverance from demons (see Mk 1:21-28; 5:1-20; 7:25-30; 9:14-29; see also 1:32-34, 39; 3:7-12); and spiritual salvation—that is, deliverance from sin (Mt 1:21; Lk 7:50; see later, Acts 27:20, 31, 34).

We didn't always draw the neat distinctions later generations did because we saw the work of God in rescuing people through Christ as a comprehensive work: physical healing and forgiveness of sin were separable but connected works (see Mk 2:1-12). Sometimes, from the viewpoint of modern people, Jesus seemed to use the idea of salvation ambiguously, as when he said that those who stood firm to the end in the context of being rescued from physical harm would "be saved" (Mk 13:13). Was it a physical rescue he had in mind, as the context might suggest, or was he looking beyond that to an eternal salvation? Jesus made it clear that the person who was sick was not always sick because he or she had sinned. Nonetheless, sickness, whether caused directly or indirectly by sin, was common in our world that, being fallen, suffered the consequences of its alienation from God.

Matthew: On one occasion I (not Jesus) quoted Isaiah 53:4, "He took up our infirmities and bore our diseases," when talking about his healing and exorcisms (Mt 8:17). Coming from that crucial servant song, it makes clear that healing is not a separate work from the cross but is crucially related to the redemption he gained there. It should also be obvious from the wider reports of his ministry that the cross doesn't ensure that everyone is going to know physical healing immediately.

Luke: Taking up the ambiguity to which Mark refers, I have an instance of that when Paul and Silas experienced the earthquake when in prison in Philippi and the jailer cried out, "Sirs, what must I do to be saved?" (Acts 16:30). I'm pretty sure he meant "saved" as in "get out of the mess I'm in"

—but they responded, "Believe in the Lord Jesus, and you will be saved" (Acts 16:31), and that's exactly what he did. A question asked on one level could be answered on another. On the other hand, there are times when the use of the word *salvation* is crystal clear. When Peter told the Sanhedrin (the Jewish council), "Salvation is found in no one else, for there is no other name under heaven given to mankind by which we must be saved" (Acts 4:12), he wasn't thinking of Jesus as a cure for a headache!

Paul: By the time I'm writing my letters, *salvation* or being *saved* was consistently used of salvation from sin and a hopeless future. That's the way I use it in a string of verses (see Rom 1:16; 8:24; 1 Cor 1:18; Eph 1:13; 2:8; 1 Tim 2:4), and it's equally the way Peter (see 1 Pet 1:5, 9; 2:2) and the Hebraist (see Heb 2:10; 5:9) use it as well.

The Hebraist: I'm not really disagreeing with that, but traces of the wider meaning of salvation still linger, as when I say that Noah's ark was built "to save his family" (Heb 11:7).

Observer: In the New Testament world human beings were viewed as whole, unified, and integrated beings and not dissected into various components, as we do today. So it shouldn't surprise us that the words *healing* and *salvation* (*sōzō, sōtēria*), although they could be used in a more restricted sense, were often used in a way that embraced the overcoming of disease, discomfort, or disorder of any sort. Healing of the body and social relationships, deliverance from social or personal ills, and forgiveness of sin were equally significant.

Mark and Luke, above, speak of the ambiguity that is seen in Jesus' healing, not because they felt that ambiguity was confusing to them but for the sake of present-day readers.[23] So in that part of their conversation we've pushed the boundaries a bit to make their meaning clear, rather than reporting words they actually said. Although they could speak of healing in a narrow sense, their view of human beings as whole, unified persons meant that they had no difficulty in seeing healing and salvation as two aspects of God's deliverance. In this way, healing becomes a model and example of eternal salvation.

---

[23]Joel B. Green, *Why Salvation?* (Nashville: Abingdon Press, 2013), 31-47.

Paul: There's more to say, as the chair mentioned. People have noticed, rightly, the way in which I, and Peter as well, write of being saved in the past, present, and future tenses. So we can quite confidently say that we "have been saved" (Eph 2:5, 8; Rom 5:12, 21; 6:22; 8:24; Gal 2:20; Col 3:1-4; 2 Tim 1:9). It's something that is settled and accomplished by the completed work of Christ. Our deliverance is sure. However, we are also in the process of "being saved" (1 Cor 1:18; 15:2; 2 Cor 2:15; 3:18). Salvation is something we must "continue to work out . . . with fear and trembling" (Phil 2:12-13) in the present, rather than being complacent about. Then, precisely because we are processing our salvation, there is more to come and we can speak of it as "the hope of glory" that we look forward to (Col 1:27; Rom 5:2, cf. 8-10). Jesus is the Savior we wait for, "who rescues us from the coming wrath" (1 Thess 1:10).

Peter: Yes, and my own writing emphasizes the present (see 1 Pet 2:2) and future dimensions of salvation (see 1 Pet 1:5, 9) rather than the past. It's not that I have any doubt about the salvation we've already received in Christ; I just express it in different language (see 1 Pet 1:3-4). My purpose in writing is to inspire people to persevere through suffering, so my emphasis is inevitably on the way the present is influenced by the future.

The Hebraist: I'm with Peter on the importance of looking forward to Christ appearing "a second time, not to bear sin, but to bring salvation to those who are waiting for him" (Heb 9:28). Salvation has a future dimension.

John: When I use the language of salvation, which I do a bit, I use it somewhat differently. I speak of Christ coming to save the world (see Jn 3:17; 12:47) and of his being the means by which people might be saved (see Jn 5:34; 10:9). I don't, though, use it in the way the other Gospels do. With Paul I rejoice that we can be certain of our salvation now, although I put it like this: anyone who believes in Jesus Christ "*has* eternal life and will not be judged but *has* crossed over from death to life" (Jn 5:24).

Where I do use the word *salvation* is in Revelation, where I'm looking forward to the future and proclaiming that "Salvation belongs to our God" (Rev 7:10; cf. 12:10; 19:1). None of this, however, is linked with with notions of healing, except in the most general and ultimate of ways.

From the Temple: Cleansing and Being Brought Near
Chair: There are a whole bunch of ideas that have their starting point in the temple, aren't there? I'm thinking of concepts like cleansing, holiness, purity, and drawing near.

Observer: Such language may be scattered in all sorts of different places rather than concentrated in one place, with the exception of Hebrews. The temple, however, as the dwelling place of God and the place where people drew near to him, was such a significant institution for Israel that it would be surprising if the New Testament didn't derive some of its understanding of salvation from what went on there, as well as from the obvious theme of sacrificial atonement.

A basic distinction made in the tabernacle was between what was holy (set apart for God's use) and what was ordinary (available for everyday use) (see Lev 10:10). Holy things had the potential to become contaminated and unclean and so needed cleansing if they were to be used in God's service. Holiness didn't describe a level of moral achievement but defined "a state of belonging to God and being dedicated to him." According to Peter Toon, "This relates directly to the Church's being called to service and sacrifice in the power of the Holy Spirit."[24] An example of this can be found when Paul addresses the Corinthians as "sanctified in Christ Jesus and called to be his holy people" (1 Cor 1:2). Their lives were anything but morally clean, but he still calls them "saints" or "sanctified"—because their calling and status in Christ, whatever the failures of their actual lives, had set them apart for God.

The Gospels use hardly any of the vocabulary of holiness, so it is largely elsewhere we need to look to see how this concept developed.

Mark: It's true we don't use holiness vocabulary much, but don't forget one incident where the wider temple picture is crucial. When Jesus died, "the curtain of the temple was torn in two from top to bottom" (Mk 15:38; Mt 27:51; cf. Lk 23:45)—a very powerful symbol of the way access to God was opened up through his death.

The Hebraist: Naturally, this perspective on salvation is close to my heart. Several relevant factors have already been mentioned, such as Christ being our high priest (see Heb 4:15–5:10) and his sacrifice bringing future salvation (see Heb 9:28); but I have a couple of fresh aspects of salvation that exploit temple imagery. First, I take up the important theme of cleansing

---

[24]Peter Toon, quoted by Colijn, *Images of Salvation*, 274.

that took place in the tabernacle or temple. People got defiled for all sorts of reasons and underwent cleansing rituals. Equally, things used in worship, bowls and utensils, got dirty and needed to be purified before being reused. I mention that "the law requires that nearly everything be cleansed with blood, and without the shedding of blood there is no forgiveness" (Heb 9:22). The exceptions to this are the minor cleansing rituals mentioned in Leviticus that involve water rather than blood—but they're secondary. So, for us, the blood of Christ cleanses our guilty consciences (see Heb 9:11-14; 10:22). How good it is to experience the removal of all the dirt and impurity of sin that clings to us so easily (see Heb 12:1) and to feel clean from the inside out! We who are impure are made pure by Christ.

A second important and not unrelated theme is that of "drawing near." Mark commented on the significance of the temple curtain being ripped apart. I develop that theme while never mentioning that event. I build instead on the foundation of the Old Testament priests who drew near to God and on the Day of Atonement were able to enter the most sacred place within the sanctuary, where God was enthroned on the ark of the covenant. Now Jesus had entered "behind the curtain . . . on our behalf" (Heb 6:19-20). What qualified the high priests of Israel to enter this most holy place was the sprinkling of animal blood, but Jesus entered using his own blood (see Heb 9:7, 11-14, 23-28). The sanctuary he entered was the real one, heaven itself, not a human model (see Heb 9:24). The significance for us is that it means we can draw near to God with unwavering confidence because of Jesus our Pioneer and Savior (see Heb 6:20; 9:12, 24-25; 10:19-22).

Paul: Those are two elements I talk about as well. When it comes to cleansing, for example, I stress the corporate rather than the individual nature of it. I talk of Christ's purpose being "to purify for himself a people that are his very own" (Tit 2:14) and of how he is currently making the church "holy, cleansing her by the washing with water through the word" (Eph 5:26). Some have read baptism into that, but if it's there, it is only as an outward sign of the inner cleansing which Christ works among us. When you look at the church, it's full of very unworthy people with skeletons in their closets; but the good news is that they have been "washed" clean from a multitude of horrible past sins (1 Cor 6:11) and so are now sanctified and justified.

I use the second idea of being "brought near [to God] by the blood of Christ" just once but in a very significant way. It means that godless, hopeless

Gentiles who had no part in the covenant of Israel are now brought in from the cold, not just to form one new people of God, but actually brought to God himself (Eph 2:13).

Peter: Before we leave this, I want to point out that I take up Leviticus 11:45 and 19:2, which instruct God's people to "be holy, because I am holy," and use that as a summary of our Christian calling (1 Pet 1:16). Our salvation involves our being distinctive and set apart to live exclusively for God.

From the Political Realm: Peace and Reconciliation

Chair: Let's move on to the question of peace and reconciliation. They take place in all spheres of relationships but often belong to the political realm. So let's deal with them under this heading. Let's start with *shalom*, that wonderful Old Testament word for "peace."

Paul: Perhaps the only real starting point for this is to acknowledge that God is the "God of peace," a well-known title for God in the early church (Rom 15:33; 16:20; cf. Heb 13:20). John says that light and love define the very character of God; that could be said of peace as well.

Luke: Well, that explains why we sometimes summed up the whole gospel by using the word *peace*. When Jesus forgave a sinful woman, he told her to "go in peace" (Lk 7:50). And Peter told Cornelius, "You know the message God sent to the people of Israel, announcing the good news of peace through Jesus Christ, who is Lord of all." The peace he meant here was the end to conflict between Jews and Gentiles, as we can see from his previous sentence: "God does not show favoritism but accepts from every nation the one who fears him and does what is right" (Acts 10:34-36).

Paul: That's definitely one of my major themes. Conflict between people is now a thing of the past, since Christ brought peace. We might even say that "he himself is our peace" (Eph 2:14). Ours is a "gospel of peace" (Eph 6:15), and we are called to live in peace with others (see Rom 12:18; Col 3:15). However, it was a peace that didn't come cheaply, because Jesus made peace "through his blood, shed on the cross" (Col 1:20).

The ramifications are immense. Personally we can enjoy peace with God, because the cause of our hostility has been dealt with (see Rom 5:1). As a result we can know peace within the deep recesses of our lives (see Rom 8:6; 14:17; 15:13; Phil 4:7). That must result in our being at peace with others (see Eph 2:14-22), whoever they are.

John: Paul's phrase "the peace of God, which transcends all understanding" (Phil 4:7) reminds me of the promise I heard Jesus make when he told us that on his departure he would leave us with peace, the like of which we couldn't experience anywhere else (see Jn 14:27). Peace, he said, was to be found "in me" (Jn 16:33).

Observer: The biblical idea of peace goes well beyond the absence of conflict and points to a state of positive well-being, as some of the verses just cited illustrate. It's a word that comes from the political realm, where warring nations found peace with each other, but it wasn't confined to international politics. Peace was needed between people at all levels of relationships and internally within individuals as well. The gospel, however, shouldn't be reduced to some sort of "feel-good" factor or contemporary pop therapy, since (a) primarily it is about peace with God, (b) the peace has been won by Christ entering the conflict, and (c), as we have seen, the good news has to do with peace between people, not just peace within an individual. It is about living an integrated life that has overcome disjointedness in any sphere and enjoys deep internal and external harmony.

The opening greeting in virtually all the New Testament letters is "Grace and peace to you." It was a conventional Greek way of starting a letter, but one that was invested with far deeper meaning than Greek culture could ever offer, because of Christ.

Chair: Reconciliation is a closely related concept, even, one might say, the same thing viewed from a different angle. The major use of the word group, outside the New Testament, is in the field of diplomacy. Therefore we place it under this heading of the gospel viewed from the political perspective.

Observer: That's true, but it is a concept that is unique to Paul, so much so that one New Testament scholar argued some years ago that it was "an interpretive key to Paul's theology," "the 'chief theme' or 'center' of his missionary and pastoral thought and practice."[25] This is perhaps an overstatement, but it recognizes the importance of the idea for Paul.

---

[25]Ralph P. Martin, *Reconciliation: A Study of Paul's Theology* (London: Marshall, Morgan & Scott, 1981), 5.

John Stott believed that the image of salvation as reconciliation was "the most popular because it was the most personal."[26] Maybe, but it would be more accurate to say, with Brenda Colijn, that "reconciliation and peace extend to all areas of life: internal, personal, interpersonal, social and even cosmic," and are not just personal.[27]

Paul: Our starting point must be our need for reconciliation with God. It arises because our sin is no light thing and turns us into God's enemies (see Rom 5:10). That means we are alienated from him and subject to his wrath (see Eph 2:3; 5:6; Col 1:21; 3:6). The "amazing grace" of the gospel is that God takes the initiative in overcoming our offenses. He alone can do this because he is the offended party; we are not in a position to ask for reconciliation. I consistently stress that our part is to receive the reconciliation God offers us in Christ, not somehow to bring it about ourselves. So note the way I use the passive voice in Romans 5:10-11: "we *were* reconciled . . . *having been* reconciled . . . through whom *we have* now *received* reconciliation."

He does not offer reconciliation because he overlooks the offense, but because he deals with it. "All this is from God, who reconciled us to himself through Christ . . . not counting people's sins against them" because, as I explain, "God made him who had no sin to be sin for us, so that in him we might become the righteousness of God" (2 Cor 5:18-19, 21).

I ought to clarify one point that has caused some debate. I write about Christ "reconciling the world" (2 Cor 5:19) and "[reconciling] to himself all things" (Col 1:20). I even mention that Israel's rejection of the gospel "brought reconciliation to the world" (Rom 11:15). Some have tied this up with 1 Timothy 4:10, where I testify that I have put my "hope in the living God, who is the Savior of all people, and especially of those who believe," to suggest I'm a universalist—that is, someone who thinks that everyone will be saved in the end. That's not so.

It should be clear from many of my other writings, mentioned elsewhere,[28] that I believe in the reality and awfulness of God's judgment at the end and

---

[26]Stott, *Cross of Christ*, 192.

[27]Colijn, *Images of Salvation*, 183.

[28]See Paul's contributions to chap. 4, 31-33, and chap. 10, 234-35.

that not all will enjoy life with God eternally. No, if you read these verses in context, it's plain that I am meaning something rather different from universalism. The urgency of persuading others to become new creations in Christ, living no longer for themselves, is obvious in 2 Corinthians 5. So I'm clearly not saying all will be saved irrespective of their response to God's offer. Reconciliation is a gift that needs to be accepted (see 2 Cor 5:20). In Colossians 1 I speak of reconciliation on a cosmic level rather than on a personal one. We need to remember that in the Roman world reconciliation was sometimes achieved by its being imposed on people—they called it "pacification"—rather than because people willingly accepted it.[29] They were reconciled to the will of Rome and enjoyed or endured the consequences of that, regardless of any personal or individual change of attitude. Colossians 1 is saying: the whole world will one day be put back right with God, whether every element of it wills and likes it or not! In 1 Timothy 4:10 ("the Savior of all people, and especially of those who believe") the word usually translated "especially" might better be translated "to be precise," "namely," "I mean."[30] So Christ is potentially the Savior of all but actually the Savior of those who believe in him.

From the Marketplace: Redemption and Canceling Debts

Chair: Although we've covered the idea of redemption from one angle above, it's fair to say that it is primarily an economic term and we should briefly revisit it in relation to a couple of other economic terms.

Paul: Agreed. Previously we viewed redemption from the viewpoint of Israel's release from slavery in Egypt, but when I say that Christ Jesus "has become for us . . . our . . . redemption" (1 Cor 1:30), I'm aware of the release from economic slavery which was enshrined in the Jubilee legislation of Leviticus 25:8-55. Those who'd fallen into debt could at last "Cry Freedom" at the Jubilee and have their debts written off if there had been no way of rescuing the situation earlier.

The other particular reference I make in this area about what salvation means is to say that in his death Christ "canceled the charge of our legal indebtedness, which stood against us and condemned us" (Col 2:14). What

---

[29]Colijn, *Images of Salvation*, 179.
[30]I. Howard Marshall, *The Pastoral Epistles*, International Critical Commentary (Edinburgh: T&T Clark, 1999), 556-67.

that debt was covers a range of things.[31] It embraces our failure to keep the law, our offenses that incur penalties, and our failure to offer God the perfect obedience that we owe him since he is our Creator. Here is a debt, however incurred, for which we were responsible; but Christ paid any price due and canceled the charges that were accruing in our accounts.

All this is consistent with the view that as Christians we are a people "bought at a price" and so are no longer free to live however we like or to submit ourselves to the expectations of others (1 Cor 6:20; 7:23; cf. Acts 20:28).

Peter: That's something I highlight once or twice. In my first letter I speak of the redemption price consisting not of perishable goods like "silver or gold" but of "the precious blood of Christ" (1 Pet 1:18-19). By the time I write my second letter I can denounce false teachers for "denying the sovereign Lord who bought them" (2 Pet 2:1). It was very natural to talk in these terms about our salvation.

From the Legal Field: Covenant

Chair: A very important idea in the Old Testament is that of covenant, of God entering into an agreement with Israel to be his special people, as we've mentioned on a number of occasions. There are in fact different covenants in the Old Testament, with Noah, Abraham, Moses, David, and so on. How does this find expression as part of the gospel?

Luke: Zechariah spoke of the coming of the Most High, meaning Jesus, and of how that demonstrated that God had "remember[ed] his holy covenant"—the one he had made with Abraham (Lk 1:72). Otherwise the only time all three of us Synoptic Gospel writers refer to the covenant is at the Last Supper, when Jesus "took the cup, saying, 'This cup is the new covenant in my blood, which is poured out for you'" (Lk 22:20). Mark speaks about it being poured out "for many" (Mk 14:24), to which Matthew adds, "for the forgiveness of sins" (Mt 26:28). Paul repeated this in his instructions about the Lord's Supper later (see 1 Cor 11:25). To be honest, covenant is more background than foreground—though Peter once referred to his audience as "heirs of the prophets and of the covenant God made with your fathers" (Acts 3:25). Oh, and Stephen also mentioned the Abrahamic covenant (see Acts 7:8, 44).

---

[31]For a discussion of the interpretations given here (law and disobedience) and other possible interpretations of what "legal indebtedness" means, see Douglas Moo, *The Letters to the Colossians and to Philemon*, Pillar New Testament Commentary (Grand Rapids: Eerdmans, 2008), 209-10.

Paul: The historic covenants were one of the immense privileges Israel enjoyed (see Rom 9:4; Gal 3:17; 4:24). They can be sure God will keep his covenant with them and take away their sins, in some way in the future, "for God's gifts and his call are irrevocable" (Rom 11:27-29). However, I'm very aware that as preachers of the gospel we are "ministers of a new covenant" (2 Cor 3:6), which is a covenant of the Spirit that leads to life rather than death (see 2 Cor 3:1-18), just as Jeremiah promised it would (see Jer 31:31-34).

John: The prize for developing this understanding of salvation surely must be awarded to the Hebraist. I don't mention *covenant* at all, although I refer to its blessings without ever using the word.[32]

The Hebraist: I'm surprised you don't all make much more of our salvation as entering a new covenant with God. Given my readership, though, it would be truly astonishing if I didn't make a lot of it. To me, Jesus is "the mediator of a new covenant" (Heb 12:24)—that is, the one who brings it into being. He's also "the guarantor of a better covenant" (Heb 7:22)—better, that is, than the old one—ensuring its complete reliability. A new covenant was needed because the old one didn't achieve its purpose (see Heb 8:7) and so has now been rendered obsolete (see Heb 8:13). The new one is "superior" (Heb 8:6) because it's built on a better foundation (see Heb 8:6). The old covenant provided plenty of sketchy illustrations pointing forward to this new one, including the importance of blood in making it effective (see Heb 9:1-21). However, the old covenant was only ever a signpost to the reality we now enjoy in having Christ as our sacrifice and high priest. He brings into being the covenant of the heart of which Jeremiah spoke (see Heb 10:16). That's the reality of the good news. It's also a great way of talking about it to those who think in traditional covenantal terms—that is to say, that we may enter into this new living covenant, or committed relationship with God, because Jesus signed and sealed the new covenant in his blood and afterward was then brought back from the dead (see Heb 13:20).

Other Concepts
Chair: I fear we've not exhausted the concepts you all press into use to explain what salvation means to people who believe in Christ. There are many more, and not always ones you'd expect. So, Paul, you use an educational

---

[32]Rev 11:19 mentions the ark of the covenant. For John's indirect allusions to covenant blessings, see Rainbow, *Johannine Theology*, 363-70.

analogy at one stage and talk about "the way of life you learned when you heard about Christ and were taught in him" (Eph 4:20-21). John, you put forward the images of having our thirst quenched (see Jn 4:13-14) and our hunger satisfied (see Jn 6:35). It seems that you were all constantly reaching for new ways of explaining the benefits of the good news to people, and that's perhaps a good example for subsequent generations to follow.

A New Power: The Holy Spirit

Chair: The good news is, as we've seen, about much more than the past fact of what Christ has done for us. The good news is that God makes it all come alive for us today through the gift of his Holy Spirit. The Spirit makes us alive in Christ and transforms us into his likeness.

I know we've already begun to explore the person of the Holy Spirit, from the viewpoint of his relationship to the incarnate Jesus,[33] but we need to think about him again more fully from the viewpoint of our experience of him and his role in our salvation. Let's look under the headings of what we know of his character, how he comes to believers, his modus operandi, and the power that he conveys to believers.

The Character of the Holy Spirit

John: There are three things I want to put on the table about the Spirit's character right away. I think we all agree on them. First, in the new age, we find a much sharper focus on the Spirit than previously, and he is undoubtedly a person, not some impersonal force. Jesus regularly made him the subject of verbs that only a person can do—*teach, remind, testify, bear witness, hear, speak, guide, glorify, confess,* and so on (see Jn 14:26; 15:26; 16:13-14; 1 Jn 4:2-3). In Revelation the Spirit "says" on many occasions (Rev 2:7, 11, 17, 29; 3:6, 13, 22; 14:13; 19:10; 22:17). Impersonal powers don't speak like this! The impression is so strong that it's natural for me to write of "*he* who is in you"[34] in 1 John 4:4.[35]

Second, although the Holy Spirit is personal, he is also a power, a life-giving power. Jesus' conversation with Nicodemus emphasizes that (see Jn 3:1-8). In it Jesus exploits the Hebrew idea of *ruach*, a word that means both

---

[33]See chap. 5, 83-85.
[34]NIV (2011) unfortunately translates the masculine personal pronoun *he* as "the one."
[35]This paragraph is dependent on Rainbow, *Johannine Theology*, 240.

"wind" and "spirit," to great effect. Creation in general and humanity in particular were brought to life by the wind/Spirit/breath of God (see Gen 1:2;
2:7). Christians are likewise born again of the Spirit, which is as mysterious
as the wind blowing. We can hear it and see its effect but are pretty ignorant
of where it's coming from or going to. The Spirit is always an animating,
invigorating, enlivening power, full of vigor and vitality.

Third, as must be evident from our earlier conversation, the Spirit is none
other than the Spirit of Jesus (see Jn 14:16, 26; 16:7, 12-15).

Paul: We can't stress too much this identity between Jesus and the Spirit:
"if anyone does not have the Spirit of Christ, they do not belong to Christ"
(Rom 8:9). It's why elsewhere I call him "the Spirit of his Son" (Gal 4:6) and
"the Spirit of Jesus Christ" (Phil 1:19).

Peter: And I similarly refer to him as "the Spirit of Christ" (1 Pet 1:11).

Mark: We—that is, Matthew, Luke, and I—make the point about the
closeness of Jesus and the Spirit the other way around. We are constantly
pointing out how the Spirit was foundational to the life and ministry of
Jesus. So we write of the Spirit being involved in the annunciation and
birth (see Mt 1:20; Lk 1:35); at his baptism (see Mt 3:16; Mk 1:9-11; Lk 3:22;
cf. Jn 1:32); temptation (see Mk 1:12-13; Lk 4:1); his miracles and ministry
(see Mt 12:28; Lk 4:14, 18; 10:21); right through to his commissioning of his
disciples (see Mt 28:19).

Luke: What's more, we refer to Jesus having taught the Spirit's empowering role for when the apostles were to face persecution (see Lk 12:12) and
to the way God will generously give the Spirit to those who ask him. He
won't hold back (see Mt 7:11; Lk 11:13).

> **Observer:** I think the character of the Holy Spirit is something we
> can learn about from the various ways the New Testament writers de-
> scribe him. Let me give a list of their descriptions, not forgetting that
> he is most frequently referred to as the *Holy* Spirit. That title occurs
> ninety-six times in the New Testament and emphasizes both his origin,
> as he partakes of the holiness of God, and his purpose, in creating ho-
> liness in Christ's followers. Otherwise they speak of him as
>
> • the Paraclete or Advocate (Jn 14:16, 26; 15:26; 16:7);
>
> • the Spirit of truth (Jn 14:17; 15:26; 16:13);

- the Spirit of life (Rom 8:2; Jn 3:5);

- the Spirit of adoption (Rom 8:15);

- the Spirit of power (2 Tim 1:7);

- the Spirit of love (2 Tim 1:7);

- the Spirit of self-discipline (2 Tim 1:7);

- the eternal Spirit (Heb 9:14);

- the Spirit of grace (Heb 10:29); and

- the Spirit of glory and of God (1 Pet 4:14).

There is also mention of "the Spirit of wisdom and revelation" in Ephesians 1:17, but there is some uncertainty as to whether this refers to the Holy Spirit (as in NIV) or to the human spirit. A similar uncertainty is found in James 4:5, which most commentators take to refer to the human spirit. The Holy Spirit is also spoken of metaphorically as

- a dove (Mt 3:16; Jn 1:32);

- wind (Acts 2:2);

- fire (Mt 3:11-12; Lk 3:16; Acts 2:3);

- a seal (Eph 1:13); and

- a deposit or guarantee (Eph 1:14).

The Coming of the Holy Spirit

Chair: So if the Spirit is the Spirit of Jesus who brings new Christians to birth and accompanies them through the world on the path of holiness, how, precisely, does he come to us? John the Baptist spoke about Jesus "baptizing" us with the Holy Spirit (see Lk 3:16; Jn 1:33; Acts 1:5), and after his resurrection John tells us that Jesus "breathed on them [his disciples] and said, 'receive the Holy Spirit'" (Jn 20:22). What does this mean?

Luke: I believe the promise of being baptized in the Holy Spirit was fulfilled on the day of Pentecost (see Acts 2:1-4). It was a promise that related to the outpouring of the Holy Spirit that occurred that day and sounded the starting gun for the new age to begin and the mission of the church to be inaugurated. This new age is often called "the last days," meaning the last and final chapter of history as we know it before the eschaton—that is, the decisive concluding events that usher in the new creation. The phrase refers to the whole time between Christ's first and his second coming—what we might also call "the church age"—not just the immediate few days before Christ returns. That seems to be how Peter understood it in his preaching, as he claimed that Joel 2:28—"In the last days, God says, I will pour out my Spirit on all people"—was being fulfilled before his hearers' very eyes (see Acts 2:17). Pentecost signaled the inclusion of the Gentiles in the gospel story and that the undoing of the curse at Babel (see Gen 11:1-9) had been set in motion, as all people heard the one gospel in their own language and formed "one new humanity," as Paul put it later (Eph 2:15).

> **Observer:** A contemporary writer has put it like this: "The Spirit had been dispensed as promised. The drought of the Spirit had ended. The longed for and expected new age had begun."[36]

Chair: But isn't the baptism of the Holy Spirit also an individual experience, and doesn't the Acts suggest this at a number of points?

Luke: Yes and no. The normal pattern, which I report throughout, is that repentance, faith, baptism. and the reception of the Holy Spirit all belong together. That's what Peter taught in his Pentecost sermon (see Acts 2:38) and was witnessed regularly, even if sometimes the sequence of those things is a bit different. It was both a personal and a corporate experience.

There are two episodes in the early church where that sequence seems to have been torn apart somewhat, giving rise to the claim that individuals should seek a special experience of being baptized by the Spirit subsequent to conversion, when repentance and faith have been exercised. I believe this is to misinterpret what was going on. Let me explain.

The first episode occurs in Samaria (Acts 8:14-17) when, after people had "accepted the word of God" that Philip had preached and been baptized in water, the apostles came down from Jerusalem and "prayed for the new believers there that they might receive the Holy Spirit, because the Holy Spirit had not yet come on any of them." That was indeed unusual, but there was a reason for it. Preaching in Samaria marked the beginning of a new

---

[36]Dunn, *Theology of Paul*, 418.

phase in the mission agenda inaugurated by Jesus at his ascension (see Acts 1:8). For centuries the Samaritans had been sworn enemies of the Jewish people, and if they were now to be reconciled to them and to God through the gospel, it was necessary that some clear and unmistakable sign be given to indicate that they were accepted on an equal footing. That's why, unusually, the coming of the Spirit on them was delayed until the apostles could, you might say, sign and seal the deal.

The second episode occurred in Ephesus (see Acts 19:1-7) and is different. The incorporation of the Gentiles into the gospel community was already clear. The dramatic coming of the Spirit on Cornelius, a Roman, and the events around it at Joppa, had signaled that for sure (see Acts 10:1-48). The only odd thing at Joppa was that the Spirit came before they were baptized with water rather than when they were baptized with water. Still, repentance, faith, baptism, and the gift of the Spirit were all closely bound up together. In Ephesus, though, it's different. From what we know, the godly people there were really John's disciples. They'd expressed repentance and been baptized according to John's rite but had not exercised faith in Jesus or even heard of the Holy Spirit. So this was not the coming of the Spirit after conversion—this was their conversion.

Paul: I concur with that. By my definition, to belong to Christ is to have the Spirit, and vice versa (see Rom 8:9). It's impossible to have the one without the other. So it's natural for me to speak about the start of the Christian life as "receiving the Holy Spirit" (1 Cor 2:12-16; Gal 3:2-3) and to see people's welcome of the gospel as evidence of the Holy Spirit at work in them (see 1 Thess 1:4-6; 2:13).

While I never speak of being baptized by the Holy Spirit as a separate and subsequent event to conversion, I do speak of the need for believers to be "filled with the Spirit." Indeed, I command it (Eph 5:18). That is a recognition of the need, continuously and daily, to surrender one's life to the control of the Spirit and to enjoy his life and to walk in his ways to the full, as outlined in Romans 8:1-17. We so easily become spiritually lethargic or slip back into old ways, foolishly resuscitating "the law of sin and death," which should be dead and buried.

Luke: I recognize that sort of language. I note several people who were "full of the Spirit" (Acts 6:3, 5; 7:55; 11:24), which marked them out for leadership and service in a special way. On one occasion, as the church was praying for Peter's release from prison (see Acts 4:23-31)—which happened, incidentally, in a miraculous manner—the whole church was "filled with the Holy Spirit." Here, as in the other cases, these periods or experiences of intensification of the Spirit led to people engaging in evangelism—that is, spreading the gospel.

The Modus Operandi of the Holy Spirit

Chair: It's evident that the Holy Spirit is to be experienced and that the basic experience is that of vitality or energizing. He is a stimulant who sustains as well as initiates our Christian lives—but how does he do this? Perhaps we can briefly list some of the many things that you write with reference to this.

John: He does so, first, by taking up residence within us: "for he lives with you" (Jn 14:17).

Second, he does so by teaching us the truth about Jesus, more and more fully (see Jn 14:25-26).

Paul: While agreeing that the Spirit becomes the resident member of the Trinity in our lives (see Rom 8:9; 2 Tim 1:14), I'd say he works in the inner core of our lives, giving us new hearts, circumcising our hearts rather than our bodies, and leading us to desire and enact a willing fulfillment of the law of Christ, rather than living under an externally imposed obedience to Moses' law. In other words, he fulfills what Jeremiah 31 and Ezekiel 36 prophesied about the coming of a new covenant (2 Cor 3:1-18; Rom 2:29).

So he sets us free (see Rom 7:6; 8:1-2; 2 Cor 3:17), but this is a freedom to love and serve, not a license for self-indulgence (see Gal 5:13).

Then he kindles religious "affections,"[37] such as love, joy, and peace, within us (see Rom 5:5; 1 Thess 1:6).

This leads to his transforming our characters (see 1 Cor 6:9-11) by providing us with spiritual energy to combat the pre-Christ way of living and strengthening our inner being (see Rom 8:1-27; 2 Cor 3:18; Eph 3:16). All this is seen as we produce "the fruit of the Spirit" in virtuous living (Gal 5:16-25).

None of this happens to us as lone disciples. He gives us the church, which he forms (see 1 Cor 12:13) and within which he then makes his home (see 1 Cor 3:16; Eph 2:19-22).

---

[37]This language is consciously chosen in deference to the great theologian and revivalist Jonathan Edwards, who wrote a classic book entitled *The Religious Affections*. First published in 1746, it is still published by The Banner of Truth Trust.

In terms of the church, he unifies it (see Eph 4:1-16), a very necessary task in view of the very different people—different in background, experiences, and gifts—who join it. A detailed explanation of our relationships in the church can be summed up under the rubric of "keep in step with the Spirit," as if we're marching in an army (Gal 5:9–6:6). This suggests how important unity is wherever the Spirit is at work.

Furthermore, the Spirit provides us with assurance (see Rom 8:15-16; Gal 4:5-7; Eph 1:3-14).

Finally, I would say that he empowers our prayers. They can sometimes be quite inarticulate, but even so they express our deep longings for God and his glory (see Rom 8:26-27).

Peter: I want to underline Paul's point about the Spirit awakening and instilling in us religious affections. I know *affections* is an old-fashioned word, but *feelings* or *emotions* can sometimes suggest something very superficial or something we should be cautious about, whereas these are deep and virtuous changes in attitude and desire that the Spirit brings about. In my first letter, I acknowledge that many of my readers won't have seen Jesus with their physical eyes, but even so they "love" him and, because they "believe" in him, they "are filled with an inexpressible and glorious joy" (1 Pet 1:8). Being a Christian doesn't lead to the suppression of emotions but rather to a deepening experience and expression of healthy emotions.

Jude: And I want to underline Paul's point about what I term "praying in the Holy Spirit" (Jude 20). Prayer needs to be inspired, enabled, and empowered by the Spirit, and that may sometimes mean we pray in unknown languages, often referred to as "tongues," with passion and even with muddled words or just groans (cf. Rom 8:26), rather than articulate poetic phrases.

John: When we are talking about the way the Spirit operates we have rightly concentrated on the way he operates in believers or in the church. Yet we dare not limit him, as if he works only there. Jesus taught us that he has a role outside the church, in the world, as well. There his approach is to convict people of their sin and convince them of Christ (Jn 16:8-11), even though they may not initially recognize him or know much about him (14:17).

The Power of the Holy Spirit

Chair: Let's shift our focus a little. I'm interested in what you might say about the power of the Spirit.

Power for Mission

Luke: The first thing I'd say is that it is a power for mission—that is, for spreading the gospel. The Spirit continued the work Jesus began (see Acts 1:1-2) through the preaching of the apostles, evangelists, and the church as a whole (see Lk 12:12; Acts 1:8; 4:8; 6:2-10; 7:55; 8:29; 9:17; 10:44; 11:24; 13:9, 52) and is still doing so (see Acts 28:31). Their preaching of the gospel was accompanied by demonstrations of the Spirit's power (see Acts 3:11–4:20; 8:4-8; 19:13-20; 28:7-10), although these miracles didn't always have a positive effect and, as Paul and Silas discovered in Philippi, could lead to persecution (see Acts 16:16-24).

Paul: The necessity of the Spirit's empowering of the preaching of the good news is something I became very conscious of. My early visit to Thessalonica set the pattern here. As I wrote to them, when I preached there "our gospel came to you not simply with words but also with power, with the Holy Spirit and deep conviction" (1 Thess 1:4-5; cf. 1 Cor 2:3-4). While some see that as implying that signs and wonders took place, I was really speaking of the effectiveness of the preaching that resulted in transformed lives and people experiencing the living God.[38] I was so aware of the Spirit's dynamic in my preaching, and of its necessity, that I could describe my ministry, and that of all gospel preachers, as a "ministry of the Spirit" (2 Cor 3:8). Whatever was accomplished was accomplished "through the power of the Spirit of God" (Rom 15:19).

Equipped with Gifts

The Spirit's work is by no means confined to the initial preaching of the gospel. He equips the church for its internal life as well as its external mission by providing its members with gifts. These came to be known as "charismatic gifts" because I use the word *charismata* to describe them, meaning that they are gifts given by God's grace (*charis*). I mention these gifts four times in my letters, and you'll immediately see that I don't present them as a fixed or closed list. There is an open-endedness and flexibility to the way I write about them, implying, at least, that these are sample lists. The living God doesn't work through bureaucratic checklists! Perhaps I can list them like this:

---

[38]For a discussion of the meaning of these verses, see Gordon Fee, *God's Empowering Presence: The Holy Spirit in the Letters of Paul* (Peabody, MA: Hendrickson, 1994), 44.

Table 2. Gifts of the Spirit in Paul's letters

Romans 12:6-8	1 Corinthians 12:8-10	1 Corinthians 12:28-30	Ephesians 4:11
prophecy	wisdom	apostles	apostles
service	knowledge	prophets	prophets
teaching	faith	teachers	evangelists
encouraging	healing	miracles	pastors/teachers
giving	miracles	healing	
mercy	prophecy	helping	
	discernment	guiding	
	tongues	tongues	
	interpretation	interpretation	

It's important to note several important things about them. The trinitarian God sovereignly distributes them (1 Cor 12:4-6). They can be described as "different kinds of . . . ," first, "gifts," since we can't demand them or earn them; second, "service," since they're given so we can serve others, not to wear as a status badge; and, third, "working" or energizing, since they serve as the fuel that mobilizes the church. The variety of gifts shouldn't cause confusion since "the same God [is] at work" in them all. They are distributed so that every member of the church has a contribution to make to the whole (1 Cor 12:7, 11, 27).

I develop the image of the church as a body, which has many parts to it and yet forms a coherent organism (see 1 Cor 12:12-26). That's a perfect picture for illustrating the way in which we're dependent not just on the more presentable, more prominent, or more visible parts of the body, but on every member of it, no matter how small or hidden. The fact that everyone has a part to play shouldn't be misunderstood as saying that anyone can teach or lead. No, as in a body, there is a certain structure to it, and parts of the body serve the body best by playing their role rather than commandeering someone else's. So God has given "first of all apostles, second prophets, third teachers, then miracles," and so on. However, unlike any other society in my world, the church doesn't go in for the worship of status. Indeed, we give "greater honor" to those parts that are usually unnoticed and overlooked as insignificant elsewhere. We know how indispensable the weaker or less presentable parts are (see 1 Cor 12:22-26).

The diversity of gifts can cause jealousy, rivalry, and division, which is why I stress how essential it is that the context in which we exercise them should be one of love—detailed, practical, down-to-earth love (see 1 Cor 13:1-13).[39]

The gifts of tongues and prophecy had particularly attracted attention and some degree of controversy in Corinth. So when I wrote to Corinth I devoted a whole section to them, explaining that both are valuable but prophecy has the edge over tongues. By tongues, I wasn't thinking of the sort of phenomenon that occurred on the day of Pentecost, which more accurately might be thought of as a gift of hearing, since "each one heard their own language being spoken" (Acts 2:6). I was thinking of speaking in an unknown language of praise and prayer. It's a beneficial spiritual exercise that I myself practice. When used in the church, though, these tongues need interpreting or else they benefit only the one who's speaking, not the church as a whole (see 1 Cor 14:6-17)—although, paradoxically, the unusual nature of such speech may have an impact on unbelievers who come into church (see 1 Cor 14:22), especially perhaps as "a sign" of the living God being present or of his judgment being at work.

To tell the truth, though, I'd rather see the gift of prophecy exercised in the church (see 1 Cor 14:18-19). That way, God's message is intelligibly communicated to the body as a whole, and even unbelievers can be convicted of their sin, right then and there, through these immediate messages from God for the congregation (see 1 Cor 14:23-25). However we work this out, we do not glorify God by worship that is chaotic or where people are shouting over one another to gain a hearing, whether tongue-speakers, prophets, or women (see 1 Cor 14:26-39). Our God is a God of order, and his character should be reflected in our worship.

This matter of giving the Spirit freedom in worship to speak spontaneously through a variety of gifts and yet to have some order to our worship involves a delicate balance. It's too easy to clamp down on the spontaneous, freedom side of the tension, or alternatively for freedom to be an excuse for chaos. That's the point I was making to the Thessalonians when I exhorted them, on the one hand, "not [to] quench the Spirit" and to allow prophets to exercise their gifts, while, on the other hand, not to be gullible and to "test"

---

[39]See further chap. 9, 213-16.

what was said, since not everything will be good (1 Thess 5:19-22). We don't want to quench the Spirit's fire, but nor should we encourage self-appointed arsonists to engage in spiritual destruction.

At Work in the Church and the World

John: All this is good, but I want to present the Spirit's work on a much wider canvas. His power is evident in both the church and the world, especially in times when the church is undergoing persecution. During such times Christians may be tempted to think that God is inactive, but my testimony is quite the opposite. The Spirit is extremely active in a number of different ways, as I demonstrate in Revelation.

First, it was because I was "in the Spirit" that I received my visions and my visionary journey unfolded (Rev 1:10; 4:2; 17:3; 21:10). Without the Spirit inspiring me, there would have been no prophecy, for he "is essentially the Spirit of prophecy" (Rev 19:10).[40] Second, he is the Spirit who addresses the churches and either encourages them to persevere or instructs them about their need to repent if they're to survive (see Rev 2:7, 11, 17, 29; 3:6, 13, 22).

Third, and perhaps most significantly, on a number of occasions he's described as "the seven spirits of God" (Rev 1:4; 3:1; 4:5; 5:6). This doesn't mean seven different spirits but one sevenfold spirit. Seven is the symbolic number for completion or perfection. There is nothing lacking in the Spirit's ministry, or in his vitality or power, even in times when the church seems to be severely challenged. One of those references is of special importance. In Revelation 5:6 I record, "The Lamb had seven horns and seven eyes, which are the seven spirits of God sent out into all the earth." That not only ties the Spirit into a relationship with God the Father and the Son, and is therefore implicitly trinitarian, but it also shows that his remit is not limited to the church. As he goes "out into all the earth" he has universal oversight and a catalytic role that progresses history toward its climax. In my final chapter he is the one, with the bride, the church, who invites those who are thirsty to "Come" and "take the free gift of the water of life" (Rev 22:17).

He indwells, transforms, and empowers both individual believers and the church, but as the Spirit of prophecy he plays a part on a much wider stage, striding throughout the world to issue the invitation of the gospel and to

---

[40]The wording comes from Donald Guthrie, *New Testament Theology* (Downers Grove, IL: Inter-Varsity Press, 1981), 569.

bring about the final act of the renewal of creation. Just as he played a vital role in the initial creation, so he is still active, playing a vital role in the new creation as well.

A NEW FUTURE: ALREADY BUT NOT YET

Chair: All this sounds very positive, and I have no desire to detract from any of it, but the truth is that our experience doesn't always measure up to our claims. We have been, in Peter's words, given a "new birth into a living hope" (1 Pet 1:3), but hope is something that is held out to be realized in the future rather than fully experienced now. So we're looking forward still to a time when God's promises will actually become complete realities. We'll look more fully into the fulfillment of that future promise later. My interest here is in our present experience in which, until the coming again of Christ, we seem to be living in-between times, with a hope that is already firm and securely established but not yet fully accomplished. I guess we shouldn't expect it to be any different, since when we were reviewing what Jesus taught about the kingdom of God we noted the "already but not yet" nature of it. Let's explore briefly how it affects our experience as Christians. There are several dimensions to look at, and no doubt we could add more; but let's stick with just five.

Paul, start us off, if you would.

In Relation to Holiness

Paul: My gospel affirms confidently that sin is dethroned in the life of a believer. It no longer has the power to keep a believer enslaved. That's the central theme of chapters 6–8 in my magnum opus, Romans. Yet, the truth is, we still do sin. Primarily this is because we fail to live up to our calling, failing to "count" ourselves "dead to sin" and to walk only in the new life Christ gives by his Spirit (Rom 6:11); but I recognize that "the world, the flesh and the devil" all conspire to make it difficult for us to do that (Eph 2:1-3). Most of my letters address the failure of the churches to exhibit the sort of behavior and relationships you'd expect from people who are living in accordance with the gospel (see 1–2 Cor; Gal 5:1–6:10; Eph 4:1–6:9; Col 3:1–4:6; 1 Thess 5:1-11). In some cases this is simply because they haven't appreciated the implications of that gospel fully enough, but we're all a work in progress, including me (see Phil 3:12-14). Fortunately, the progress is in God's hands, and he will complete his work of reconstructing us on "the day of Christ Jesus" (Phil 1:6). Then we will be fully transformed.

John: I echo Paul on this, even if I'm writing pastorally in 1 John to a different audience and not seeking to explain the theology of sanctification. I highlight the same tension. On the one hand, "No one who is born of God will continue to sin" (1 Jn 3:9). That isn't arguing for absolute perfection but stating that the stranglehold of sin is broken and we simply can't claim to be followers of Jesus if we happily go on sinning. On the other hand, the realistic position is that we do sin; we delude ourselves if we claim otherwise. However, "if we confess our sins, he is faithful and just and will forgive us our sins and purify us from all unrighteousness" (1 Jn 1:9). So, although we are God's children now, we're not yet perfect. "But we know that when Christ appears, we shall be like him, for we shall see him as he is" (1 Jn 3:1-2).

In Relation to Our Spiritual Experience

Paul: I think the area where we are most conscious of the tension between the "already but not yet" is that of our spiritual experience. We experience so much of God and his grace now, and yet we have not fully entered into all God has for us and experience it all somewhat unevenly now. That's why I highlight that the Holy Spirit "is a deposit guaranteeing our inheritance until the redemption of those who are God's possession" (Eph 1:14), as if our redemption is still future. I refer once or twice to the idea of the Spirit as a deposit or an inheritance we've yet to receive (see 2 Cor 1:22; 5:5; Eph 1:18; Col 1:12; 3:24).

Peter: You'll find I make the same use of our future inheritance at the start of my first letter (1 Pet 1:4).

John: I'm in danger of repeating myself here. Knowing God is something we can be sure of now, especially through the ministry of the Holy Spirit (see 1 Jn 2:20-21; 3:1, 24; 4:7-14), and yet, in the verse I just quoted, we know there is much more to come that we won't experience until we see him face-to-face (see 1 Jn 3:2).

Paul: Yes, and our present experience of God is definite and genuine, but only partial and, to be honest, somewhat fitful. We're not always living lives of unalloyed praise, are we? We're often grappling with the much more mundane. Take the Thessalonians as an example. They really did turn from worshiping idols to serving the living God (see 1 Thess 1:9), but then immediately faced suffering and persecution as a result (see 1 Thess 2:17–3:5). Wasn't life in Christ supposed to be one of continuous joy? And then, to cap it all, some of their fellow believers died before Christ had returned. They weren't expecting that; their hope of his return was much more immediate. So I had to write and explain more fully how it all fit together and how we had to live in the light of his return, however postponed that might be (see 1 Thess 4:1–5:13). We're on the way—on the right path—but we haven't reached the destination yet.

In Relation to Mission

Chair: The puzzle here, as Paul has just implied, is that we have good news, but not everyone welcomes it. Why? To add to the dilemma, Matthew tells us that when Christ was ascending he commissioned us to "make disciples of all nations," speaking, at the same time, of all the authority he had been given "in heaven and on earth" (Mt 28:18-19; cf. Acts 1:8). So why is missionary progress so tough and halting?

Matthew: If we remember the parables Jesus told about the advance of his kingdom, such as the ones I gather together in chapter 13 of my Gospel, you won't find this so surprising. Jesus taught us to expect that the advance of the kingdom would often be hidden and would meet obstacles en route.

Luke: Well, those obstacles certainly took many forms. I note in Acts that there was opposition from authorities (see Acts 4:1-21; 5:17-42; 12:1-19); hypocrisy in the church (see Acts 5:1-11); division (see Acts 6:1-7); persecution (see Acts 7:1–8:3); harassment and people disrupting the preaching (see Acts 16:16-40; 17:5-9); procrastination (see Acts 17:32); slow progress with only tiny communities being formed, even though we could claim that "all the Jews and Greeks who lived in the province of Asia heard the word of the Lord" (Acts 19:10); plots (see Acts 20:3); and even storms and shipwrecks (see Acts 27:13–28:16). In spite of all this, "the word of God spread" (Acts 6:7) and even flourished.

> ## THE WORD OF GOD GREW
> Acts 9:31; 11:1; 12:24; 13:49; 19:20.

Paul: In addition to all that, I noted the obstacles of Satan closing doors (see 1 Thess 2:18) and the discouragement of disciples turning back and becoming apostates (see 1 Tim 1:20; 2 Tim 1:15; 4:10, 14). Yet, for all that,

"God's word is not chained" (2 Tim 2:9) and will go on spreading until the time when everything is brought into harmony with God himself (see Eph 1:10; 1 Cor 15:28).

> **Observer:** Although the New Testament writers never quote it, they share Isaiah's vision of the day when "the earth will be filled with the knowledge of the LORD as the waters cover the sea" (Is 11:9).

In Relation to Ethics

Paul: Picking up my earlier comments about Christians who continued to live lives that were not truly consistent with the gospel, I guess we should say that I devote much space in my letters (and I'm not alone in doing this) instructing Christians how to live in this "in-between" time. We have a great vision of our future lives, when we will be totally transformed and live in the full light of God's presence, but in the meantime we have to live in the real world of politics, hierarchies, families, idols, retribution, sexual promiscuity, and so on.

This is really the running theme of my first letter to the Corinthians. Their major problem was that they lived as if they had already arrived in the new creation and so conventional, "earthly" rules didn't apply to them. This is called "over-realized eschatology" in the trade. Consequently, I was trying to teach them to live within the present reality while not reneging on the future vision.

The issues are widespread, but let me give just a sample by referring to two of them. Take the complex issue of "head-covering" in worship as an example, which I deal with in chapter 11. What it boiled down to was that some of the Christians in Corinth were so convinced they'd already arrived that none of the normal cultural marks of decorum or wisdom applied to them. So they pushed their freedom in Christ to the limits and dispensed with any signs of social respectability by allowing their men to pray with covered heads and their women to pray without restraining their hair in any way. All this did was send out signals to others that they were licentious or immoral. Rather than commending the gospel as a path to freedom, it raised unnecessary barriers for people and prevented them from grasping a gospel that, we have to admit, was scandalous enough on its own terms (see 1 Cor 1:18-25). So, while they were quite right that such cultural signals ultimately didn't matter as far as the eternal future was concerned, they were quite wrong to apply it prematurely in this way to their behavior as they did.[41]

We still live in a world of cultural codes and currents that take some negotiating. It doesn't mean we'll always let culture determine our behavior. There will be times when we stand against our culture, as our teaching on sexual ethics often clearly demands. However, we have to discern when it matters and when it doesn't as far as spreading the good news is concerned. We may have a right to do anything, "but not everything is beneficial" (1 Cor 6:12). One day we'll be free of such constraints, but we're not there yet.

A second, briefer, example might be the emphasis I make on leading a peaceable and quiet life (see 1 Thess 4:11; 1 Tim 2:2). There were lots of things wrong with the Roman government, and, as John shows in Revelation, it could become oppressive and demonic. That shouldn't stop us, though, from recognizing that God has given us the institution of government for a good reason (see Rom 13:1-7), and a less-than-perfect government is better than the unrestrained forces of anarchy, which only results in chaos. So, rather than challenging everything, we need to know when to pick our battles, as I did in Philippi (see Acts 16:37-39), and when quietly to submit. The government of our world won't be perfect until God takes his throne and rules over all. The determining factor is always what will enhance the progress of the gospel and the welfare (*shalom*) of the people.

We must never dilute our vision of the future and, indeed, must prepare ourselves for it by living now as we will live then, insofar as we can; but we must also recognize that we can't live now exactly as we will then. We presently face limitations, especially, for example, because our bodies will continue to decay until they rise to their immortal state in the resurrection. Other constraints are imposed on us by law and culture, which we need sensitively to negotiate our way through—sometimes, where no gospel truth is at stake, living within unwelcome constraints and sometimes protesting against them and refusing to compromise.

---

[41]A fuller explanation of this position can be found in Roy E. Campa and Brian S. Rosner, *The First Letter to the Corinthians*, Pillar New Testament Commentary (Grand Rapids: Eerdmans, 2010), 499-541; and Derek and Dianne Tidball, *The Message of Women*, The Bible Speaks Today Bible Themes (Nottingham, UK: Inter-Varsity Press, 2012), 210-34.

In Relation to Spiritual Warfare

Peter: I'd like to raise the issue of spiritual warfare. One day the battles will be over, but in the meantime we're in the midst of them. I'm aware that "the devil prowls around like a roaring lion looking for someone to devour." We're in a spiritual battle, that's the truth of it, and we need to be alert to that and not unaware of Satan's schemes (see 1 Pet 5:8).

Luke: There was certainly plenty of evidence of that when the apostles first preached the gospel. Satan's strategies are very varied, but one obvious one is that of the demonic activity that the apostles encountered on several occasions (see Acts 5:16; 8:7; 16:16-18; 19:11-20).

Paul: This really is another illustration of the "already but not yet" tension we live under, isn't it? We're absolutely confident that the cross of Christ has defeated the forces of evil (see Col 2:15), and yet they're still on the loose and at work in our world (see Eph 1:21; 2:1-3; Col 1:13-16). It's not our job to defeat Satan or his subordinates: Christ has done that; but we do have a responsibility to use the resources God has given us to protect ourselves as we wield the sword of truth, by which I mean the gospel. There's a whole range of spiritual armor at our disposal and meant for our protection, which I outline in Ephesians 6:10-17 and mention more briefly in 1 Thessalonians 5:8. And in addition to all that there is the overall weapon of prayer (see Eph 6:18). We must remember in all this that we're not fighting in the normal human way, so we're not talking about passing laws, putting people in prison, using deceitful propaganda, raising military forces, or enforcing conversions by the sword. It's a battle of an altogether different kind we're talking about—a spiritual one—and we fight with spiritual weapons.

John: And the good thing is that we already know the outcome of the battle. God wins. Indeed, he's already won the decisive battle through the cross and resurrection (see Jn 16:33). What we're experiencing is just a mopping-up operation. The day will come, though, when evil in all its forms will be banished from the universe and the devil and his coconspirators will be "thrown into the lake of burning sulfur . . . [and] will be tormented day and night" (Rev 20:10). No wonder we cry, "Hallelujah!"

CONCLUSION

Chair: That's been a very wide-ranging conversation about how the good news applies to us in the present. We began by seeing that it offered us a new freedom, atonement from sin, a new relationship with God through our union with Christ, and a new standing before God, since we are now justified. Then we opened up the discussion to consider several of the major concepts that help us understand the nature of the salvation we experience. After that we explored the new power of the Holy Spirit, who makes all this real to us and brings us alive in Christ, before honestly admitting that we're caught between times and haven't yet entered fully into all that God has in store for us.

All that focused on our salvation. We'll continue our conversation by asking how we can make it our own. How do we begin this life in Christ, and what follows from our starting the journey?

8

How Do We Make
the Good News
Our Own?

Chair: We have good news. Jesus is the good news. He's also the one who brings it to us. He's both message and messenger. Having heard the good news, we need to look at the other side of the coin and ask, as they did at Pentecost, what we must do to receive this good news and make it our own. How tragic to see this good news merely as a historic revelation or factual account of Jesus and not benefit from it personally. So how can we enter into it, and what are the implications of doing so for our ongoing lives?

God remains true, whether we respond to him or not. Paul gives us an example of that by pointing out that Israel's unfaithfulness to God didn't "nullify God's faithfulness" (Rom 3:3-4). Even so, we must respond if we are to allow God's salvation to achieve its purpose in our own lives. To use the example we find in Hebrews, the people of Israel were given the good news of God promising them rest, "but the message they heard was of no value to them, because they did not share the faith of those who obeyed" (Heb 4:1-2). The Hebraist encourages us to believe the good news and so obtain the promise God makes.

But how? In this discussion we'll look at the questions of the initial stages of the Christian life and the importance of being part of a community of fellow believers.

THE GOSPEL REQUIRES A RESPONSE

Mark: As the author of what might claim to be the earliest discipleship manual (apart from some of Paul's letters), let me draw attention to the various themes that crop up in my Gospel that answer your question about how we enter the Christian life.

First, Jesus invites us to follow him (see Mk 1:17; 2:14; 8:34; 10:21), not in the sense the crowd did as curious spectators, but as committed disciples. "To follow" was to become a learner, walking in the shoes of a master. Typically, when Bartimaeus was healed of his blindness, he "followed Jesus along the road"—in other words, he became a disciple (Mk 10:52). The women were the most faithful disciples of all, following him from Galilee to the cross (see Mk 15:41). I think every Gospel writer would put that at the top of the list.

> ### PARALLEL VERSES ABOUT FOLLOWING
>
> Mt 4:19-22; 8:19-22; 9:9; 10:38; 19:21, 27-28; 20:34; 27:55; Lk 5:11, 27-28; 9:23, 57-62; 14:27; 18:22, 43; 23:49, 55; Jn 1:43; 6:66; 8:12; 10:27; 12:26; 13:36-37; 21:19-20, 22.

Second, we are to "have faith" or "believe" (Mk 9:23; 11:22). Faith seems to be present when God is at work (see Mk 2:5; 4:40; 5:34; 10:52).

Third, we are invited to repent (see Mk 1:14-15; 6:12), which isn't so much about feeling sorry for our sin, although that must come into it, but finding a new direction in life and changing course so we go the way of Jesus (more on that later).

Fourth, Jesus spells out that following him involves taking up our cross (see Mk 8:34; Mt 16:24; Lk 9:23).

Fifth, Jesus talks about entering or receiving the kingdom (see Mk 10:15, 23-24). The only way to become a citizen in this kingdom is to become like little children—that is, to forgo our rights and consider ourselves as having no claims, depending totally on the mercy of God.

Luke: I have two things to add to what Mark has just said. First, incidents like the one Mark just mentioned of Bartimaeus "[following] Jesus along the road" after his healing (Mk 10:52) gave rise to the early Christians being described as those "who belonged to the Way" (Acts 9:2).

The other thing is to stress that Christians were *disciples*, which means "devoted learners" and "followers." Disciples, as Mark said, attached themselves to a master and learned from him, not in a sedentary classroom setting, but on the road. They learned to imitate their teachers in their beliefs, attitudes, and actions. This title is the most-used description of what it is to be a Christian: it crops up 268 times in the Gospels, and I use it twenty-three times in Acts.

John: Although my Gospel is different in style, here's an area where there is a great deal of overlap. I'd want to emphasize one thing and add two little things to what's been said. The thing I want to emphasize is the need to believe in Jesus. You can't start the Christian life without this belief, and the Christian life is marked by continually exercising it. *Believing* is my word for "exercising faith." I only use *faith* once (Jn 12:42), but I speak of *believing* over eighty times. So the words *believe* and *believing* are scattered throughout my Gospel. Famously I wrote, "For God so loved the world that he gave his one and only Son, that whoever believes in him shall not perish but have eternal life" (Jn 3:16). And my reason for writing was so that "you may believe that Jesus is the Messiah, the Son of God, and that by believing you may have life in his name" (Jn 20:31). Note, I connect believing with my great theme of "life": Jesus came that people "may have life, and have it to the full" (Jn 10:10). We can never experience that quality of life apart from believing in Jesus.

My two little additions are, first, that to believe in Jesus is to "receive" him and welcome him into your life, just as you would a permanent resident in your home (Jn 1:12). Therefore those who ask, "Have you received Jesus?" are using the language of my Gospel and inviting us not to ignore him, mistake his identity, or, worse still, reject him altogether.

The second is this: when Jesus stood up to the bullying religious mob and took the side of the accused adulterous woman, he said to her what he'd say to anyone whom he forgives: "Go now and leave your life of sin" (Jn 8:11). I don't use the words *repent* or *repentance*, but that's exactly what Jesus was inviting the woman, and us, to do.

THE ESSENCE OF THE RESPONSE:
REPENTANCE, FAITH, AND BAPTISM

Chair: While there may be several ways the Gospels describe what's involved in starting a journey with Jesus, the key elements in the preaching and writing of the early apostles are those of repentance and faith.

Repentance

Peter: They're fundamental. Luke gives a summary of my Pentecost sermon. When people asked me what they were to do as a result of what I had told them about Jesus, I replied, "repent and be baptized, every one of you, in the name of Jesus Christ for the forgiveness of your sins. And you will receive the gift of the Holy Spirit" (Acts 2:38). Repentance means to change one's mind about Jesus and so to change the direction of one's life; baptism is the expression of our trust in him; and that is sealed, as Paul might say, by the gift of the Holy Spirit. Although on occasions these three seem to have been a little disconnected in the way people experienced them, they are, in reality, all of one accord.[1]

Luke: In inviting people to repent on that first day of the new church age, Peter was repeating the challenge he'd heard Jesus frequently issue, as Mark mentioned just now. Jesus had not come "to call the righteous, but sinners to repentance" (Lk 5:32). He wove instruction about repentance into a lot of his teaching (see Lk 13:5; 15:7, 10; 16:30), and at the end he told his disciples that "repentance for the forgiveness of sins will be preached in his name to all nations" (Lk 24:47). It was a challenging call to think afresh about God, to live a different life, not hanging on to old stubborn patterns of sin, but leaving them behind to find new life under Christ's rule.

Matthew: My use of the word *repent* follows Luke's very closely (see Lk 4:17; 11:20-21; 12:41; 21:32).

Mark: As mentioned, *repent* is one of my headlines! It's there in bold print in the opening pronouncement Jesus made about the purpose of his coming (see Mk 1:15). I'd simply add that when Jesus sent out his disciples to spread the good news, "they went out and preached that people should repent" (Mk 6:12).

> **CALLS TO REPENT IN ACTS**
>
> 3:19; 5:31; 8:22; 11:18; 20:21; 26:20.

Luke: It was certainly a key part of the preaching of the first apostles. They were always calling on people to turn around, leave their sin, and follow Christ, with Paul even saying, just on one occasion, that God "*commands* all people everywhere to repent" (Acts 17:30).

---

[1]See further chap. 7, 163-66.

Paul: It's interesting you recall that, Luke, because *repentance* isn't a word I use much in my own writings. Because I mention it only five times (Rom 2:4; 2 Cor 7:9-10; 12:21; 2 Tim 2:25), some have claimed I "had little interest in the subject."[2] However, when I say that the Thessalonian converts "turned to God from idols to serve the living and true God" (1 Thess 1:9), well, that's repentance by another name. Similarly, my idea of justification involves a total reorientation of one's life and results in an entirely new mindset, which, again, is another way of talking about repentance.

The Hebraist: Perhaps repentance was preached so much that we almost took it for granted in our writings. I, for example, list it as foundational to the Christian life and speak of it as a one-off irrevocable commitment to Christ (see Heb 6:1, 6), but I don't talk of it otherwise.

Peter: Repentance remained central to my preaching from the day of Pentecost onward, even if I'm largely silent about it. You can gauge its importance to me, though, by recalling what I said in my last letter: "The Lord is not slow in keeping his promise. . . . Instead he is patient with you, not wanting anyone to perish, but everyone to come to repentance" (2 Pet 3:9).

John: I don't use the word in my Gospel, but it's fairly important in Revelation, although used somewhat differently. My concern is twofold. First, I do not present repentance as a one-off turning to God (although I don't deny the importance of that), but as something the church needs to do whenever she falls into sin, so that she might restore her love for and dedication to the one who died and is alive forever more (see Rev 2:5, 16, 21-22; 3:3, 19). Second, I point out that many of the troubles in the world are designed to move people to repentance for their sin, but rather than causing repentance they strengthen people's resistance to God (see Rev 9:20-21).

Faith

Chair: So repentance is one element in our response to the good news. What about the other element of faith? What have we got to say about that? I think it has a fairly uncomplicated meaning to start with, but then, as time goes on, you begin to use it in more nuanced ways.

Mark: Yes, Jesus mentions faith far more than repentance and in the straightforward sense of actively placing one's trust in God or believing in Christ his Son, not as a one-off but as a dynamic and ongoing stance in life.

---

[2]Donald Guthrie, *New Testament Theology* (Downers Grove, IL: InterVarsity Press, 1981), 589.

Jesus was constantly calling people to exercise this faith in all sorts of dire and impossible circumstances (see Mk 1:15; 4:40; 5:36; 11:22, 31; 16:11-14). It was always a lively quality that found expression in some practical way, such as prayer (see Mk 11:22-24). Faith released Jesus' power to work miracles (see Mk 2:5; 5:34; 9:23-24; 10:52; 11:23-24). Conversely, a refusal to believe in him as God's Son could be a real hindrance to God displaying his power (see Mk 6:5-6).

Luke: Matthew and I mention one thing that Mark doesn't, and that's the way Jesus stressed that it was not the quantity of faith that mattered but that faith even as small as a mustard seed, proverbially the smallest seed in the world, could result in great miracles (see Lk 17:5-6; Mt 17:20). Jesus certainly had an arresting way of teaching in using

> ### MATTHEW STRESSES THE CONNECTION BETWEEN FAITH AND MIRACLES
>
> 6:30; 8:10, 26; 9:2, 22, 29; 13:58; 14:31; 15:28; 16:8; 17:20; 21:21.

such hyperbolic language. Behind the claim lies the unspoken thought that it is not the size of our faith that's important but where we put whatever little faith we have. It needs to be placed in him.

John: I use the word *faith* only once (Jn 12:42), but I have a great deal to say about believing, which is the same thing, as some of Mark's verses above show. Remember, the reason I wrote the Gospel was that readers "may believe that Jesus is the Messiah, the Son of God" (Jn 20:31). When I wrote that I used a continuous tense, because believing isn't a one-off commitment so much as a continuing trust in Jesus, especially when the going gets tough—as it did for many of my readers.

What's important, as Luke has just said, is not belief in itself but where you place your belief, who you believe in. As I constantly emphasize, it is having faith in the person of Jesus that matters. Those famous words of Jesus, "You believe in God; believe also in me" (Jn 14:1; see also 4:53; 8:30; 12:11), highlight that. Sometimes I talk about believing the message, but to believe the message is to believe in the messenger, Jesus himself. Once I talk about believing in his "name"—but the "name" simply stands for the person it belongs to (Jn 1:12). Salvation, or, to use my favorite term, eternal life, comes through believing (see Jn 1:12; 3:16; 6:40). Belief is so central that my common way of talking about the disciples is to say that they are "believers"—a term I use some eighty-four times in one way or another.

My first letter carries on the same theme: "Who is it that overcomes the world? Only the one who believes that Jesus is the Son of God" (1 Jn 5:5); and "I write these things to you who believe in the name of the Son of God so that you may know that you have eternal life" (1 Jn 5:13).

Luke: The apostles' early preaching underlined the main point John has just made. Faith was about having faith in the person of Christ, as when Paul told his suicidal jailer in Philippi to "Believe in the Lord Jesus, and you will be saved" (Acts 16:31; see also 11:17; 14:23; 20:21; 24:24). Occasionally I use the shortcut in Acts and say they believed "the message" (Acts 4:4; 17:11-12) and assume people would know that the message is the message about Jesus. On a couple of occasions I even summarize the whole message in terms of "the faith" (Acts 6:7; 13:8), just as Jesus himself once did (see Mt 24:10) and as Paul was going to do again in his later writings, as I'm sure he'll explain.

Before he does so, though, I want to add another element to our discussion. Faith was a quality that was particularly expected of leaders. Stephen was exemplary because he was "full of faith" (Acts 6:5), and so was that remarkably encouraging character, Barnabas (see Acts 11:24).

Paul: Thinking about it, I would say there are four main ways in which I write about faith. First, and preeminently, I use it to talk about justifying faith. Let me give you some headline verses:

- Romans 3:25: "God presented Christ as a sacrifice of atonement, through the shedding of his blood—to be received *by faith.*"

- Romans 5:1: "Therefore, since we have been justified *through faith,* we have peace with God through our Lord Jesus Christ."

- Galatians 2:15-16: "We . . . know that a person is not justified by the works of the law, but *by faith* in Jesus Christ. So we, too, have put our faith in Christ Jesus that we may be justified *by faith* in Christ and not by the works of the law, because by the works of the law no one will be justified."

- Ephesians 2:8: "For it is by grace you have been saved, *through faith*—and this is not from yourselves, it is the gift of God."

We have already explored some of the dimensions of this from the viewpoint of justification.[3] Here we simply want to say that the way to receive God's justifying grace is to trust in Christ and have faith in his life, cross, and resurrection.

Second, faith is the heartbeat of our Christian lives throughout. We do not begin with faith and graduate to something else, but live constantly by faith (see Gal 2:20), from the beginning to the end of our Christian experience. I offer a fuller exposition of this in Galatians 3:1-14, but the theme of living by faith crops up regularly. Faith, with hope and love, is one of the great cardinal virtues of the Christian life. And as I reminded the Corinthians, "we live by faith, not by sight" (2 Cor 5:7).

> **FAITH AS THE HEARTBEAT OF THE CHRISTIAN LIFE**
>
> Rom 12:3; 14:1-2, 23; 16:26; Gal 5:5-6; Eph 3:12, 17; Col 1:23; 1 Thess 1:3; 3:2, 7; 2 Thess 1:3-4, 11; 1 Tim 1:4; 2:15; 3:13; 4:12; 6:11-12; 2 Tim 1:5; 2:22; 3:10.

Third, I write about the special gift of faith in 1 Corinthians 12:9. This is not the justifying faith without which no one can be a Christian, but a special degree of faith given to some by the Holy Spirit—perhaps for believing, against all odds, that God will work in certain ways in particular situations, or to enable a person to hold on when he or she is facing extremely challenging circumstances. Though I include it in my list of "manifestations of the Spirit," it's not something I develop.

> **FAITH, HOPE, AND LOVE**
>
> 1 Cor 13:13; Col 1:4-5; 1 Thess 1:2-3; 5:8.
> Faith and love only:
> Eph 1:15; 2 Thess 1:3; 1 Tim 1:5, 14; 2 Tim 1:13.

Fourth, as Luke commented, in my later writings I refer to "the faith," not so much in the sense of an active quality but as a title for a settled set of beliefs (1 Tim 1:2, 19; 3:9; 4:1, 6; 6:10, 12, 21; 2 Tim 3:8; 4:7). However, that should not be seen as an entirely new development, since I referred to "the faith" in my earlier writings as well (1 Cor 16:13; 2 Cor 13:5; Gal 1:23; Col 2:7).

---

[3]See chap. 7, 139-41.

I think you'll find the essentials of my teaching about faith all contained in the letter to the Ephesians. There I speak of faith as

- the distinguishing mark of the Christian ("for us who believe," Eph 1:19);

- how one initially responds to the gospel (see Eph 1:13, 15);

- the only means of appropriating grace (see Eph 2:8);

- the continuing stance required of a believer (see Eph 3:12, 17; 6:16); and

- shorthand for the body of Christian doctrine (see Eph 4:5, 13).

Chair: Do any of the rest of you have anything to add? Is that how you all see it?

The Hebraist: Actually, I contribute a slightly different perspective on faith. My starting point is to spell out what others assume and to define what we mean by faith, rather than take it for granted: "faith is confidence in what we hope for and assurance about what we do not see" (Heb 11:1).

On that basis, I reflect on the way a host of "ancients" shaped their lives by their faith. I mention some obvious characters who accomplished immense feats for God, such as Noah, Abraham, and Moses (see Heb 11:7-19, 23-28), who all in their individual way believed what most normal people thought impossible. I also mention some lesser characters who equally took risks on the basis of faith even when the evidential proof most would require was absent. Here I talk about people like Abel, Enoch, and Rahab (Heb 11:4-6, 31). In fact, the examples of those who acted on a promise they had not yet received are so numerous that I'm reduced to shooting off a long list at the end of this chapter (Heb 11:32-37). Their lives might have proved to be nothing more than empty, misguided dreams, except that, as I've explained up to this point in my letter, the promises all came true with the coming of Jesus.

My real message in all this is simple: "without faith it is impossible to please God, because anyone who comes to him must believe that he exists and that he rewards those who earnestly seek him" (Heb 11:6).

James: I too have a somewhat different approach to the subject. As a Christian wisdom writer, I stand in the tradition of those who are concerned about a practical, working belief. So, as I spell out in 2:14-26, I want to stress the futility of faith that is not actively translated into living actions. The punch line is this: "faith without deeds is dead" (Jas 2:26); in fact, it was probably never alive. Faith without works is stillborn. I don't want to see faith that is useless, inactive, and unproductive; I want to see faith that is active, productive, and, because it is alive, fruitful.

Observer: Many have subsequently tried to drive a wedge between Paul's teaching on faith and that of James. On the face of it, there are some tensions between them. They both draw on their Jewish heritage and use Abraham to illustrate their teaching, but do so in opposite ways. So for Paul, Abraham is an example of faith (see Rom 4:1-25), whereas for James, he is an example of works (see Jas 2:20-24). However, much of the tension is resolved by understanding that they are addressing different questions.

Paul is concerned about the incorporation of the Gentiles with the Jews into the one new people God has brought into being through Christ. In explaining this, he questions the reliance the Jews have shown on their works of the law, such as circumcision, dietary laws, and sabbath observance. When James, on the other hand, speaks of the law, it is not these aspects of the law he has in mind so much as the moral aspects of the law, with its emphasis on living justly and its concern, for example, for orphans, widows, and the poor. Paul stresses in his writings that genuine faith will lead to good works (see Rom 1:5; 16:26; Gal 5:13-14; 6:1-10; Phil 1:11; Col 1:10; 1 Thess 1:3; 2 Thess 1:11). I can hear James applauding all this.

James's target is different from Paul's. He is aiming at those who claim an intellectual faith, like the demons (see Jas 2:19), but never let it affect the way they behave. If James doesn't focus on faith as Paul does, it's not because he considers it irrelevant; rather he assumes it (see Jas 2:17, 20, 26). It's the nature and quality of faith that concerns him, rather than the necessity of it.

As Douglas Moo has written, "The difference between Paul and James consists in the *sequence* of works and conversion. Paul denies any efficacy to pre-conversion works, but James is pleading for the absolute necessity of post-conversion works."[4] In other words, this is like Paul

---

[4]Douglas Moo, *James*, Tyndale New Testament Commentary (Leicester: Inter-Varsity Press, 1985), 102.

denying that we can be justified by the works of the law of Moses but saying that, having been justified, we must fulfill the law of Christ.[5]

There are other themes they have in common. For example, they both assert that God chooses the poor, the weak, and the lowly to be the true agents of his salvation and heirs of his kingdom. In 1 Corinthians 1:26-29 and James 1:9-10; 2:5-6, they clearly echo each other. In this and other ways Paul and James are complementary to each other, rather than in conflict with each other.[6]

Baptism

Chair: Let's move on. Judging from Peter's response to the crowd on the day of Pentecost, another vital element in people responding to the gospel is baptism (see Acts 2:38). Yet it seems that the New Testament as a whole doesn't make too much of it. What, then, can we say about baptism?

Matthew: The most obvious starting point is that Jesus himself was baptized by John "the baptizer," as we Synoptic Gospel writers all record (see Mt 3:13-17; Mk 1:9-11; Lk 3:21-22). Mark, typically, gives us a very concise account, and on this occasion Luke follows him. I add something to their accounts. When Jesus went to be baptized by John, John resisted his request, saying, "I need to be baptized by you, and do you come to me?" John could see the infinite superiority of his cousin Jesus and was presumably anxious that, by submitting to a baptism that symbolized repentance, Jesus would be admitting he too needed cleansing from personal sin. Jesus' reply was interesting: "Let it be so now; it is proper for us to do this to fulfill all righteousness." By this I think Jesus meant that he wasn't admitting personal sin but he did want to identify fully with the sinful human beings he had come to save.

We all note the affirmation Jesus received from his Father in heaven at his baptism, which took the form of a dove descending and a voice interjecting. The dove was God's Spirit descending on Jesus and empowering him for ministry. The voice was God affirming the special nature of Jesus' sonship and his pleasure in him.

---

[5]See chap. 7, 126-31.
[6]For an excellent exposition of these issues, see Richard Bauckham, *James*, New Testament Readings (New York: Routledge, 1999), 120-40.

John: While I don't actually record the act of Jesus' baptism itself, I do allude to it (see Jn 1:32-34) and quote John the Baptist as contrasting the nature of his baptism in water with the baptism Jesus would administer later in the Holy Spirit.

I don't explicitly mention any theological interpretation of baptism in my Gospel, although some have been keen to find allusions to it in all sorts of places, like in the conversation Jesus has with Nicodemus (see Jn 3:5). What I do note, however, is that Jesus' disciples baptized those who followed him (see Jn 3:22–4:2), so it wasn't a practice confined to John by any means.[7]

Matthew: Absolutely. And that leads to the commission Jesus gave to his disciples at his ascension to "go and make disciples of all nations, baptizing them in the name of the Father and of the Son and of the Holy Spirit, and teaching them to obey everything I have commanded you. And surely I am with you always, to the very end of the age" (Mt 28:19-20). He instructs them to baptize disciples in the name of the Trinity, even though the doctrine of the Trinity seems to have been fully developed only later; but, as we've seen, all three persons of the Trinity were involved in Jesus' own baptism, and it is a logical outworking of teaching about God that is implicit throughout the Gospels.

Luke: Yes, whatever the theology of baptism—to which I'm sure we'll come with Paul's help—I'd want to emphasize that from the day of Pentecost onward the early church quite naturally practiced it. It wasn't an issue. It was the accepted expression of conversion and the way someone was initiated as a follower of Jesus into the Christian community. Baptism, of course, had a pre-history in Judaism, and Christians made these ritual baths their own, filling them with new meaning. Three thousand were baptized at Pentecost (see Acts 2:41), using every available public pool in Jerusalem to do so! The treasury official Philip spoke to on the Gaza road immediately realized that as a new convert he should be baptized (see Acts 8:36), as did Cornelius whom Peter visited (see Acts 10:48). The Philippian jailer was baptized in the early hours of the morning, straight after his conversion to Christ (see Acts 16:33). The rest of his household followed suit, since in those days the father of the house determined the religious identity and commitment of the house as a whole; because he had become a Christian, his household became a Christian household.

---

[7]John 3:22 suggests Jesus himself baptized, but 4:2 explains it was done by his disciples.

Paul's letters paint the same picture (see 1 Cor 1:13-16), even if he distances himself somewhat from actually having conducted baptisms so people didn't focus on him but on Christ and his gospel.

Chair: So, Paul, help us out. What is the meaning of baptism?

Paul: The relatively simple action of dipping someone in water[8] actually turns out to be a very rich symbolic act with multiple levels of meaning. At the most straightforward level it is taking a ritual bath, and you take a bath to wash yourself clean. So it captures the cleansing from sin that goes on when we're reborn and renewed by the power of the Holy Spirit (see Tit 2:14; 3:5).

At another level, in burying someone in water and raising him or her up again we're replaying what happened to Jesus, who died, was buried, and on the third day was raised to life. Yet we're doing more than replaying it: we're actually joining with Christ, uniting ourselves with him, by undergoing, albeit symbolically, what he underwent that first Easter. In our case, it signals death to the old sin-driven way of life, the burial of that Christless way of living, and our rising again to live in the power of Christ's risen life. That's how I explain it in Romans 6:1-4, and it's what I take for granted in Colossians 2:12.

Observer: Some have also seen a recapitulation of Israel's story in this. In N. T. Wright's words:

> What is not normally recognized is that, here in Romans, Paul tells a version of the very same story [of the crossing of the Jordan]. . . . Romans 6 describes how Christians come through the water of baptism (like the Red Sea) and thus leave behind the land of slavery and enter upon a new freedom (like leaving Egypt and setting off for the promised land).[9]

If so, this adds a further depth to our understanding of baptism. Baptism signals our liberation from bondage and entry into our promised land.

Paul: There are two other aspects of the symbolic meaning of baptism I refer to. So, third, baptism is a rite of initiation into the church. I remind the Corinthians that "we were all baptized by one Spirit *into* one body" (1 Cor

---

[8]The Greek word *baptizein* (to baptize) means to dip, to immerse, to submerge.
[9]N. T. Wright, *Paul for Everyone: Romans, Part 1: Chapters 1–8* (London: SPCK, 2004), 99.

12:13).[10] Every social group has some rite of entry, and Christians are the same. Inevitably some have seen this as the equivalent of the older Jewish rite of circumcision, and there is obviously some relationship between them, as I take for granted in Colossians 3:10-12. There are, however, also some crucial differences, the chief of which is that baptism is not restricted to eight-day-old males but is undergone by both males and females who wish publicly to identify themselves as disciples of Jesus the Christ.

Fourth, and finally, I use another aspect of the way the rite is practiced to point out its spiritual meaning. When people are baptized, they set aside one set of clothes and dress in a new set after emerging from the water. They don't go around dripping wet. Several times I build on this to teach that becoming a Christian is about putting off one wardrobe and putting on a new one. That's in my mind when I write about "putting off" one way of life and "putting on" a new way of life, as I do in Ephesians 4:25–5:20 and Colossians 2:11; 3:5-14. It's there in Romans 13:14 and Galatians 3:27 as well, where I write of Christians as those who have clothed themselves with Christ. We need to dress in the wardrobe he gives and wear the uniform that sets us apart from the crowd.[11]

Chair: Well, that probably covers it, doesn't it, since not too much is said about baptism in the New Testament?

Peter: I'd just like to add that I see it as crucial in our experience of salvation, and I refer to it as "the pledge of a clear conscience toward God" (1 Pet 3:21). So while God the Holy Spirit meets us in baptism, it is also an expression of our commitment to him.

The Hebraist: My only allusion to it is to try to ensure that the outward act of washing our bodies is entirely consistent with our inner experience—namely, of "having our hearts sprinkled to cleanse us from a guilty conscience" (Heb 10:22). The one without the other is incomplete and doesn't make sense.

BELONGING TO THE NEW COMMUNITY

Chair: The mention of baptism as a rite of entry into the church leads us nicely to talk about the new community of Christ, the church. Among you

---

[10]NIV (1984) and NRSV translate the Greek *eis* as "into." This straightforward translation is to be preferred to NIV (2011), which uses the more complex "so as to form one body."
[11]See further chap. 9, 218-20.

Gospel writers only Matthew mentions the church, leading some to say that Jesus never intended to found a church. Strictly speaking, I suppose the church, as we understand it today, didn't come into being until after Pentecost.

Matthew: I mention the church twice because by the time I wrote my Gospel the church had been formed and my Gospel is addressed to the church, as well as to a wider audience. So I took Jesus' teaching about the way the community of his disciples is to live and quite legitimately updated his vocabulary, without changing what he said, by using the word *church* (*ecclesia*). *Ecclesia* isn't a particularly religious word, although that's what it has become. It's the normal word for a gathering or assembly of any kind. The church is distinguished from other assemblies because it gathers around Jesus.

After Peter had publicly claimed Jesus to be the Messiah, Jesus said to him, "I tell you that you are Peter, and on this rock I will build my church" (Mt 16:18). In some ways it's a puzzling statement. What was the rock on which Jesus would build? *Rock* was obviously a play on Peter's name (*Petros* means "rock"), so he might well have meant he would build his church on Peter himself as the leading apostle and on all that Peter would teach and preach. Peter won't mind me saying, though, that if this was what he meant, it was an extraordinary sign of God's grace. He'd be trusting the future of his movement into the hands of an all-too-human and, at the time at least, somewhat unstable individual! However, God has always demonstrated his power and grace by using such fallible human beings, so it's entirely possible that that is exactly what he did mean. Others, though, aware of the dangers of putting forward one individual like this, have suggested that "this rock" refers not so much to Peter himself as to the confession he had just made that Jesus was "the Messiah, the Son of the living God." Regardless of whether it refers to Peter personally or not, it certainly refers to this foundational belief.

The other place where I mention the church comes in 18:17, where I am presuming the community is already formed and is faced with the issue of how to deal with a member who sins. Jesus taught us to deal with such offenses personally, member to member, and to keep them known to as small a group as possible unless the offender became stubborn and resisted all attempts at resolution. In that case, eventually the matter should be told "to the church"—but that was the last resort, not the first.

I immediately add something Jesus said that shows the influence of the synagogue on the early Christian community. To form a synagogue you need to have ten men to make up its critical mass; but Jesus said that bar was set too high and that where just "two or three gather in my name, there am I with them" (Mt 18:20). That "two or three" included women. So if you think *discipleship*, you must also think *church*.

John: None of the other Gospels uses the word *church*, but that doesn't mean the idea is absent. My Gospel may be read as individualistic in its orientation, but read it carefully and you'll see that I don't believe a disciple can ever have a solitary, individual relationship with God apart from other believers. Throughout, Jesus assumes the existence of the community we call the church. A wedding is never a solitary affair; a miracle is never the cause of a private celebration; a conversion always leads to public confession. No vine consists of one branch; no sheepfold has only one sheep in it. Relationship, as we saw before, was at the heart of his vision for the disciples after his departure from the world.[12]

CHURCH AS FAMILY

Mt 12:46-50;
23:8; 28:10; Mk
3:31-35; 10:29-31;
Lk 8:19-21; 22:32.

Luke: John has put his finger on it. One verse in my Gospel sums it up: "Do not be afraid, little flock, for your Father has been pleased to give you the kingdom" (Lk 12:32). That saying involves a flock of sheep, a family under a father's care, and a kingdom that is made up of citizens. These are images that are found throughout Jesus' teaching.

Peter: I think we're putting the cart before the horse a little here. Great as it is to start the discussion with what Jesus taught, there is something prior that we need to take into account. God's desire for a people who were particularly in tune with him and who would do his work in the world didn't start when Jesus came; it goes back to Adam and Eve, to Noah, and especially to the call and election of Abraham (see Gen 12:1-3) and the age of the patriarchs. It particularly takes shape after the exodus, when God inaugurated a new covenant with Israel in which he said, "if you obey me fully and keep my covenant, then out of all nations you will be my treasured possession. Although the whole earth is mine, you will be for me a kingdom of priests and a holy nation" (Ex 19:5-6). Israel failed to live up

---

[12]See chap. 5, 82-85.

to the promise but God never set aside his plan. Consequently, I see the church as very much in line with those historical purposes of God and in continuity with Israel. That's why I can say of the church that it is "a chosen people, a royal priesthood, a holy nation, God's special possession, that you may declare the praises of him who called you out of darkness into his wonderful light" (1 Pet 2:9).

Paul: True, the church is central to the purposes of God and therefore right at the heart of my mission. I was never about converting individuals; my calling was to plant communities of believers by the power of the Spirit. I believe "Christ loved the church and gave himself up for her" (Eph 5:25). So the church is no optional extra for believers. To be in step with God means being part of his church.

My letters are mostly addressed to those communities and deal with their beliefs and practices. So I have a lot to say about the church, some of which will come out later. Much of the time, when I use the word *you* I'm using it to refer to a group rather than an individual.[13] But let me suggest three elements by way of clueing you in to what I say.

First, I typically use the word *church*—which I do some 114 times—to apply to the local community of believers, not to any wider group beyond the local church (see Rom 16:5; 1 Cor 1:2; 1 Thess 1:1; 2 Thess 1:1; Philem 2; and so on). If I want to speak of a wider network of churches, I don't use the single word *church* but the plural (see 1 Cor 16:1, 19; 2 Cor 8:18-19; 11:28; Gal 1:2; 1 Thess 2:14; and so on). Only on three occasions do I use the word *church* to refer to the collective body of believers in general (1 Cor 10:32; 15:9; Gal 1:13). When I do so I certainly don't have in mind any organizational structure or institution, like the denominations that subsequently developed. It's true that in my later writings my view of the church is heightened, and I speak of the place the church has in the universal and heavenly purposes of God (Eph 1:22; 3:10; 5:23-27, 29, 32; Col 1:18; 3:12), but I never lose the local focus.

That leads me to the second clue, which is best seen in my use of the image of the church as a body, which I develop in 1 Corinthians 12:12-31 and use differently in Ephesians 4:16 and Colossians 1:18; 2:19. The important

---

[13]Sadly, the English language no longer distinguishes between *you* plural and *you* singular, and this can lead to a distorted understanding of Paul's writings in which the church becomes less significant than it is and the individual is made to shoulder all sorts of responsibilities and privileges that rightly belong to the church as a whole.

point to grasp is that bodies are living and integrated organisms composed of different members who are intricately and vitally related to one another. A body isn't a collection of individuals who "do their own thing." It's an organism whose members depend on each other and function together.[14] This proves a great challenge to those who don't want to sacrifice their individual autonomy.

The third clue to my intricate and multifaceted view of the church is this: I see the church as the herald of the age to come. We are what later theologians have called "an eschatological community"; that is to say, we anticipate and demonstrate in our life together now, albeit imperfectly, the life we will live in the new age, when Christ has returned and renewed our fallen creation and when God rules completely. We are a community with a memory, and we look back regularly to the cross as that which constitutes our life; but we're also a community of anticipation, since we do this "until he comes" (1 Cor 11:26). Our future destination governs our present lives. As I explained in the very forward-looking letter to the Ephesians, the purpose of the cross was "to create in himself one new humanity out of the two, thus making peace" (Eph 2:15). We're a showcase of that "one new humanity" now, even though God won't bring it to fulfillment until everything is brought into unity through Christ (Eph 1:10). If we understand this, we'll know we can't possibly live conflict-ridden, self-centered lives that are unclean or harbor resentments. Ours is the privilege of giving people a sample of the *shalom* to come.

Chair: Paul, we'll return to other things you have to say about the church in a moment. Let's continue laying some foundations by asking others if they have any preliminary points to add.

The Hebraist: I'm bifocal in my writing about the church. Looking through one lens, I see Paul's view of the church as a local gathering and stress how vital it is to persevere in meeting together and not to let the social pressures get in the way of our doing so. Incidentally, I also put this in the context of Christ's return. We need to meet with each other "all the more as you see the Day approaching" (Heb 10:25). That leads me to some very practical

---

[14]The most insightful illustration I've come across about this is the comment of Michael Griffiths in *Cinderella with Amnesia: A Practical Discussion of the Relevance of the Church* (London: InterVarsity Press, 1975), 54: "The crucial point . . . is surely that a congregation is more than an aggregation, *that a body is something quite different from a pile of minced meat!*" (emphasis mine).

comments about respecting the church's leaders who currently have some spiritual responsibility for us (see Heb 13:7, 17).

Viewed through another lens, however, I have almost a mystical view of the church, seeing it both as "a great cloud of witnesses" who encourage us to remain faithful (Heb 12:1) and as made up of those who join the joyful worshiping multitude of angels and whose names, unseen, "are written in heaven" (Heb 12:22-24).

James: I don't suppose it will surprise people if I say my approach is quite simple. My background leads me to see the church as if it were a synagogue—I actually use that word for the church in 2:2—whose leadership is in the hands of the community elders, while at the same time being a community of equals where we pray for "each other" (Jas 2:1-13; 5:13-16).

John: My letters are particularly concerned about distinguishing between the true and the false church, and I deal with the harsh reality that not all who initially put their faith in Christ continue with him or continue to believe or practice the right things. Sadly, some even leave the church (see 1 Jn 2:19; 3 Jn).

In Revelation I have a very different agenda, but the book has the church at its heart in so many ways. Very near the beginning (see Rev 2:1–3:22) there are letters from Jesus to seven churches in Asia that leave us in no doubt about the continuing importance to God of the local church. And far from the church being a tiny minority that is likely to be extinguished by a hostile political power, my vision of heaven shows it to be a very large international worshiping community that grows to be universal in its embrace (see Rev 5:9-14). In the light of that and of their destiny, persecuted Christians are called to persevere (see Rev 7:9-17), knowing that God is not neglecting them. As they struggle, they're encouraged to listen to the voice of the prophets, a very significant leadership role for any church undergoing suffering (see Rev 10:7; 16:6; 18:24; 22:6-9). Like others, I see the church as the community of the future, and I encourage people to pray that that future may arrive soon (see Rev 22:20).

The Church and Israel

Chair: Let's explore some particular dimensions of our understanding of the church more fully. Peter drew attention to the continuity between Israel and the church. Can we be more precise? What role does Israel continue to have?

Paul: While we may see the church today as "the Israel of God" (Gal 6:16), it is vital we don't write Israel off as having no further part in God's plans. I write about this extensively in Romans 9–11, which, although many don't understand this, is really the crux of the letter. I point out that God's word hasn't failed (see Rom 9:6), that God is never unjust (see Rom 9:14), that he is sovereign in mercy (see Rom 9:16-21) and that his "gifts and his call are irrevocable" (Rom 11:29). However, to my great grief (see Rom 9:2), since I am one of them, Israel rejected the path of belief, choosing to trust in their own righteousness rather than in the promise and gift of God's righteousness (see Rom 9:30–10:4) that reached its focal point in Christ (see Rom 10:5-21).

Israel's rejection is not, however, final. In fact, a remnant always believed (see Rom 11:1-10). Currently it is the Gentiles who are coming to faith, but they're like a wild branch being grafted onto an olive tree while the unbelieving Jews, the branches that naturally belong to the tree, are broken off (see Rom 11:11-24). That should be a warning to the Gentile believers not to become presumptuous about their position! All this is designed "to make Israel envious" so that they experience the riches God intended for them (Rom 11:11-12). So don't write off the Jewish people as having no further part in God's plans. God longs to have mercy on all, Jew and Gentile alike (see Rom 11:32). We've not got to the end of the story yet, and I firmly believe that God will not go back on his word to them.

> **Observer:** The interpretation of Romans 9–11 is among the most difficult in the New Testament. While it is clear that it *rules out* any "replacement theology"—that is, any argument that says the church has supplanted Israel and they no longer have any part in God's future plans—what it *rules in* is not so clear.
>
> The key question is what Paul means by "Israel." Some take it to refer to ethnic Israel, whereas others point out that Paul defines Israel as those who believe God's promise. He says this explicitly in Romans 9:6-8: "not all who are descended from Israel are Israel"; "it is not the children by physical descent who are God's children, but it is the children of the promise who are regarded as Abraham's offspring." So this would not seem to be a carte blanche promise about ethnic Israel being restored— far from it. Identifying the current secular state of Israel as the fulfillment of these prophecies therefore has no basis in this text.

Old Testament references to Israel's restoration (see Is 60–65; Ezek 35–48) must first be understood to prophesy the time when Cyrus permitted Israel to return from exile to Judea in 638 BC. These prophecies must then be read in the light of the coming of Christ, since "no matter how many promises God has made, they are 'Yes' in Christ" (2 Cor 1:20). His mission and the gospel of God's grace are universal in scope (as in reality they always have been). So they cannot serve as a template for a territorial, nationalistic people.

Metaphors of the Church

Chair: Let's return in our thinking about the church to something simpler. I note, Paul, that when you're talking about the church you often resort to a variety of images. What are they?

Paul: The value of images is that they are often quite self-explanatory. So I describe the church as follows:

- The temple of the living God (see 1 Cor 3:16-17; 2 Cor 6:16-18; Eph 2:21). It is the dwelling and home of our trinitarian God.

- The body of Christ (see 1 Cor 12:12-31; Eph 4:16; 5:23, 30; Col 1:18; 2:19). As mentioned earlier, this highlights the way there must be unity and coherence in all our diversity and how we need one another. It also illustrates how we function under the direction of Christ, our head.

- The field of God (see 1 Cor 3:9), which stresses that it is God's life-giving power that matters and produces growth, not human leaders or organization.

- The bride of Christ (see 2 Cor 11:2; Eph 5:25-27). This image always points forward to the wedding day and the way the bride prepares herself for it. John also uses the image to anticipate the future (see Rev 19:9).

- The army of the Spirit (see Gal 5:25–6:5). The image is more implicit than explicit, but throughout these verses I'm using military terminology. In Ephesians 6:10-18, and more briefly in 1 Thessalonians 5:8, I speak of our spiritual armor, which obviously builds on the idea of the church as God's army, albeit a very different one from the armies of this world.

- The household of God (see 1 Tim 3:15), with all that implies about how a household organizes itself and how each member has a place in serving the whole. Another allusion to that image is found in 2 Timothy 2:20-21.

- The pillar and foundation of truth (see 1 Tim 3:15). Houses need to be built on decent foundations and have strong pillars to support the upper floors and roofs, or else they collapse. The church equally needs strong foundations (see Eph 2:20-21) and pillars to make it secure, and these are found in "the truth," by which I mean the gospel and apostolic teaching (see Col 1:5; see also 2 Jn 1, 2, 4).

Practices of the Church

Chair: Let's be practical. What does the church do, and how does it function?

Ordinary Practices

Luke: I give an insight into this in one of the earliest glimpses of the church, as it wasn't long after Pentecost, in Acts 2:42-47: "They devoted themselves to the apostles' teaching and to fellowship, to the breaking of bread and to prayer." Those were their priorities. Almost as a by-product they did "many wonders and signs," and many were converted. They had no "church" buildings of their own, so they did all this in public, "in the temple courts," and in their own homes. Through sharing what they possessed, they made sure no one was in need. The rest of Acts illustrates the way this all developed, such as when the Greek-speaking widows felt themselves neglected "in the daily distribution of food," an oversight that was immediately corrected by the apostles (Acts 6:1-6).

Paul: I'm certainly not unique in referring back frequently to that original mandate of the church; it is woven throughout my writings. So to give some examples:

- The apostles' teaching in 1 Corinthians 7:10; 11:23-24; Ephesians 2:20; 2 Timothy 1:11-14. (See also 2 Pet 1:12-21; Jude 3.) Galatians gives us an insight into how the apostles' teaching was clarified and firmly established.

- Fellowship (see further below).

- Breaking of bread (again, see further below).

- Prayer in Romans 12:12; Philippians 4:6-7; Colossians 4:2-3, 12; 1 Thessalonians 1:2; 5:17; 1 Timothy 2:1-3, 8; and Philemon 4. Others write about it too, like James (Jas 5:13-18) and Jude (Jude 20). Moreover, we don't just write about it; we practice it. You can find a number of our prayers scattered throughout our writings (see Eph 1:15-22; 3:14-21; Phil 1:9-11; Col 1:9-13).

- Sharing common life. I write extensively about this, and about how it applied once the church had moved out of Jerusalem and became a scattered, international body, in 2 Corinthians 8–9. It is also mentioned elsewhere by me and by others (e.g., see 1 Thess 2:8-9; 1 Tim 5:3-16; Jas 1:27; 1 Jn 3:17-18).

- Worship/praising God is dealt with in 1 Corinthians 14:26-33; Ephesians 5:19; and Colossians 3:16.

- And having an evangelistic impact is evident in 1 Corinthians 14:24-25 and Philippians 2:14-16.

"ONE ANOTHER"

Love: Jn 13:34-35; Rom 12:10; 13:8; Eph 4:32; 1 Thess 4:9; 2 Thess 1:3; Heb 13:1; 1 Pet 1:22; 3:8; 1 Jn 3:11, 23; 4:7, 11-12; 2 Jn 5.

Accept: Rom 15:7.

Instruct: Rom 15:14; Eph 5:10; Col 3:16.

Agree: 1 Cor 1:10.

Encourage: 2 Cor 13:11; 1 Thess 4:18; 5:11; Heb 3:13; 10:24-25.

Bear with: Eph 4:2; Col 3:13.

Submit: Eph 5:21.

Forgive: Eph 4:32; Col 3:13.

Admonish: Col 3:16.

Confess: Jas 5:16.

Offer hospitality: 1 Pet 4:9.

Walk in the light: 1 Jn 1:7.

Let me expand a little on fellowship, if I may. Fellowship (*koinōnia*) means sharing or participating with each other. It doesn't describe a superficial give or take but is a deeply relational word about joining with others in something you have in common. The idea of fellowship crops up all the time, but in my writings one of the best ways to understand it is to note the frequent use of the word translated "one another" (*allēlōn*). The Christian church was never designed to be a hierarchical institution where things flowed from the top down (other than from the headship of Christ). It was meant to be a community of believers where we shared life together. If you chase through the frequent use of this word *allēlōn*, you'll soon get the idea.

I guess one of the routine practices of the church that developed was the taking of an offering, especially for the needs of others rather than for the running of the church's organization. I gave brief instructions about it in

1 Corinthians 16:2—instructions I had already given the Galatians (see
1 Cor 16:1)—where I told them that their giving should be regular: "on the
first day of every week"; considered: "each one of you should set aside";
proportional: "in keeping with your income"; and elsewhere I add: "cheerful"
(2 Cor 9:7). I relate all this to Christ in the context of a full exposition of the
theology of the offering in 2 Corinthians 8–9.

Special Rites: The Lord's Supper

Chair: There were two things Jesus commanded his disciples to do. One
was to practice baptism and the other was to break bread together. We
looked at baptism just now.[15] What can we say about the Lord's Supper?

Luke: It was one of the practices that the early Christians adopted from
the start. I refer to it as "the breaking of bread" (Acts 2:42, 46). In some respects it was just like eating an ordinary supper. Every day people would give
thanks to God and then break off some bread from a loaf they were sharing
(see Acts 20:11; 27:35). As they did so, however, it came to carry a deeper
meaning and reminded them of Jesus' Last Supper with his disciples and
how he said to them, "This is my body given for you; do this in remembrance
of me" (Lk 22:19). The meal developed into something special, especially
after Christ, on the evening of the resurrection, broke bread with the two
disciples from Emmaus, which enabled them to recognize who he was (see
Lk 24:30). So it became a special act of worship and remembrance.

Mark: Yes, Matthew and I agree with Luke about this Last Supper that
Jesus ate with his disciples (see Mk 14:12-26; Mt 26:17-30; Lk 22:7-38). We
may differ on some of the details, but we don't differ on the substance. This
was a Passover meal, and the Passover liturgy is quite complex, so it is no
wonder we pick up various elements of it. You, Luke, to take a minor point,
seem to suggest Jesus served the cup before he broke bread (see Lk 22:17-19),
but there were four cups passed around at the Passover, so it's not a problem.

We all agree this was a Passover meal and was therefore a celebration of
God's great act of liberation and salvation for Israel. We also agree that Jesus
invested the meal with an entirely new significance by identifying the bread
as his body and the wine as his blood. This was a pretty explicit claim that it
was the sacrifice of his body and the shedding of his blood that was going to
inaugurate the new and greater act of liberation from sin. So Jesus commanded

---

[15]See chap. 8, 189-92.

us to repeat this meal in memory, no longer of Moses and the exodus, but of himself. He himself was the new Passover Lamb. He told us his blood had initiated a new covenant, one which would replace the old one. This is a theme, as we know, that the Hebraist expands on at great length.

He did say one strange thing during the meal, which was that he wouldn't drink the cup again "until that day when I drink it new in the kingdom of God" (Mk 14:25). He was obviously pointing to the future, to the time when the kingdom of God he had inaugurated and done much to bring in during his lifetime would be more fully realized. He was probably pointing to the end time when he would participate in what John calls "the wedding supper of the Lamb" (Rev 19:9).

Chair: Talking of John, isn't it true, John, that you don't record this Last Supper?

John: You're right. I don't record the Last Supper in the way the other Gospel writers do, although I do mention the occasion (see Jn 13:1-38). I'm captivated by the way, when we met for that last meal, Jesus took the role of the servant and washed his disciples' feet. We should have been doing it to him, but he taught us a very powerful lesson in love, service, and humility that evening, even though he knew that events were about to unfold that would lead to his crucifixion shortly afterward.

Having said that, my Gospel alludes to the Last Supper elsewhere. When Jesus fed the five thousand it gave rise to a theological debate in which Jesus uttered some astonishing words. "Unless," he said, "you eat the flesh of the Son of Man and drink his blood, you have no life in you" (Jn 6:53). That's clearly a variation on a theme, isn't it? And then after the resurrection he had a meal with us on the lakeshore in Galilee, where he "took the bread and gave it to [us]" (Jn 21:13), which is also an echo of that Last Supper.

Paul: I mention it only once (see 1 Cor 11:17-34), possibly because it was widely practiced and readily understood. It was often only when things went wrong, as they did in Corinth, that we addressed an issue; that's why I deal with it in my letter to them. However, it wasn't "central"[16] to our thinking. You'll note I'm not at all interested in who "presided" (pompous word!) at the Last Supper, what "liturgy" was used, any details of the "ritual" or order of it, or even if it was

---

[16]Caird says that "there is no evidence that it was central to the thought or to the worship of the early church." George Caird, *New Testament Theology*, ed. L. D. Hurst (Oxford: Oxford University Press, 1994), 228.

something separate from an ordinary meal or a love feast tacked on. It was, or should have been, a community meal, friends celebrating together. Since they messed it up, I had to remind them what it was all about. It's an amazing meal that looks in several directions at once. It causes us to look:

- upward to Christ, since it is about participation in him (see 1 Cor 10:14-17);
- backward to tradition (see 1 Cor 11:23) and, more significantly, to the cross: "you proclaim the Lord's death" (1 Cor 11:26);
- forward to the coming of the Messiah: "until he comes" (1 Cor 11:26);
- inward to our own spiritual state: "Everyone ought to examine themselves . . ." (1 Cor 11:28-32); and
- outward to those who sit at the meal with us (see 1 Cor 11:33-34). That was the real problem at Corinth! The supper that should have united them was being used to emphasize their social divisions, with one group showing disrespect to another by their eating habits. Such behavior had to be corrected or else the whole point of the death of Christ, where we all stand as equals, receiving his forgiveness through faith, would have been denied.

Observer: The forward dimension of the supper is consistent with the future messianic banquet that crops up in a number of ways throughout Scripture from Isaiah 25:6, through the teaching of Jesus (see Lk 14:1-23, esp. v. 15), to the book of Revelation (see Rev 19:9).

Chair: The truth is, the Lord's Supper isn't mentioned anywhere in the New Testament documents other than in the passages we've looked at.

The Energy of the Church

Chair: Let me ask, on a different note, what fuels or energizes the church? The church isn't just a human club where people gather around a common interest, is it? It's more than that.

Luke: Well, you can't read the Acts without seeing the answer to that is very clearly that the church is different, and it is the Holy Spirit who makes the difference. The living God, through his Spirit, is the one who gives the growth and enabled the word, as I often put it, to grow or spread (see Acts 6:7; 12:24; 13:49; 16:5; 19:20).

Paul: Too true. It is "only God . . . who makes things grow" (1 Cor 3:7). The church takes its cue in everything from Jesus and grows because it is united to him (see Eph 2:21-22); but that life of Jesus is mediated to the church by the Holy Spirit. As the temple of God, the church is infused by the life of his Spirit (see 1 Cor 3:16). The triune God is the one who energizes the church by distributing gifts to its members, as mentioned before, enabling them to serve one another and accomplish his work (see 1 Cor 12:4-6). Consequently, to change the analogy, we must "keep in step with the Spirit" (Gal 5:25). And our teaching must be sensitive to what the Spirit says (1 Tim 4:1).

So, while the church is unavoidably a human institution, and the flaws of that are all too obvious, the church is also the place invigorated and empowered by God himself.

Leadership in the Church

Chair: Since you mention it is a human organization, Paul, let's explore the question of leadership a little. We've learned that the church is a community, but even communities have structures and leaders. They need them to survive. The church is often spoken of as a family, but families have structures, with parents taking the greater share of responsibility within them. Is there a pattern of leadership that God has given to the church?

Mark: We surely must begin by acknowledging the importance of the apostles in this. When Jesus "appointed twelve that they might be with him and that he might send them out" (Mk 3:14), he was self-evidently appointing the counterparts of the twelve tribal heads of Israel. He made it clear that on the one hand they were to stay close to him, and on the other hand they were to go out as his emissaries.

Luke: And the story of the early church confirms the significant role the Twelve played in its foundation and growth. When Judas betrayed Jesus, he left a vacancy in the apostolate, and they immediately sought to replace him so that the number twelve was maintained (see Acts 1:15-26). These apostles, the "sent ones," took the lead in those initial days. However, even though they were in a unique position, it wasn't long before they began to share their leadership with others, sometimes as a result of their own initiative, sometimes because events overtook them.

A quick survey of my history of the early church refers to "seven men" being chosen to share in the leadership of the church in Jerusalem (Acts

6:1-6). Though appointed to "wait on tables," it's not long before we read of them doing other things. Stephen performed miracles, provoked opposition, and became the church's first martyr (see Acts 6:8–8:1). Philip goes off to preach in Samaria, and through his "unauthorized" work a church is planted there (see Acts 8:4-17). Paul, Barnabas, and others in the church at Antioch who were "prophets and teachers" are inspired by the Holy Spirit to start a new missionary work to the Gentiles (Acts 13:1-3), without referring everything back to Jerusalem first. In the churches they planted, they "appointed elders" (Acts 14:23), so a local leadership emerges. Meanwhile, back in Jerusalem, James the half brother of Jesus is taking the lead and is working alongside the apostles and other elders there (see Acts 15:1-21). Leadership seems to have something of a Jewish complexion to it, but equally seems to be flexible according to need.

Paul: I endorse Luke's picture. My writings portray a complex, multilayered pattern of leadership. The apostles remain vitally important (see Eph 2:20). I, in fact, was chosen by the Lord to join them in my special role as an apostle to the Gentiles, even though I wasn't one of the original twelve (see 1 Cor 15:8). Indeed, given my background as a persecutor of the church, God's calling on my life was a special mark of his grace and example of the gospel at work transforming lives (see 1 Tim 1:12-17).

Yet there are so many other things to say. One element of leadership is that God equips certain people to exercise particular kinds of leadership, not only as foundational apostles but also as "the apostles, the prophets, the evangelists, the pastors and teachers" (Eph 4:11; see also Rom 12:6-8; 1 Cor 12:28).[17] Sometimes *apostles* refers to the Twelve, and sometimes, as here (cf. Rom 16:7), to a wider group of pioneer missionary church planters.

Then local churches recognized "overseers and deacons" (Phil 1:1) as their leaders. Here the word for overseers is *episkopoi*, sometimes translated as "bishops." The elders Luke referred to above were called *presbyteroi*, a more familiar Jewish term for the same thing.

We also need to acknowledge the important leadership role of householders who hosted the church in their homes. These people such as Lydia, Aquila and Priscilla, Stephanas, Chloe, Nympha, and Philemon— women as well as men—led in a countercultural way (see Acts 16:11-15;

---

[17]See further chap. 7, 168.

18:24-28; 1 Cor 1:11, 16; 16:15-16, 19; Col 4:15; Philem 1-2). As householders they would normally have expected to be served, and yet they gave themselves in service to others without being jealous of their status; such is the transforming power of Christ. But don't be deceived: in serving they exercised leadership.

There were also other people who acted as patrons of the church, such as Phoebe (see Rom 16:1), and colleagues such as Barnabas who undertook a tremendous amount of leadership responsibility without ever having an official title. Then, when I was more limited in my ability to travel, I made use of some younger men, such as Timothy and Titus, who went and exercised leadership on my behalf without having a title or "official position."

Toward the end of my ministry, leadership may have settled down somewhat and mainly, but not exclusively, consisted in local churches having elders or overseers

> ### THE MINISTRY OF BARNABAS
>
> Acts 4:36; 9:27; 11:22-26, 30; 12:25–13:3, 7, 42-52; 14:1-28; 15:1-41; 1 Cor 9:6; Gal 2:1, 9, 13.

and deacons, as is reflected in 1 Timothy 3:1-12 and Titus 1:5-9. Here I use interchangeably the words *presbyteroi*, the familiar Jewish term, and *episkopoi*, which has more of a Greek background. I'm more concerned about the leaders' characters and abilities, which qualify or disqualify them from the task, than I am about their titles.

While the early church undoubtedly went in the direction of stable leadership, the contrast between the pattern seen in the earlier and later church should not be overdrawn. I refer to the role of the Spirit proportionately as much in Ephesians, a later letter, as I do in my earliest letters, such as 1 Corinthians or Galatians. Some want to contrast strongly initial charismatic ministry with later ministry based on "offices," but I resist that. In my earliest letters, such as Philippians, I write to the whole church but pick out "the bishops and deacons" for special mention. In my later writings I have a fair amount to say about the Holy Spirit empowering ministry, and I mention gifts like those of prophecy and apostolic commissioning (see 1 Tim 4:14; 2 Tim 1:6-7, 14; 4:1-8). The apostolic writings as a whole do not lay down a clear pattern or ecclesiastical structure but suggest that the Spirit shapes and reshapes ministry according to the demands of context and time.

Peter: None of us is really interested in providing a manual for church government. So when I touch on this issue I assume, as does James, that the church is led by elders (see 1 Pet 5:1; Jas 5:14), typical of its Jewish roots. Like Paul, I'm much more concerned about the character of the elders and the way they lead, rather than any job description they might fulfill.

The Hebraist: Given my conviction that there is no continuing earthly priesthood, but only one new great high priest who serves us (see Heb 4:15–5:10; 7:1–8:13), you'll not be surprised that I don't concern myself with details of human leadership. When I do refer to leaders in the church, I don't use a religious word to do so but simply use the normal word for rulers or leaders (*hēgemōn*), which we would use of governors, generals, or business leaders. I believe that, like those secular leaders, they have an authority that should not be undermined; but I too am concerned that their lives should be worthy of imitation and that they are people who are accountable for their leadership, something other rulers too easily forget (see Heb 13:7, 17).

The Mission of the Church

Chair: We should finally give our attention to the mission of the church.

Matthew: Yes. In view of his universal authority as the risen Lord, Jesus commissioned his disciples to "go and make disciples of all nations." He explained this would mean baptizing people in the name of the Trinity and "teaching them to obey everything I have commanded you" (Mt 28:19-20).

Luke: My sources highlighted that they were to preach "repentance for the forgiveness of sins" "in his name to all nations" and to witness to the things they had seen (Lk 24:47). He repeated that emphasis on "witnessing" to him "to the ends of the earth" when he took his leave from them (Acts 1:8). Their commission was to speak about what they had seen and heard.

John: I remember Jesus saying to his disciples on the evening of the resurrection, "As the Father has sent me, I am sending you" (Jn 20:21). That suggests it was more than just preaching and involved "signs," since earlier he had said that "whoever believes in me will do the works I have been doing, and they will do even greater things than these, because I am going to the Father" (Jn 14:12). It's hard to imagine he could have meant "greater in kind," since he raised the dead, like Lazarus, so he must have meant "greater in extent." His ministry was that of one person in one country; they would be many witnesses in many countries, and so "greater."

Matthew: That certainly fits with the way he sent out the Twelve and later a wider group on practice missions during his lifetime (see Mt 10:1-42; Mk 3:13-19; 6:7-13; Lk 9:1-6; 10:1-20). They not only preached repentance but saw miracles and exorcisms taking place—the signs of the kingdom—as well. So preaching and powerful actions went hand in hand.

Luke: Yes, and that certainly continued into the early days of the apostolic mission, as we've drawn attention to before.

Mark: True, but Jesus cautioned them not to get too excited about the miracles and warned them that people would seek for the signs but miss what those signs pointed to—in other words, signs alone wouldn't bring people to have faith in him (see Mk 8:11-12). Luke and John, you both comment on that as well (see Lk 10:13-16; Jn 4:48; 12:37).

Chair: Once again, however, there is something of a surprise in the rest of the New Testament, since mission isn't mentioned as such, and certainly none of you ever repeats Christ's command to "go and make disciples" subsequently. Why not?

Paul: I guess the primary answer to that is that we didn't have to keep telling people to do it; they just got on with it. It was part of their DNA to speak to others about Jesus. Look, for example, at my letter to the Philippians. I commend them for their "partnership in the gospel" (Phil 1:5); remark on the courage my imprisonment had given others "to proclaim the gospel without fear" (Phil 1:14); recognize that lots were preaching the gospel but not always for the best motives (Phil 1:15-18); and try to strengthen their resolve to shine like stars in "a warped and crooked generation" as they held out the word of life (Phil 2:15).[18] Even when rebuking two women who were falling out with each other I reveal that they had "contended at my side in the cause of the gospel" along with many others (Phil 4:2-3). That gives a positive glimpse of how evangelism was a natural part of congregational life.

Furthermore, you'll get an insight into what happened if you remember the story of the founding of the church at Colossae. Epaphras, who was converted through my preaching in Ephesus, went back home to Colossae

---

[18]Phil 2:14-16 echoes both Jesus telling his disciples they were "the light of the world" (Mt 5:14) and Daniel's comment that "those who are wise will shine . . . like the stars for ever and ever" (Dan 12:3). The verb *epechontes* may mean either "hold on to" or "hold out." The former refers to perseverance and the latter to evangelism.

and quite naturally preached the gospel there (see Col 1:7). He didn't have
to wait for authorization or special instruction to do what came naturally.
And when talking to the Colossians about my own proclamation of the
gospel, I encourage them also to "make the most of every opportunity" to
spread the message of grace (Col 4:4-6).

Luke: Yes, I testify to the way people were naturally spreading the good
news. Those who were scattered by persecution spread the word wherever
they went, at first only to Jews but soon to Gentiles as well (see Acts 11:19-20).

Peter: In case there's any doubt about this, remember how, on the one
hand, I tell wives how to win over their unconverted husbands "without
words" (1 Pet 3:1-2), and then, on the other hand, tell everyone to "always be
prepared to give an answer to everyone who asks you to give the reason for
the hope that you have" (1 Pet 3:15). Every believer was intent on winning
others over to allegiance to Jesus Christ.

Observer: As mentioned in the Introduction, the New Testament
has been described as "the documents of a mission" and essentially
"missionary theology."[19] It first reports the mission of Jesus and then
"the mission of his followers called to continue his work by proclaiming
him as Lord and Savior, and calling people to faith and on-going commitment to him, as a result of which the church grows."[20]

There are currently many debates about the nature of mission, which
is often construed today as working for social justice or engaging in
social and political reform. The basis for this lies in the total sweep of
God's revelation in Scripture: for example, in Isaiah 58:1-14; in Micah
6:8, where the concern for justice is evident; in the "Nazareth Manifesto"
(see Lk 4:16-21); and in Jesus' many acts of compassion and healing, as
well as his teaching in parables such as that of the good Samaritan (see
Lk 10:25-37). All these texts and all Jesus' actions and teaching give us
an understanding of what the kingdom of God looks like in reality.

Living in the context of the Roman Empire, the early church would
have had no realistic opportunity to challenge social injustices directly,
engage in politics, or set up wide-scale compassion ministries (although

---

[19] I. Howard Marshall, *New Testament Theology: Many Witnesses, One Gospel* (Downers Grove, IL:
   InterVarsity Press, 2004), 34.
[20] Ibid., 35.

they did this in-house: see Acts 6:1-6; Gal 6:10; 1 Tim 5:12-16). Their actions alleviated the poverty of their fellow believers (see 2 Cor 8:1–9:5) but didn't explicitly confront the empire's economic system, which was responsible for causing a great deal of poverty and in which people's lives and liberty were always precarious. Much of their teaching ultimately overthrew institutions like slavery, as will be mentioned later.[21] They never saw themselves as "bringing in the kingdom" or reforming this world so as to bring it to a state of perfection by human effort. This was the work of God himself, beyond anything humans could do.

What is clear is that the early Christians saw their primary responsibility as that of preaching the good news about Jesus, variously expressed, which focused on the forgiveness of sins, reconciliation with God, liberation to a new life, transformed living that didn't have self at the center, hope for the future beyond the grave, and the ultimate healing of our broken world when Christ returns.[22]

Chair: Okay, we've given the church a fair introduction, even if there is a lot more we could say.[23] Let's think now about what it means in terms of our lifestyles to be a gospel people.

---

[21]See further chap. 9, 220.

[22]See further, James D. G. Dunn, "Methodology of Evangelism in the New Testament: Some Preliminary Reflections," in Jon C. Laansma, Grant Osborne, and Ray Van Neste, eds., *New Testament Theology in the Light of the Church's Mission: Essays in Honor of I. Howard Marshall* (Eugene, OR: Wipf & Stock, 2011), 25-40.

[23]For an excellent introduction to Paul's teaching about the church, see James W. Thompson, *The Church According to Paul: Rediscovering the Community Conformed to Christ* (Grand Rapids: Baker Academic, 2014). Thompson is concerned about the superficial and partial understandings of the church as mirrored in many recent discussions that see it as a business corporation, seeker-friendly, missional, emerging, and so on.

9

What Does It Mean to Live as a Good News People?

Chair: Every community has its own identity and distinguishes itself from others by adopting a particular way of life. A crucial element in this concerns ethics. The Jewish people were marked out by practicing circumcision, sabbath observance, dietary regulations, temple worship, and keeping various moral laws. Christians belong to an international, multiethnic community where most of that no longer makes sense. Baptism is perhaps the equivalent of circumcision, although significantly different from it. Food laws have been made redundant, although we have our own special meal in the Lord's Supper—but that's not exactly an equivalent. Sabbath observance has been replaced by Sunday worship, because of the resurrection, but you all seem very cautious about making too much of special days. So presumably what distinguishes Christians from others is essentially our moral and ethical living. Do I understand correctly?

Paul: Correct. There are two things to keep in tension here. First, we are a people who have been given freedom in Christ, and the last thing any of us should do is subject ourselves to various human traditions or laws (see Gal 5:1; Col 2:20-23), like those that involve days and diet, circumcision or ceremonies. However, that doesn't mean we are free to live as we like. We are to use our freedom not "to indulge the flesh [but] rather [to] serve one another humbly in love" (Gal 5:13). That is why I am able to champion freedom and at the same time instruct the church "how to live in order to please God" (1 Thess 4:1-2).

A major principle might be said to be this: Christian living is the outworking of the gospel in our everyday lives. So, for example, at the heart of the gospel is the message of God reconciling us. As a result we must live in reconciled relationships with others, as I pointed out to the Corinthians and Ephesians (see 2 Cor 5:11-21; Eph 2:11-22).

Chair: Thanks for starting us off like this, Paul. Can we put some flesh on that introduction? One thing that seems to permeate all your writing is the overriding importance of love.

THE PRIORITY OF LOVE

Mark: Since I am the one who talks about love least—in fact, just once—let me state clearly that love was at the heart of Jesus' teaching. After loving God, Jesus taught that the second great commandment was to "love your neighbor as yourself" (Mk 12:31; Lk 10:27). In saying this he was quoting Leviticus 19:18, so the love ethic was not new, but he developed it in new ways.

Matthew: The culture of the time dictated that you loved only those who would love you in return. Reciprocity was at the heart of all relationships. Jesus, however, insisted we should love even our enemies and show kindness to those from whom we would get nothing in return (see Mt 5:43-48; Lk 6:27-36). Loving like this, Jesus said, is the way to "be perfect," by which he meant to be mature, a master of the trade of being a Christian, if you like, rather than without any sin at all.

Luke: I recall him adding that such love would mean we were truly "children of the Most High, because he is kind to the ungrateful and wicked. Be merciful, just as your Father is merciful" (Lk 6:35-36). That's astonishing. Our concept of God was that he was a God of justice who would punish the ungrateful and wicked, not be gracious to them.

John: I totally agree. For me the crucial teaching moment about love came at the Last Supper when Jesus instructed us with the words, "A new command I give you: love one another. As I have loved you, so you must love one another. By this everyone will know that you are my disciples, if you love one another" (Jn 13:34-35).

Paul: The love command is constantly seeping through in my writing. Let me give you just a few examples:

- "Love must be sincere.... Be devoted to one another in love" (Rom 12:9-10).

- "Let no debt remain outstanding, except the continuing debt to love one another, for whoever loves others has fulfilled the law" (Rom 13:8).

- "For the entire law is fulfilled in keeping this one command: 'Love your neighbor as yourself'" (Gal 5:14).

- "Walk in the way of love, just as Christ loved us and gave himself up for us as a fragrant offering and sacrifice to God" (Eph 5:2).

- "And this is my prayer: that your love may abound more and more" (Phil 1:9).

- "And over all these virtues put on love, which binds them all together in perfect unity" (Col 3:14).

- "May the Lord make your love increase and overflow for each other and for everyone else, just as ours does for you" (1 Thess 3:12).

- "Flee the evil desires of youth and pursue righteousness, faith, love and peace" (2 Tim 2:22).

We could go on. If you want to see more, look at Philippians 2:2; Colossians 3:12; 1 Thessalonians 4:9-10; 1 Timothy 1:5; 6:11; 2 Timothy 1:7; Titus 2:2, 4; and Philemon 7, 9—to name just a few!

Love, of course, has many dimensions to it but means nothing unless it is a practical virtue. I spell out some of those practical dimensions in 1 Corinthians 13, deliberately placed between two chapters that deal with issues of tension and conflict in Corinth.

1 CORINTHIANS 13:4-7

"Love is patient, love is kind. It does not envy, it does not boast, it is not proud. It does not dishonor others, it is not self-seeking, it is not easily angered, it keeps no record of wrongs. Love does not delight in evil but rejoices with the truth. It always protects, always trusts, always hopes, always perseveres."

The Hebraist: I'm no less insistent on the need for love than my colleagues are, even though I mention it only once (Heb 10:24). It is an aspect of living at peace with others and of the holiness without which "no one will see the Lord" (Heb 12:14).

James: I take up the relation between law and love to which Paul has referred and say that to love your neighbor as yourself is to "keep the royal law found in Scripture" (Jas 2:8). The rest of my letter might be seen as an applied commentary on what it means to keep that royal law.

Peter: As with everyone else, for me love is fundamental (2 Pet 1:17). I urge people to "love one another deeply, from the heart" (1 Pet 1:22) and to "love the family of believers" (1 Pet 2:17). And I repeat this command twice more (1 Pet 3:8; 4:8), adding on the latter occasion that "love covers over a multitude of sins."

John: Anyone who's read my first letter will immediately recognize that love is a major theme. In one respect my letter is a meditation on Jesus' command to his disciples to love one another. I'm concerned to show the integral connection between God's loving us, our loving God, and our love for our brothers and sisters. These three dimensions of love are inseparable: "we know and rely on the love God has for us. God is love. Whoever lives in love lives in God, and God in them" (1 Jn 4:16). We love him "because he first loved us" (1 Jn 4:19). His love was made known to us in that "Jesus Christ laid down his life for us" (1 Jn 3:16). Our love needs to be equally tangible and practical and not a matter of mere words (see 1 Jn 3:17-18). However, rather than selecting odd points from my writing, the best way to understand it is to read 3:10-18 and 4:7-21 slowly and carefully.

I briefly return to the same topic in my second letter, verses 5-6.

Jude: I want to point out that, although many people see my letter as harsh and judgmental, I wish my readers "mercy, peace and love . . . *in abundance*" (Jude 2) and actually write to encourage them to "keep [themselves] in God's love" (Jude 21). And yet, without any contradiction, I can be very opposed to those who were destroying the church. Love isn't the same as sentimentality, and true love sometimes requires conflict to be engaged in and discipline to be exercised.

Observer: While love is unquestionably the platform on which Christians are called to work out the living of the gospel, it is surprising that some writings do not mention it. Acts never uses the word. Revelation emphasizes endurance rather than love. As seen above, Mark and Hebrews mention it just once.

For this reason, when Richard Hays wrote his seminal *Moral Vision of the New Testament*, he drew back from making love one of the three focal images that "bring the moral vision of the New Testament canon into focus" and enable us to determine unity within the apparent diversity of the New Testament. He also wisely cautioned that "the ethics of love is often but a cover for what is fundamentally an assertion of ethical relativism."[1] Any Christian ethic of love needs to define love in a robust way that centers on the cross, not only as God's self-giving for us, but also as the means by which sin is dealt with to the satisfaction of a holy God.

The focal images Hays chose instead, which have given rise to much debate, were community, cross, and new creation.

Luke: Without wishing to outstay my welcome on this topic, I want to point out how much Jesus stressed the way in which love needed to be shown to those who were generally considered as of no importance in society: the poor, disabled, unclean, and outsiders. In doing this he was living out the radical vision the Old Testament had for the poor or vulnerable (see Deut 24:10-22; Zech 7:9-10). It was most obvious to me in Jesus' most epic sermon (see Lk 6:17-26; Mt 5:1-10) and in his response to the unclean intruder in the Pharisee's house (see Lk 14:1-24), but it is present throughout his teaching. It is also seen in his actions of healing the unclean, whether the uncleanness was that of a crippled woman (see Lk 13:10-13) or of a tax collector who had betrayed his nation (see Lk 19:1-10). Poverty took many forms, but Jesus confronted them all with love.

I don't think my colleagues would disagree with this, given, for example, what Paul wrote about remembering the poor (see Gal 2:10) and what James wrote about the fate of the rich who didn't show respect for the poor (see Jas 5:1-6).

KINGDOM OF GOD LIVING

Chair: Love was at the heart of Jesus' ethical teaching, but he had much more to say than that, didn't he? Much of his teaching is found in condensed form in what Matthew records as a sermon preached on a mountainside (see Mt 5:1–7:29) and Luke recalls as a sermon on a level place (see Lk 6:17-49). You both say he directed his teaching to his disciples. This was how citizens of his kingdom were to live. And yet he was saying this in the presence of a

---

[1]Richard B. Hays, *The Moral Vision of the New Testament: A Contemporary Introduction to New Testament Ethics* (New York: T&T Clark, 1997), 202-4.

large crowd, because the way of living he advocates contains huge wisdom for everyone, disciple or not.

Matthew, you give us the fuller version, so can you lead us through what he said?

Matthew: Yes, happily, Chair. Without covering every detail that disciples of Jesus need to work through carefully, point by point, here's the outline.

First (see Mt 5:3-12; Lk 6:17-26), he announced that true blessing—that is, happiness or fulfillment—in life is found only if we turn conventional wisdom on its head. Conventional wisdom speaks of happiness being found in wealth, independence, a carefree life without sadness, where you look after your own interests, watch your own back, and strive to be on top. Jesus, though, said that the blessed life was one where you were poor in spirit, where you knew what it was to mourn, to act meekly, to have a hunger and thirst for righteousness, to be merciful and pure, to work for peace, and to persevere in suffering. This was the way God had decreed it and had made the world to function.

Second, having told his disciples they were to be salt and light in the world (see Mt 5:13-16), he unpacked the way in which he hadn't come to do away with the law so much as to demonstrate in his own life and teaching what it truly meant (see Mt 5:17-20). This led him to a series of illustrations in which the requirements of the law were intensified by being driven inward (see Mt 5:21-37). So it was no longer a question of proscribing murder, but hate; no longer proscribing adultery, but lust; no longer swearing oaths, but being truthful through and through. We were no longer to be a people who demanded our rights and insisted on retaliatory justice, but instead a people who generously and freely gave, even loving our enemies (see Mt 5:38-48; Lk 6:27-36).

Third, that theme of going below the surface of our behavior to unmask our true motivations continued (see Mt 6:1-18). We were to give to the needy but not for show; to pray, but not so that others would think us spiritual; to fast, but so as no one would know. It was while he was talking about prayer that he gave us a model prayer to follow (see Mt 6:9-13; Lk 11:1-4). All this was because we were investing, not in what was seen in the here and now, but in the life to come, storing up, as he put it, "treasures in heaven" (Mt 6:19-24). It also meant we didn't need to worry about anything, since God would provide if we had our priorities right (see Mt 6:25-34).

Fourth, Jesus developed the subject of relationships. Our relations with others weren't to be destroyed by our arrogantly judging them while ignoring our own faults (see Mt 7:1-6; Lk 6:37-42). We were to develop our confidence in God our Father through prayer (see Mt 7:7-12; Lk 11:5-13).

Finally (see Mt 7:13-27; Lk 6:43-49), by using a series of contrasts— narrow and wide gates, true and false prophets, genuine and fake disciples, wise and foolish builders—he set out the choice we make between two paths, just as we find repeatedly set out in Israel's ancient wisdom, such as Psalm 1, for example.

THE BAPTIZED LIFE

Chair: OK, let's look at other approaches. Paul, you seem to relate your ethical teaching to baptism. As mentioned when discussing baptism,[2] you exploit the image of people undressing for baptism and clothing themselves with a new set of clothes after their burial in water.

Paul: Yes, I do. Let me explain a bit more. To me it seems a graphic way of describing how, when we are baptized, we don't go on living as we did before but have started a new life, which includes new patterns of behavior. It's like putting on a new uniform, if you like, one in which we are distinguished as Christians not by the clothes on our back but by the way we walk through life—that is, in a manner that fits the gospel we believe. You'll see this call to "live a new life" in Romans 6:4, Ephesians 4:1, Colossians 3:7-8, and 1 Thessalonians 4:1.

The main places where I use the baptismal clothing image are these:

- "Rather, clothe yourselves with the Lord Jesus Christ, and do not think about how to gratify the desires of the flesh" (Rom 13:14).

- In Ephesians 4:22-25 I write about this twofold action of undressing and dressing: "Put off your old self . . . put on the new self." Several features of the larger context are noteworthy. I set it in a devastating critique of the futility of Gentile living (see Eph 4:17). I explain that our ethical living is a restoration of God's image in us, since we are "created to be like God in true righteousness and holiness" (Eph 4:24). And I am careful to balance the negative teaching about things to discard with the positive teaching about patterns of behavior and character traits to adopt. So typically I

---

[2]See chap. 8, 192.

advise, "Steal no longer, but . . . work," "Do not let any unwholesome talk come out of your mouths, but only what is helpful for building others up," and so on (Eph 4:28-29).

- "Put to death . . . rid yourself of . . . put on the new self . . . clothe yourselves" (Col 3:5-14). Just as our clothes have several layers, so we're called to discard the outer layers of sinful actions and the inner layers of wrong attitudes and get dressed in new attitudes and actions.[3] Note, this only makes sense in the context of the new community and of relationships within the church (e.g., see Col 3:11, 15-16). It's not about individualistic living.

- My comment in 1 Corinthians 12:13—"baptized . . . so as to form one body"—also points out that the baptized life is a corporate or communal life, not a question of solitary character reformation. In fact, many of the qualities mentioned in these passages are relational qualities and are only intelligible if worked out in the church.

On several occasions I describe the kinds of lives baptized Christians should be living (see Gal 5:16-26; Eph 4:25–5:20; Phil 2:1-11; Col 3:5-17). We should shun anything to do with religious idolatry, sexual immorality, unbridled desires of any kind, selfish ambitions, and reactions that lead to conflict and a lack of forgiveness. Instead we should be cultivating the qualities that I describe as the fruit of the Spirit—that is, the outworking of the life of the Holy Spirit within us. That fruit is "love, joy, peace, forbearance, kindness, goodness, faithfulness, gentleness and self-control" (Gal 5:22-23). Elsewhere I particularly stress the need to be truthful, to forgive each other, and to be thankful.

Peter: My first letter provided suitable instruction for a baptismal service. Although there are several places where I get close to saying something similar to what Paul's just been saying, especially in my emphasis on love (see 1 Pet 1:22), my agenda is somewhat different. My readers were people who were suffering for their faith, often quite unjustly, so I am writing to encourage them to persevere and to teach them how to react in these particular circumstances. In my second letter, though, I say something somewhat akin

---

[3]Eugene Peterson captures its meaning beautifully: "You're done with that old way of life. It's like a filthy set of ill-fitting clothes you've stripped off and put in the fire. Now you're dressed in a new wardrobe. Every item of your new way of life is custom-made by the Creator, with his label on it. All the old fashions are now obsolete. . . . Dress in the wardrobe God has picked out for you." Eugene Peterson, *The Message* (Colorado Springs: NavPress, 2002).

to Paul's "fruit of the Spirit": I urge Christians to "make every effort to add to [their] faith goodness," and then successively to add knowledge, self-control, perseverance, godliness, mutual affection, and love (2 Pet 1:5-8). We can only do that, however, because "His divine power has given us everything we need for a godly life through our knowledge of him who called us by his own glory and goodness" (2 Pet 1:3). We're not having to supply the resources for our growth in the faith ourselves; it all comes from him.

"IN THE LORD": CHRISTIAN HOUSEHOLD ETHICS

Chair: There is another point at which you come very close together. Paul and Peter, you both set out what has been called a "household code." The household was the basic building block of Roman society and was composed of several generations of the family, with slaves, work colleagues and sometimes friends attached. Contemporary moral philosophers wrote about how these relationships were to be regulated, and I guess the early Christians wanted to know what changes might be involved in becoming a Christian household.

Paul: Yes, there was the potential for a lot of misunderstanding here, and some were beginning to apply their freedom in Christ in the wrong way, as if it was no longer necessary to respect any of those who had ruling positions in the house. That way anarchy would soon reign.

So, in Ephesians 5:21–6:9 and, more briefly, in Colossians 3:18–4:1, I set out to compose a Christian household code. I address the three typical sets of relationships you'd find in such an ethical code: husband and wife, parents and children, and masters and slaves. Under the call to mutual submission I instruct wives to "submit" to their husbands and husbands to love their wives "just as Christ loved the church and gave himself up for her." Children should obey their parents, but parents had an equal responsibility to train them wisely and not discourage them with harsh treatment. Slaves should continue to obey their masters, even if they were brothers or sisters in Christ. They needed to remember that they were working not only for a human master but for Christ; but then masters should not take this as license to treat their slaves as they liked, whatever the law permitted, because they were accountable to their own master in heaven.

Chair: All that sounds pretty socially conservative and reinforces the authority of the people who have power.

Paul: Well, a careful reading of what I wrote would question that interpretation. Yes, I am advocating an approach that encourages social stability. That's a good thing. In a later writing I encouraged Christians to pray for those in authority, however much we may differ from them, "that we may live peaceful and quiet lives," because, as I believe, this "pleases God our Savior" (1 Tim 2:2-3).

At the same time I've introduced various elements into my household code that totally change its nature when compared with those codes found outside the gospel community. For a start, I directly address the so-called weaker partners—the wives, children, and slaves—as people in their own right, rather than merely addressing the heads of the household or addressing those "weaker" partners through them.

Second, I inject "the Lord" into the code, and that sets an altogether different tone from what you'd hear elsewhere. This is not a charter for abuse that permits husbands, fathers, and masters to exercise authoritarian control over their "weaker" partners. The love husbands are to show their wives is a self-sacrificial love equal to that seen on Christ's cross. He was the one who accepted abuse; he didn't dish it out! Fathers are to instruct their children "in the Lord"; you can't be educating children in love and not practice it! Masters have no special privileges because they are masters; they are accountable to the Lord, "and there is no favoritism with him." Submission, as I said just now, is to be mutual, not one way (see Eph 5:21). It is to be voluntary, not enforced, imitating the very life Jesus himself lived—which was not one in which he demanded his rights or was self-assertive or self-protective, but he voluntarily gave himself for others, resulting in their salvation.

Peter: I have little to add to that. In my version of the household ethical code (see 1 Pet 2:18–3:7) I mention only slaves, wives, and husbands, and address their particular circumstances. Many slaves were suffering unjustly, and, at the time, many wives were behaving like the "new women" in Rome and abusing their freedom in Christ by spending on expensive, showy fashion items, as if that was what made them beautiful, and by living independently from their husbands.[4] A key word throughout my letter is *submit*.

---

[4]This issue is also reflected in 1 Tim 2:9-10. For background details, see Bruce Winter, *Roman Wives, Roman Widows: The Appearance of New Women in the Pauline Communities* (Grand Rapids: Eerdmans, 2003). For a fuller exposition of the relevant passages, see Derek and Dianne Tidball, *The Message of Women*, The Bible Speaks Today Bible Themes (Nottingham, UK : InterVarsity Press, 2012), chaps. 18–19.

Relationships are at their healthiest when we submit to one another, just as Paul said, following the example of Christ (see 1 Pet 2:21-25).

> Observer: For the reasons given, the New Testament household codes are more socially radical than they seem at first sight. The constant reference back to Christ changes the nature of them, setting limits and transforming the quality of relationships. The early Christians did not live in democratic societies, and the ability of people to change society by political action was inconceivable to them and outside of their experience. Nonetheless, eventually the practice of these ethical codes led to the profound transformation and demise of practices such as exposing unwanted children, slavery, and patriarchy in the Roman Empire.

THE RE-APPROPRIATED LAW

Chair: The New Testament writings cover a range of ethical topics including the power of the state and how to relate to it; how to deal with injustice; wealth; divorce; violence; sex; and women in various roles, not just as wives. We will need to leave a detailed discussion of those to another conference, but can we approach the subject by asking whether as gospel people we have a law to obey?

Paul: We looked at this from a different angle earlier,[5] but it is probably helpful to look at it again in relation to particular ethical topics.

To recap briefly, Christians are never told they are to obey, observe, keep, do, rely on, or boast about the law, meaning the Mosaic law. Christ has fulfilled that law for us (see Rom 8:1-4). Yet "everything that was written in the past was written to teach us" (Rom 15:4), and we are called to "fulfill the law of Christ" (Gal 6:2; cf. 1 Cor 9:21), which is also called the law of faith or of the Spirit (see Rom 3:27; 8:2). Christ frees us to live under this new kind of law, whose hallmarks are love, service, and wisdom, as we spelled out above. Wisdom is crucial (see Rom 16:19; 1 Cor 3:18; 6:5; Eph 5:15; Col 4:5).

This means Christians often will live in harmony with the Mosaic law to a greater or lesser extent, but don't slavishly follow it all, nor think that salvation comes from obeying it. We've seen how Christians treat the sabbath

---

[5]See the major discussion in chap. 7, 126-31.

differently and are no longer bound by the dietary laws; but let's take another example, that of tithing.

Tithing is enshrined in the Mosaic law (see Lev 27:30-33; Num 18:21, 25-28; Deut 12:4-6, 11; 14:22-29; 26:12), but none of us approaches the subject of giving as gospel people by reference to the tithe. Rather, in my extensive discussion of giving in 2 Corinthians 8–9, I approach it in an entirely different way. I speak of the "grace of giving" (2 Cor 8:7) that is patterned on the self-giving of Christ (see 2 Cor 8:8-9). I encourage generosity, rather than mechanical giving, and establish the spiritual principle that "whoever sows sparingly will also reap sparingly, and whoever sows generously will also reap generously" (2 Cor 9:6). I claim that giving is a matter of freedom, not compulsion, and that every believer should give after reflection, and should do so gladly (see Cor 9:7). The point of contact with the Mosaic law is found in this: when people gave their tithe they had to trust God to look after the rest of their needs, as do we when we give our offering. We do so believing that "God is able to bless [us] abundantly, so that in all things at all times, having all that [we] need, [we] will abound in every good work" (2 Cor 9:8). It's worth emphasizing that God doesn't bless us for our own personal enjoyment but for "good works." You see how different that is from the law of the tithe? I believe in a God who "richly provides" for us (1 Tim 6:17).

Even when I am writing about sexual ethics, as I frequently do, I never tell people "to obey the laws (of Moses) against adultery, incest, prostitution, sexual immorality, homosexual relations, and so on."[6] That's just not the way I come at it. Nonetheless my instructions are deeply influenced by that law, and we come to the same conclusion about these issues via a different route. You'll see that if you compare Leviticus 18 with 1 Corinthians 5:1-13 on incest; with 1 Corinthians 6:18-20 on sexual immorality; and with Romans 1:26, 1 Corinthians 6:9, and 1 Timothy 1:10 on homosexual practice.

James: Though much more shaped by my Jewish heritage than most, I adopt exactly the same approach as Paul. My ethical stance is governed by my reading of Leviticus 19. I allude to it at least four times in 2:8-13 and have other general allusions as well to the law of Moses. However, I never

---

[6]Brian Rosner, *Paul and the Law: Keeping the Commandments of God*, New Studies in Biblical Theology (Downers Grove, IL: InterVarsity Press, 2013), 196.

seek to reimpose the Mosaic law on Christians and write instead of "the royal law found in Scripture" (Jas 2:8) and "the law that gives freedom" (Jas 2:12). And I place all this in the wider context of a discussion of "wisdom" (Jas 3:13-18).

THE IMITATION OF CHRIST

John: There is a simpler approach to determining what it means to live as a gospel people, and that is to say that we are to imitate Christ.[7] For example, at that Last Supper when Jesus washed his disciples' feet, he told us that, since he had done so as our Lord and Teacher, we should follow his example and do the same for each other (see Jn 13:14). At several points in those last days he compared our experience with his own and instructed us to behave in the way he did (see Jn 13:12-17; 15:18-25; 17:20-23). We were to stay close to him so we could "bear much fruit" (Jn 15:1-8). This led me to write later that "whoever claims to live in him must live as Jesus did" (1 Jn 2:6). In short, Christian living is about imitating Jesus.

Paul: True enough. That's the line I take in telling the Philippians they need to learn humility in their handling of one another. The whole point of that great hymn about the humility and exaltation of Christ is that they should follow the example of Christ (see Phil 2:5-11). That's also the point of my telling the Romans to "clothe yourselves with the Lord Jesus Christ" (Rom 13:14). If they did that, they'd live as he lived. It's why I commended the Thessalonians for being "imitators of us and of the Lord" (1 Thess 1:6)[8] and advocated the path of imitation to others as well (see 1 Cor 11:1; Eph 5:1).

Peter: Same here. My argument that we should submit to others, even when it is unjustly demanded, is based on the example of Christ. "Christ," I write, "suffered for you, leaving you an example, that you should follow in his steps" (1 Pet 2:21). He is more than an example—he's our Savior—but he's not less than our example. We're called to imitate him.

---

[7]This approach has been advocated and discussed at length recently in Richard A. Burridge, *Imitating Jesus: An Inclusive Approach to New Testament Ethics* (Grand Rapids: Eerdmans, 2007).

[8]For a discussion of Paul's invitation for Christians to imitate him (see 1 Cor 4:16; 11:1; Phil 3:17; 2 Thess 3:7, 9), see Linda Belleville, "'Imitate Me, Just as I Imitate Christ': Discipleship in the Corinthian Correspondence," in Richard N. Longenecker, ed., *Patterns of Discipleship in the New Testament* (Grand Rapids: Eerdmans, 1996), 120-42.

Observer: Having examined all the imitation texts in some depth, George Caird concluded that the morality it led to didn't fit

any stereotyped pattern; it consists rather of learning from Jesus an attitude of mind which comprises sensitivity in the presence of God and to the will of God which is the only authority, a constant submission of personal interest to the pursuit of that will in the well-being of others, and the confidence that, whatever the immediate consequences may appear to be, the outcome can be safely left in God's hands.[9]

Chair: This may appear simple, but it proves a profound and all-embracing, comprehensive rule. In summary, Christian living has Christ as its center.

---

[9]George Caird, *New Testament Theology*, ed. L. D. Hurst (Oxford: Oxford University Press, 1994), 203. See pp. 197-203.

WHAT DOES THE GOOD NEWS SAY ABOUT THE FUTURE?

Chair: It is evident that we have not reached the end of the story yet. Jesus clearly hasn't finished what he began. The good news hasn't run its full course yet. From the earliest days (see Acts 1:11) the disciples of Jesus have been taught to believe there is another chapter to follow, when Jesus will return and initiate the final act when God will rule "all in all" (1 Cor 15:20-28). Let's establish, first of all, where this belief started and its general features before exploring some more detailed questions.

THE BELIEF IN JESUS' COMING AGAIN

> ### THE COMING AGAIN OF THE SON OF MAN
>
> Mt 10:23; 16:28; 25:31; 26:64; Mk 9:1; 14:62; Lk 9:26; 17:24, 30.

How Common Is the Belief?

Matthew: Jesus himself taught both explicitly, at length, and implicitly that he would come again, presupposing it, for example, in parables such as those of the ten virgins (see Mt 25:1-13), the bags of gold (see Mt 25:14-30), and the sheep and the goats (see Mt 25:31-46). He often spoke of the separation that will take place on the final day and the judgment God will exercise on humanity.

The most detailed picture he gives takes the form of an apocalyptic address. "Apocalyptic" is a type of literature that has visions of the future, which it describes in cosmic terms. Jesus spoke at length like this, as we all record (see Mt 24:1-51; Mk 13:1-37; Lk 21:5-38). His disciples were admiring the temple one day when Jesus somewhat shockingly said to them that the day was coming when "not one stone here will be left on another" (Mt 24:2). They obviously wanted to know more. So a little later they asked him a double question: "When will this happen, and what will be the sign of your coming and of the end of the age?"

Jesus' initial reply (see Mt 24:4-14) informed them that the signs of the end would involve false messiahs, wars, famines, earthquakes, persecution, increase of wickedness, declining love, and the preaching of the gospel in all nations. He went on to say (see Mt 24:15-29) that when they saw the temple defiled (by "the abomination that causes desolation," as foreseen by Daniel—see Dan 9:27; 11:31; 12:11), it was time to get out! Awful suffering would follow, and events of cosmic proportions, as if the sun and moon were having their light extinguished, would be triggered. All this would, however, herald the coming of the Son of Man (remember, that was Jesus' favorite title for himself) on the clouds of heaven with power and great glory. Again, the language reminds us of Daniel 7:13-14, where God establishes the universal and everlasting rule of "one like a son of man." Jesus then warned his disciples to keep alert for the signs that this time is near (see Mt 24:32-35).

As the conversation went on, Jesus expanded on "that day" when the Son of Man would come, and he announced that only God knew when that would occur (Mt 24:36-51). The angels didn't know, nor even did the Son. Only the Father knew. So he told them to stand out from the crowd who lived as if nothing would ever change and encouraged them to "keep watch," for his coming would occur without warning, just as when a thief burgles a house. He wasn't saying: suspend everything, and do nothing but speculate about my coming. Far from it. He was saying: while going about your ordinary business, keep on your toes!

Observer: By its nature, apocalyptic literature is not easy to interpret, and these passages (see Mt 24; Mk 13; Lk 21) have caused interpreters great problems. Three basic interpretations have been offered.

The first interpretation, traditional among evangelical Christians, is that the whole discourse refers to the second coming of Christ at the end of time. Much effort has therefore been expended in reading the "signs of the times" to estimate how close we are to that day dawning. Negatively, people have gotten excited when wars, famines, and earthquakes have occurred because they think it means the second coming is about to happen! Positively, it has provided motivation for world mission, since another sign is that "this gospel of the kingdom will be preached in the whole world as a testimony to all nations" (Mt 24:14), and only after that will the end come. Those who advocate this interpretation argue that the predictions Jesus gave have yet to be fulfilled in full, so this discourse cannot refer to some event that has already happened.

At the opposite end of the interpretive spectrum are those who argue that this has nothing to do with the second coming of Christ in the traditional sense but is a prophecy of the destruction of Jerusalem and its temple, which occurred in AD 70.[1] These interpreters point out that the question the disciples ask is in fact a question about the destruction of the temple rather than one about some distant event. Many details fittingly describe the Jewish experience at that time, which was "the end of the age" as far as the Jewish nation was concerned. Matthew 24:14 is no barrier to this interpretation since by AD 70 the gospel had been widely preached by the apostles and their successors across the earth. Verse 30 might be said to have been fulfilled through God's judgment on Judea at that time. This interpretation also explains Jesus' saying that "this generation will certainly not pass away until all these things have happened" (Mt 24:34). Several who adopt this view believe that the second coming of Christ is taught elsewhere; they just do not think Jesus is teaching it here.

The third interpretation argues that Jesus is answering two different questions posed in verse 3.[2] The first question asks, "When will *this* happen?" and refers to when the destruction of the temple will take place. Jesus answers this in verses 4-35. The second is a longer-range question and asks, "*And* what will be the sign of your coming and of the end of the age?" According to this view, Jesus turns to answer this

---

[1]The most notable scholar who interprets it in this way is N. T. Wright, *Jesus and the Victory of God* (London: SPCK, 1996), 339-68.

[2]One of the chief and best exponents of this view is R. T. France, *Matthew*, Tyndale New Testament Commentary (Leicester: Inter-Varsity Press, 1985), 333-52; and *The Gospel of Matthew*, New International Commentary on the New Testament (Grand Rapids: Eerdmans, 2007), 896-946.

second question only at verse 36, where he says, "But about *that* day or hour no one knows . . ." So the first question and answer relate to the destruction of the temple and the events of AD 70 and could be anticipated by Jesus' hearers if they were discerning about the times in which they lived; but, following that, the second question and answer relate to the second coming of Jesus as the Son of Man at an unknown time, a belief that would be reaffirmed and explored more fully in later writings. The different language used in the two sections supports this view. The first answer relates to "those days," plural, whereas the second answer talks of "that day or hour," singular. The second answer speaks in verses 37 and 39 about the *coming* (*parousia*) of the Son of Man as "universally clear," whereas his first answer describes the events leading up to the fall of Jerusalem as quite confusing and a contrast with his ultimate coming.[3]

John: I don't venture into this area in my Gospel because I'm more concerned, as you know, about the experience of eternal life here and now. It's plain, though, that I believe in Christ's return. I record Jesus promising his disciples, "I will come back and take you to be with me that you also may be where I am" (Jn 14:3). And in talking with Peter on the lakeshore after his resurrection, Jesus used the phrase "until I return" (Jn 21:23) without feeling any need to explain it. It was obviously part of his original teaching, even if I don't explore it much.

Luke: The angels told the apostles on Ascension Day that the "same Jesus . . . will come back in the same way you have seen him go into heaven" (Acts 1:11), so they were certainly expecting him to return. They believed themselves to be living in "the last days" (Acts 2:17), by which they meant the last chapter of God's plan for the earth and humanity as we know it. Peter explained that the next step would be that the Messiah would remain in heaven "until the time comes for God to restore everything" (Acts 3:21). And they taught that Jesus had been appointed the "judge of the living and the dead," which implies a future day of accountability (Acts 10:42). Their main concern, however, was to get people to acknowledge that Jesus was God's Messiah who had already inaugurated the last days that they could join in now.

---

[3]France, *Gospel of Matthew*, 890.

Paul: From the beginning to the end of my ministry, I taught that Jesus would return. Having said "the Lord himself will come down from heaven, with a loud command" to raise the dead and meet the still-living saints "in the air," I went on virtually to repeat Jesus' own words that "the day of the Lord will come like a thief in the night." As Jesus said, it will all happen suddenly, so we need to be prepared (1 Thess 4:16–5:11). To the Philippians, while warning about the judgment some face, I comment that "our citizenship is in heaven. And we eagerly await a Savior from there, the Lord Jesus Christ" (Phil 3:20). If you go to the other end of my writings, to a much later letter like Titus, I'm still talking excitedly about the Lord's return. In Titus 2:13 I describe "the appearing of the glory of our great God and Savior, Jesus Christ" as our "blessed hope."

I have lots more to say about it in-between and in different ways, but I'm sure we'll unpack some of that in a moment.

The Hebraist: The return of Christ certainly undergirds my thinking. I too believe these are the "last days" (Heb 1:2), and I fully expect that Christ "will appear a second time" to complete the work of salvation his cross began (Heb 9:28). I see that approaching day as one of the main incentives to persevering in the Christian life (see Heb 10:25).

James: Even I, who am often accused of being a lightweight theologian, refer to "the Lord's coming"[4] and how we need to be patient for it, since only then will justice be done. Don't think I'm postponing it to some indefinite future, however: I believe it is imminent, which is why I say his "coming is near" and "the Judge is standing at the door!" (Jas 5:7-9).

Peter: James's view dovetails with mine. I adopt a strong forward look, believing that "the end of all things is near" (1 Pet 4:7), and when that occurs the injustices of this world will be righted and those who have suffered unjustly will be vindicated.

I write more fully about what all this means in my second letter, using the familiar image of the Lord coming "like a thief" (2 Pet 3:10). With Jude I use graphic, apocalyptic language to stress that his coming will be a day of judgment for the disobedient, ungodly, and unrighteous, and a day when the godly will be rescued from their troubles (see 2 Pet 2:1-22; Jude 5-16). It will be payback time.

---

[4]This does not specifically say that the Lord who comes is Jesus. The language is derived from the Old Testament teaching about "the Day of the Lord." See further chap. 10, 232.

In that letter I do a couple of other things as well. I offer an explanation, or rather several explanations, for what seems to be a delay to Christ's return. Cynics say the world is fixed and the future won't hold any surprises for us; but a moment's reflection on the world's story up to now proves otherwise (see 2 Pet 3:1-7). Skeptics judge things by our own experience of time, but God doesn't live within our time frames (see 2 Pet 3:8-9). Having removed some obstacles, I then explain, again using graphic apocalyptic language, that Christ's return will involve nothing less than the re-creation of the whole universe, the heavens and the earth, so that it becomes a new creation "where righteousness dwells." Since this is where we are heading, we should get in practice for living in that environment now. That means only one thing: we must "make every effort to be found spotless, blameless and at peace with him" (2 Pet 3:11-18).

John: In thinking about the future, don't forget the coming of the antichrist. One day the great big antichrist will appear, perhaps the one Paul calls "the man of lawlessess" in 2 Thessalonians 2:1-12, was it, Paul? However, we don't have to wait for the ultimate antichrist to come, since his spirit is already here and his representatives are at work (see 1 Jn 2:18, 22; 4:3).

There may be several things that are unclear about the antichrist, but I am absolutely clear, along with the others, that Jesus is going to appear again, and we need to be sure that we can "be confident and unashamed before him" when he comes (1 Jn 2:28–3:3). The second coming of Christ is one of the biggest incentives to holiness and purity there is.

Revelation, of course, is built on the premise that Jesus is returning. It first gets a mention in 1:7 when I quote from Daniel 7:13. The last mention comes in 22:20 where Jesus himself gives us the reassurance "Yes, I am coming soon," to which we respond using the well-known prayer of the early church, "Amen. Come, Lord Jesus" (see also Rev 22:12; 1 Cor 16:22).

How Is His Return Described?

Chair: So we've established that the return of Christ is taught from the beginning. However, the phrase "the second coming" doesn't actually occur in the New Testament. We owe that phrase to Justin Martyr (AD 100–165). Given that you don't describe it as a second coming, what words do you use to speak about it?

The Hebraist: If I may say so, Chair, that's a little pedantic, since I say "he will appear a second time" (Heb 9:28). That's pretty similar language.

Paul: Yes, and let me say the words I use to describe it and indicate where others use the same description. There are four terms I use:

- It is a *parousia*, an appearance or arrival after a period of absence, a term that was used especially in relation to a royal visit or the appearance of a Greek deity (see 1 Cor 15:23; 1 Thess 2:19; 3:13; 4:15; 5:23; 2 Thess 2:1, 8; also Mt 24:27, 30, 37, 39; Jas 5:7; 2 Pet 1:16; 3:4, 12; 1 Jn 2:28).

- It is an *epiphaneia*, meaning "manifestation" or "appearance." I'm the only one to speak of it like this (see 2 Thess 2:8; 1 Tim 6:14; 2 Tim 4:1, 8; Tit 2:13).

- It is an *apokalypsis*—that is, "a revelation," "disclosure"—in which the true identity of Jesus is revealed for all to see (see 1 Cor 1:7; 2 Thess 1:7; also 1 Pet 1:7, 13; 4:13; and, used differently, Rev 1:1).

- It is also "the day of the Lord" (*hē hēmera tou kyriou*). This draws on the rich Old Testament roots of the concept (such as Is 13:6, 9; Ezek 13:5; 30:3; Amos 5:18-20; Zeph 1:7, 14) and applies them to Christ (see 1 Cor 1:8; 5:5; Phil 1:6, 10; 2:16; 1 Thess 5:2; 2 Thess 2:2).

- *Parousia* and *hē hēmera tou kyriou* are used interchangeably in 2 Thessalonians 2:1-2, 8.

Did They Change Their Minds About the Imminence of the Second Coming?

Observer: Scholars have recently suggested that with the passing of time there was a dampening of eschatological fervor in the early church and their belief in the second coming was relegated to the distant future. James Dunn, for example, writes of the apocalyptic strand in the New Testament where in 1 and 2 Thessalonians; 1 Corinthians 7:26-31; 15:51-57; Mark 13; and Revelation an imminent *parousia* is prominent: "Evidently, Paul's proclamation had led his converts to believe that the eschatological climax was very imminent indeed."[5] However, in Paul's later writings, it is argued, the imminence of Christ's return is played down and eschatology becomes more and more about realized eschatology—that is, about what we can already experience of the future.

---

[5]James D. G. Dunn, *Unity and Diversity in the New Testament: An Inquiry into the Character of Earliest Christianity* (Philadelphia: Westminster Press, 1977), 325.

The evidence for this argument is as follows. The deaths of believers, which had been such a surprise in 1 Thessalonians 4, had already become the accepted norm by 1 Corinthians 15:51. Paul was no longer certain he would be alive to witness the second coming in his present body (see Phil 1:20-26). Colossians 3:4 mentions the appearing of Christ but "without urgency," and the sense of already being raised with Christ is stronger. In Ephesians, "there is still a looking forward to a future consummation," but only after several generations. And in the pastoral letters belief is still strong (see 1 Tim 6:14; 2 Tim 1:12, 18; 4:1, 8; Tit 2:13) but lacks urgency, even though Paul[6] writes of his time as the "later times" (1 Tim 4:1). Overall, "the sense of expectation of an imminent End is wholly lacking and the *parousia* is not even mentioned."[7] Luke's rendering of Mark's apocalypse is said to postpone the expectation of Christ's return. For example, Luke 21:8 specifically uses Mark's comment about the false prophets who claim "the time is near" to stress the need for perseverance. John's Gospel, as mentioned, advocates the most realized eschatology of all. And 2 Peter is concerned to explain the delay in Christ's return and introduces a new chapter in explaining its postponement. This justification of postponement goes hand in hand with the church being more at home in the world and less in conflict with it.

Some scholars see the shift as more radical than others. Those who argue for the dampening of expectation are sometimes in danger of imposing a predetermined framework on the texts. Dunn, for example, sees both Romans 13:11-14 and Philippians 3:20 as evidence of "non-urgent" texts, but is there any justification for doing so? In Philippians 4:5 Paul asserts, "The Lord is near." The differences may be accounted for simply on the grounds of Paul getting older and increasingly realizing that he was unlikely to be alive when Christ returned, rather than of any greater change in the doctrine of eschatology.[8]

---

[6]Those who argue for the delay in expectation often do not accept that Paul wrote the pastoral letters but use them as evidence of the way the thought of the Pauline school was developing.
[7]Dunn, *Unity and Diversity*, 346.
[8]Donald Guthrie, *New Testament Theology* (Downers Grove, IL: InterVarsity Press, 1981), 811.

The Manner of His Coming

Chair: Let me try to summarize on your behalf what you seem to agree on about the manner of his coming. It will be

- personal (see Acts 1:11; 1 Thess 4:16);

- physical (see Acts 1:11; Rev 1:7);

- visible to all (see Mt 24:27, 30; Col 3:3-4; Tit 2:13; Rev 1:7);

- sudden and unexpected (see Mt 24:37-44; 25:1-12; 1 Thess 5:1-3; Rev 3:3; 16:15); and

- glorious (see Mt 24:30; Phil 2:9-11; 1 Thess 3:13; 4:16; 2 Thess 1:7, 10).

THE REASONS FOR HIS COMING

Chair: Let's be more specific and spell out what will be accomplished when he comes. Paul, I think you have a neat way of setting out the key reasons for his return in Philippians 3:17-21. It's not that you're the only one to make these points—it's just that you have a concise way of putting it. Perhaps we can use that passage as a framework and add in other voices as we go.

Paul: Thank you, Chair. The first reason for his return is this:

Judgment Will Be Executed

I allude to it briefly here, saying the destiny of those who live as enemies of the cross of Christ is "destruction" (Phil 3:19). I don't rejoice in that. When I speak of those who are at enmity with God, I do so with tears. This points to a final catastrophic judgment when God's wrath will descend once and for all on evil and those who perpetrate it will be banished forever.

God's wrath is no minor theme in my theology. I refer to it frequently in Romans. People are already experiencing it because of their behavior, but judgment is more than the impersonal outworking of the consequences of people's actions in the here and now: it is the personal act of the righteous Judge at the end (see Rom 1:18-32; 2:5, 8; 4:15; 5:9; 9:22; 12:19). It will include everyone; no one will be exempt (see Rom 14:10). Right will triumph in the end. In the meantime, as I mentioned, God uses imperfect human governments to exercise something of his wrath against wrongdoing (Rom 13:4).

The theme of judgment runs through my other letters too. Perhaps I'm at my fiercest on the topic in 2 Thessalonians 1:5-9. Mostly I'm rightly quite reserved about the nature of it while leaving people in no doubt how serious and dreadful it will be (see Eph 2:3; Col 3:6; 1 Thess 1:10; 2:16; 5:9).

Matthew: That's in line with Jesus himself, who both accepted and endorsed the Jewish framework that said there would be a day of reckoning at the end. It's found in his parables (see Mt 13:36-43, 47-50; 22:1-14; 25:1-13, 31-46) and in his more direct teaching (see Mt 5:21-22, 29; 7:2; 12:36; 23:33).

John: Agreed. I present Jesus' mission while on earth as essentially a positive one of bringing salvation, but nonetheless God's judgment was real and already in progress (see Jn 3:17-18). As far as future judgment was concerned, the Father had already put that in his Son's hands (see Jn 5:22-27).

Luke: Judgment was certainly an element of apostolic preaching (see Acts 10:42; 17:30-31), but what was even more striking was the fact that God's judgment could be experienced with immediate effect. I'm thinking of the time Ananias and Sapphira dropped dead because of their deception (see Acts 5:1-11), of Herod's death (see Acts 12:19-23), and of even the threat of judgment that caused Simon the sorcerer to repent (see Acts 8:18-24). God's judgment was terrifying.

The Hebraist: Paul tends to speak about "God's wrath." I speak of judgment, even eternal judgment (see Heb 6:2; 9:27; 10:27). It's the same belief, but my choice of words focuses strictly on the event rather than attributing it to God's anger at sin. I use more picturesque language at one point where I mention that Christ is currently sitting "at the right hand of God" biding his time waiting "for his enemies to be made his footstool" (Heb 10:12-13).

Peter: We writers of the general letters stand shoulder to shoulder on this. Speaking for all who wrote the shorter, general letters, we talk of judgment, punishment, destruction, and perishing. In my letters, note especially 2 Peter 2:9-11. Previously, in 1 Peter 3:19-20, I'd alluded to the judgment that occurred in Noah's day. James

> **OTHER REFERENCES TO JUDGMENT**
>
> 1 Pet 4:5; 2 Pet 2:1, 3, 12; 3:7, 9, 16.

writes of judgment in 5:9 of his letter; John in 1 John 4:17; and Jude, in a letter that has some overlap with my second letter, writes about it more fiercely than any of us in verses 6-16.

Jude: Well, the situation was desperate and the future of the church severely threatened. I draw on some examples from earlier Scriptures and other writings and specify that those who are guilty of rejecting or perverting the grace of God will "suffer the punishment of eternal fire" (Jude 7).

John: Thank you, Peter, for mentioning my reference to the judgment in my first letter. It might be worth pointing out that I mention the continuing reality of the day of judgment immediately after saying that "God is love." His love should "drive out fear" of the judgment, but we need to live in love, and so have God live in us, if this is to be so (1 Jn 4:16-18).

However, I really wanted to point out that I think that I, not Jude, can claim the prize for the most extensive graphic writing in this area! The visions of Revelation contain the story of judgment, as well as of the deliverance and vindication of God's suffering people. The judgments work themselves through the successive cycles of human experience, symbolized by the opening of the seals (see Rev 6:1-17; 8:1-5), the blowing of the trumpets (see Rev 8:6-12; 11:15-19), and the pouring out of the bowls (see Rev 15:1–16:21). This pattern recurs until the climax is reached with the ultimate downfall of Babylon (the symbol for all anti-God cities and governments) in Revelation 18–19. The triumph of the Lamb over Babylon results in the downfall of "the beast" and "the false prophet," who are "thrown alive into the fiery lake of burning sulfur," while the kings of the earth who had opposed God "were killed with the sword" (Rev 19:19-21).

The final defeat of evil takes place after the millennium, when the dead, "great and small," face the "great white throne" of God to receive his verdict on the basis of "what they have done" during their lives (Rev 19:5; 20:11; 22:12). Paul and I agree that judgment is always on the basis of "what they have done." If you don't believe me, see what Paul wrote in 2 Corinthians 5:10. So is this a message that we are saved by our works after all? No. Justification means that God brings his future verdict forward and so declares those who are "in Christ" already not guilty—but behavior and works still matter. It is not that they are irrelevant. Being "in Christ" necessarily involves living to please him.[9]

Incidentally, I speak of judgment at the "great white throne" of God (Rev 20:11), and Paul speaks of "the judgment seat of Christ" (2 Cor 5:10), but don't

---

[9]N. T. Wright, *Paul for Everyone: 2 Corinthians* (London: SPCK, 2003), 58.

drive any wedge between us. What happens there signals the ultimate triumph of God and the defeat of all evil, since not only is everything contrary to God banished from his new creation, but "death," the penalty for sin, "and Hades" are "thrown into the lake of fire [together with] anyone whose name [is] not found written in the book of life" (Rev 20:11-15). The language may be graphic and apocalyptic, but nothing less can convey the reality and awfulness of God's just judgment.

Chair: Let me add some footnotes before looking at the second reason for Jesus' return. The first is to underline the fact that those whose names are written in the book of life, Christians themselves, will also face judgment, as Paul reminded us in 2 Corinthians 5:10. For them, it won't be a matter of condemnation but of evaluation.[10] Their salvation will not be in doubt, but the way they have lived as justified people and the value of the work they have done for Christ will be appraised. This is also spoken of in 1 Corinthians 3:12-15. You weren't embarrassed, were you, Paul, to think in terms of rewards for work done (see Gal 6:7-9; 2 Tim 4:8)? You're quite capable of putting different nuances on the one word *judgment*.

The second note is simply to be up-front about this: there can be no salvation without judgment. They are inseparable—opposite sides of the same coin. For the weak, defenseless, vulnerable, and victims to receive justice, those who have abused and mistreated them have to be dealt with. Expand that beyond the narrow question of social justice to embrace the whole spectrum of sin, and you will see why God's judgment is necessary.

Observer: A contemporary writer pithily remarked that we must see "judgment as the triumph of God's grace."[11]

Chair: Lastly, none of your writings supports the idea of universalism— that all will be saved in the end, regardless of whether or not they have repented in this life or believed in Christ. None of you suggests that there is any opportunity to put matters right after death. Rather the reverse. As the Hebraist put it, "people are destined to die once, and after that to face

---

[10]I owe this contrast to Paul Barnett, *The Second Epistle to the Corinthians*, New International Commentary on the New Testament (Grand Rapids: Eerdmans, 1997), 276.

[11]Michael F. Bird, *Evangelical Theology: A Biblical and Systematic Introduction* (Grand Rapids: Zondervan, 2013), 306-7. He has adapted this from Donald Bloesch, *The Last Things: Resurrection, Judgment, Glory* (Downers Grove, IL: InterVarsity Press, 2004), 213.

judgment" (Heb 9:27). The only universal there is is a universal offer of salvation to all people now.

Believers Will Be Vindicated

Paul: This is implicit rather than explicit in the paragraph in Philippians 3:17-21, but the second reason is that believers who are despised as fools—or worse, persecuted—for believing now will be vindicated then. By contrast with those whose "destiny is destruction," I write that "our citizenship is in heaven. And we eagerly await a Savior from there." When Jesus comes to the rescue, our true identity will be revealed and we will no longer be despised. The persecution, contempt, and injustice we've suffered will be over.

Elsewhere I mention this explicitly. It will be time "for the children of God to be revealed" (Rom 8:19), when our true identity will no longer be hidden but we "will appear with him in glory" (Col 3:3-4), and when relief will come and the tables be turned on persecutors of the church (2 Thess 1:6-10).

The Hebraist: I want to back up that point about citizenship. I play a lot with that idea, believing that Christians will eventually receive "a kingdom that cannot be shaken" (Heb 12:28) in contrast to all the cities or kingdoms to which people belong in this world. Those cities seem so attractive, but they'll surely pass away. When I reflect on the great heroes of the faith, I give many examples of people who were mocked by their contemporaries because they believed a promise that hadn't yet been delivered (see Heb 11:1-14). However, their tormentors were fooling themselves, since the pleasures they experienced were only fleeting, whereas the rewards for those who believed God's promises were substantial and, for us too, will never pass away.

Salvation Will Be Completed

Paul: I draw attention to this when I say that "we eagerly await a Savior from [heaven]" (Phil 3:20). We spoke earlier about the way we have already begun to experience salvation, but it's obvious to everyone that we haven't entered into the full experience of it yet.[12] In fact, when I wrote that, I was languishing in a prison cell and my next move might well have been to face an executioner's sword! The church, though in pretty good shape, wasn't yet perfect, and there was ample evidence that its members were not yet fully

---

[12]See chap. 7, 172-77.

redeemed (see Phil 1:15-18; 4:1-3). We were looking forward to the day when we'd all be free from the struggles of this life, totally free from sin, and enjoying the blessing of God's immediate presence in his new creation.

I described this to the Ephesians as our having received to date only the "deposit" or "down payment" of our salvation—but that deposit does guarantee "our inheritance" until the full redemption of those who are God's is put into effect (Eph 1:14). And what a rich and "glorious inheritance" it is (Eph 1:18)! I often encouraged people to look to their future inheritance (see Col 1:12; 3:24; Acts 20:32; Rom 8:18; 2 Cor 4:17-18).

Peter: I identify with that inheritance language and make the point that, unlike human inheritances that may not fare well over time or that can be devalued with inflation, our inheritance in the risen Christ is one that will "never perish, spoil or fade" (1 Pet 1:4).

The Hebraist: I use a single word for that: our inheritance is "eternal" (Heb 9:15).

John: I don't use the word *inheritance*, but I do employ all my God-given imaginative skills to describe what entering into it is going to be like. In Revelation 21:1–22:5 I try to describe the indescribable and capture something of what it will mean to live in the continuous presence of God and experience salvation completely.

Creation Will Be Healed

Chair: John's comment connects us to the next reason for Christ's coming again. It's not just so that individuals can be saved but so that creation itself can be healed. Paul, how do you tackle this?

Paul: In Philippians 3:21 I put it like this: when the Savior returns he will have "the power that enables him to bring everything under his control." I guess that needs unpacking a little. As a result of human sin, our present creation has gone wrong and is no longer fully functioning under God's authority. Therefore it is disjointed, broken, and discordant.[13] When Christ returns, however, the harmony of creation will be restored, and God will be in his proper place as the sole and unchallenged conductor from whom every instrument in the cosmic orchestra takes its cue.

The hope of that day is expressed in a number of ways:

- "Creation itself will be liberated from its bondage to decay" (Rom 8:21).

---

[13]See chap. 4, 39-43.

- When Christ comes, "the end will come, when he hands over the kingdom to God the Father after he has destroyed all dominion, authority and power. . . . [Then] the Son himself will be made subject to him . . . so that God may be all in all" (1 Cor 15:24, 28).

- God's purpose "to be put into effect when the times reach their fulfillment [is] to bring unity to all things in heaven and on earth under Christ" (Eph 1:9-10).

- "And through him [the Son] to reconcile to himself all things, whether things on earth or things in heaven, by making peace through his blood, shed on the cross" (Col 1:20).

> **Observer:** Eugene Peterson grasped the meaning of this brilliantly when he translated Colossians 1:20 as "Not only that, but all the broken and dislocated pieces of the universe—people and things, animals and atoms—get properly fixed and fit together in vibrant harmonies, all because of his death, his blood poured down from the cross."[14]

Peter: My vision of the future is similarly one where it's not only individuals who get saved; it's painted on a much wider canvas than that. I foresee the wholesale re-creation of the heavens and the earth—in other words, of the entire cosmos—when the Lord returns like a thief (see 2 Pet 3:10-18).

John: I can't add much more to what's already been said, but yes, my vision too is of "a new heaven and a new earth," epitomized by a new and magnificently beautiful Jerusalem (Rev 21:1–22:11). Cities, exemplified by Babylon, had been human centers of opposition to God throughout history; but now, at long last, God's chosen city, Jerusalem, epitomizes the remaking of all creation, free from all imperfection and evil. It will become, as originally intended, the place where God lives among his people.

Our Bodies Will Be Transformed

Chair: That's going to be quite a day! The amazing thing is the connection between the re-creation of the cosmos and the re-creation of our own bodies. Paul, we owe this thought particularly to you. Perhaps you bring it

---

[14]Eugene Peterson, *The Message* (Colorado Springs: NavPress, 2002).

out because, by all accounts, you don't enjoy the best of health or the most robust of physiques?

Paul: Leaving my personal health aside, it's true this is an element I draw attention to because it's all part and parcel of what will happen at Christ's return. In Philippians I say that his return "will transform our lowly bodies so that they will be like his glorious body" (Phil 3:21). I reflect on that elsewhere too—for example, in 2 Corinthians 5:1-10. I talk most enthusiastically about it, however, in 1 Corinthians 15:42-44. There I contrast our present bodies with our resurrection bodies. It's the difference between the earthly and the heavenly, the perishable and the imperishable, dishonor and glory, weakness and power, the natural and the spiritual, the mortal and the immortal. The change will happen "in a flash, in the twinkling of an eye, at the last trumpet" (1 Cor 15:51-52). I really can't wait.

> **Observer:** All this can be summed up in saying that the return of Christ leads to "the consummation of all God's promises."[15]

Chair: All that makes me want to pray that ancient prayer "*Marana tha*," "Come, Lord!" (1 Cor 16:22; Rev 22:20), and to "speed its coming" by living a holy life (2 Pet 3:12).

THE SIGNS OF HIS COMING

Reviewing the Signs

Chair: Jesus instructed his disciples to be alert to the signals that would indicate he was coming again so they would be ready (see Mt 24:32-35, 42-44; Mk 13:28-31, 33, 35; Lk 21:29-30, 36). What are those signs?

Mark: We've already been over this ground to some considerable extent as far as I and my fellow Gospel writers are concerned. Perhaps I can just refer people back to our earlier discussion.[16] I think, though, that Paul and John might well have some interesting things to add.

Paul: Well, I faced the situation where the Thessalonians didn't pick up my teaching accurately and rather misinterpreted the implications of Christ's imminent return. They were, as we've said, rather taken aback when some

---

[15]Thomas R. Schreiner, *New Testament Theology: Magnifying God in Christ* (Grand Rapids: Baker Academic, 2008), 802.
[16]See chap. 10, 226-31.

of their number died before it had happened (1 Thess 4:13). They were over-excited about it and thought that, if he was returning that soon, it didn't matter how they lived, so they lived somewhat irresponsibly (see 1 Thess 5:4-11). Some even gave up working and became disruptive nuisances in the church rather than productive members of the community (see 2 Thess 3:6-13). So I was trying to get them to "settle down" a bit (2 Thess 2:1-2; 3:12). In fact, both my teaching and my example should have led them to live in the exact opposite way to the way they were living. If Christ was coming again, they needed to live "sober" lives characterized by faith, love, and hope (1 Thess 5:7-8). That's basic apostolic teaching. You'll find Peter adopts the same approach in 2 Peter 3.

Peter: I couldn't agree more.

Paul: I point out that before Christ appears again there will be an almighty rebellion and "the man of lawlessness" will be "revealed, the man doomed to destruction" (2 Thess 2:3). As I explain (see Thess 2:4-12), he will set himself up in arrogant opposition to God, even seducing people into worshiping him rather than the living God who alone is real and authentic. In fact, his rebellion against God only personifies in one powerful person the climax of a long-running history of rebellion that is already active. It's symptomatic of the way Satan works—but thank God that the lawlessness is currently being restrained! When the restraint is removed, this rebellion will reach its climax. People will be deluded by him en masse. In fact, he'll even engage in counterfeit miracles. But then he'll meet his end when Christ appears in "splendor" and he's destroyed, and his devotees perish with him.

Observer: There has been much speculation as to the identity of "the man of lawlessness," a term which is unique to Paul. John's "antichrist" (1 Jn 2:18, 22; 4:3; 2 Jn 7) is usually thought to refer to the same person, although there are some differences of emphasis between them. Even so, like the "man of lawlessness," the antichrist is in rebellion against God, is a deceiver, and personifies a long-running process of apostasy. John also uses the word *lawlessness* (1 Jn 3:4).

The "man of lawlessness" was a familiar figure in Jewish history. Antiochus Epiphanes (215–163 BC) and the Emperor Caligula (AD 12–41) both desecrated the Jerusalem temple in rebellion against God in ways that matched 2 Thessalonians 2:4. These historical examples were well known, and little further explanation was needed for the original readers of the letters.

While some want to depersonalize the image and interpret it as applying to an institution or to political structures, which by extension it does, the language of the apostles strongly suggests it will be a person. However, no dictator, tyrant, psychopathic ruler, or anti-God despot rules without having the political, economic, and some sort of religious machinery to legitimize and bolster his or her authority.

John: It would be wrong to try to map the visions of Revelation exactly onto what Paul sets out as the future. My visions don't function as a linear timetable. They're poetry, not prose. There is, though, a considerable meeting of minds between us. Throughout Revelation I describe:

- the successive working of lawless evil in our world and its attendant horrors (see Rev 6:1–16:21);
- the blame lying with Satan, the dragon, the beast, and Satan's other subordinates (see Rev 2:9, 13; 3:9; 12:3, 7-9, 13-17; 13:1-18; 19:20; 20:2)
- who receive blasphemous worship (see Rev 13:3-10)
- because people are sucked in and deceived by their counterfeit wonders (see Rev 13:3-4);
- but even so, God is still in control throughout (but see esp. Rev 4:1–8:5)
- until Satan and all his forces are utterly defeated and destroyed (see Rev 18:1–20:15).

Chair: So there are a number of "signs of the end" we might look out for, but you never write of them in such a way as to allow us to set out a timetable. That means we have to be alert at all times.

The Millennium

There is one short passage in Revelation, John, about the millennium, which people have often made the center of their prophetic systems.

John: Yes, it is interesting that the few verses I wrote in Revelation 20:1-10 should have become the focus of so much discussion. They come after I have described the defeat of the beast and the kings of the earth by the word of God (see Rev 19:1-21), and so people have read them as describing the next chapter in history, the one that will occur immediately before the creation of the new heaven and the new earth. Remember, though, that my visions are not intended to map out a linear future timeline of history but to inspire people who are suffering for their faith to persevere, whatever the time.

Put simply, I envision a time when Satan and the dragon will be under lock and key for a thousand years. You'll remember that my numbers are never meant to be exact but are rounded and symbolic, so this speaks of a very long period. After that, they are released and create havoc on the earth again for a short time before being conclusively captured and thrown into the lake of burning sulfur, where "they will be tormented day and night forever and ever" (Rev 20:10).[17] It is intended to be good news. The emphasis, as always, is on God being ultimately in control all along and irrevocably in control at the end of time. My writing is designed to give pastoral encouragement rather than set out a predictive timetable.

Observer: Those who have tried to place the various things said regarding Christ's return into a coherent time frame have often been governed by their understanding of the millennium (see Rev 20:1-10). There are three basic positions with regard to the millennium, with numerous variations within them.

Amillennialism identifies the millennium with the church age, with the figure of "a thousand years" standing for "a long time." The gospel is what is keeping Satan under lock and key, unable to roam as freely as he would like. There is no future millennium period to look forward to since we are experiencing it now. The next thing to happen will be the return of Christ, the resurrection of all, and the judgment, followed by the assignment of an eternal destiny to all. This does not quite do justice to the threefold nature of the passage that speaks of Satan's imprisonment, Satan's release, and then Satan's defeat.

Postmillennialism sees the millennium as the goal to which we are heading on earth and teaches that, when the gospel has made progress and its preaching has transformed the world so as to bring it to live according to God's standards, the world will enjoy his millennial blessing. It is after the reaching of this goal, which will last for a long

[17]The threefold movement is analogous in terms of a game of chess to check, stalemate, and then checkmate.

time but not necessarily a thousand years, that Christ will return and the final sequences of the end times will be initiated. Postmillennialism is optimistic in nature and fits with Enlightenment ideas of progress. It was the inspiration for the modern missionary movement through the ministry of people such as Jonathan Edwards, one of the leaders of the eighteenth-century Evangelical Revival.

Premillennialism has been the most popular recent view among evangelicals. It offers the most literal understanding and draws on many different strands of prophetic texts to present a composite picture of the future, which includes a definite thousand-year period of bliss. It comes in many forms but generally believes that the world will degenerate further morally until the final stages of the end are triggered. Therefore it is somewhat pessimistic about the present time. Its name comes from the fact that it teaches Christ will return after a period of tribulation (see Rev 7:14; Dan 9:24-27) to reign for a thousand years on earth with his saints and preside over a restored earthly kingdom of Israel. Satan will be bound during this time but will rally troops of unbelievers for one last push against Christ before he is finally defeated. One popular version among dispensationalists—those who distinguish various dispensations in history, including those of Israel and the church—believes there will be a "secret rapture" of saints prior to the tribulation. For this reason it is called "pretribulation premillennialism."

This view depends on piecing together a variety of prophetic texts that originally address some very different times, contexts, and issues and that do not always naturally fit together. It is, however, the most immediately exciting interpretation, especially since some see the establishment of Israel in 1948 as a pivotal event not only in world history but also in fulfillment of biblical prophecy. Its literal interpretation of Revelation 20, though, does raise some severe exegetical difficulties.

The main point of the New Testament on the subject, however, discourages speculation about the timing of Christ's return and encourages Christians always to persevere in a state of alert readiness so that they can greet Christ without shame whenever he comes (see Mt 24:42; Mk 13:34-37; Lk 12:40; Eph 5:8-17; 1 Thess 5:4-11; Jas 5:7-9; 1 Jn 2:28; Rev 22:20).

DEATH AND IMMORTALITY

Chair: A couple of times we've touched on one issue that demands more attention, and that is death. We've mentioned it in passing before—when discussing, for example, the Thessalonians, who were surprised people in their assembly had died before Christ returned, or John's mention of a second death. Let's ask some more questions about it and give some brief answers, please.

What Is Death?

Paul: Death has been understood in different ways down the years, but to Christians there is only one issue that really matters: death is "the wages of sin" (Rom 6:23). It all goes back to the Garden of Eden (see Gen 3:3, 19-24). It is both the consequence of and a penalty for our rejection of God and his commands. It is a "divine judgment on human disobedience"[18] (see Rom 5:12-14; Eph 2:1-5). "The sting of death is sin" (1 Cor 15:56).

Given this, human beings react to death as to an enemy, which it is (1 Cor 15:26). It seems to be so final and, unless there's something beyond, it seems to render life so futile. We can fulminate against it, and may even be able to postpone it for a bit, but in the end we can do nothing about it. We will all die because of our sin.

James: The rest of us say the same, usually more briefly. I say, "sin, when it is full-grown, gives birth to death" (Jas 1:15).

How Does the Resurrection Impact Death?

Paul: The point about the resurrection of Jesus is that it breaks through the death barrier and defeats it. By rising from the dead, he showed that death wasn't the last word nor need it be the most powerful force in our lives. He died and then rose because it was impossible for death to keep him, the eternal life-giver, secured in his tomb. He was stronger than death. And the significance of this is that his resurrection wasn't just about what happened to him; it was about bringing the old order, in which death had been undefeatable, to an end. It was about Jesus rising so he could become the first of many to do so, the first pickings of a much greater harvest to come (see 1 Cor 15:21-23; Col 1:18).

So death remains an enemy to humanity, but it is now a tamed, defeated enemy we need no longer fear because we look forward to sharing in Christ's

---

[18]John Stott, *The Cross of Christ* (Leicester: Inter-Varsity Press, 1986), 65.

resurrection. No wonder I sing about it: "Death has been swallowed up in victory. Where, O death, is your victory? Where, O death, is your sting?" (1 Cor 15:54-55).

Of course, we still mourn the severing of relationships that occurs in this life, as we're separated by death from those we love. It would be inhuman to pretend otherwise. However, we "do not grieve like the rest of mankind, who have no hope" (1 Thess 4:13). The resurrection has more than blunted the edge of death.

Peter: At the start of my letter to the exiles I say the same thing: "Praise be to the God and Father of our Lord Jesus Christ! In his great mercy he has given us new birth into a living hope through the resurrection of Jesus Christ from the dead" (1 Pet 1:3).

What Happens to a Believer at Death?

Chair: There seem to be two different things said about what happens when a believer dies. On the one hand, some texts suggest an immediate transference into the presence of God. Jesus said to the repentant criminal on the cross, "Truly I tell you, today you will be with me in paradise" (Lk 23:43). Paul, you say you'd "prefer to be away from the body and at home with the Lord" (2 Cor 5:8) and "I desire to depart and be with Christ" (Phil 1:23). On the other hand, Paul, you also write to the Thessalonians that "the dead in Christ will rise first" (1 Thess 4:16), which suggests they spend some time in the grave awaiting the return of Christ. Which is it?

Luke: Let's listen carefully to Jesus' words on the cross, as I believe they were reliably reported to me. He seems deliberately to have said that the penitent would be with him "in paradise." Originally, *paradise* was a word for a park, a place where someone waited before being admitted to the presence of a king. We know that Jesus went to "the realm of the dead" following his crucifixion, which the Jews called "Hades" (Acts 2:27, 31). Peter says so in 1 Peter 3:19-21. Stephen's prayer for God to receive his spirit as he was martyred may refer to this place of waiting in anticipation of the resurrection (see Acts 7:59). This may suggest a temporary or intermediate state between death and resurrection, before believers enter their final destiny in the new creation.[19]

---

[19]See discussion in J. Richard Middleton, *A New Heaven and a New Earth: Reclaiming Biblical Eschatology* (Grand Rapids: Baker Academic, 2014), 227-37.

Paul: This really isn't an issue to which I give a great deal of attention. My writing here is incidental and more by way of pastoral encouragement than focused, extensive doctrinal exposition, and so you may pick up a varying tone in what I say, depending on the situation I'm addressing. I spoke to Felix about the general resurrection ahead that all will face (see Acts 24:14-15). I'm happy to use the familiar imagery that when a believer dies he or she has "fallen asleep," but one shouldn't build too much on that by way of detailed

> ### DEATH DESCRIBED AS "SLEEP"
>
> Mt 9:24; Mk 5:39; Lk 8:52; Jn 11:11-13; Acts 7:60; 13:36; 1 Cor 11:30; 15:6, 18, 20, 51; 1 Thess 4:13-15; 5:10.

construction. It's a metaphor that indicates that a person is no longer conscious of this world but will awake to another. To argue that it implies there is a gap between death and waking up is to miss the point. What should eclipse all our lesser questions is the assurance that after death the believer becomes conscious of being in the Lord's presence.

What Did Jesus Mean When He Said a Believer Would Never Die?

Chair: It was at Lazarus's tomb, when Jesus described him as "asleep," that Jesus also claimed to be "the resurrection and the life"; but then he added somewhat enigmatically, "The one who believes in me will live, even though they die; and whoever lives by believing in me will never die" (Jn 11:25-26). That seems a bit self-contradictory. John, you reported it: What did he mean by it?

John: To appreciate my Gospel you have to have some understanding of the artistry of words and figures of speech. This is not a contradiction; it's a paradox. Jesus is saying in a striking manner that, on one level, believing in him will not prevent someone from dying a natural death, but, on a deeper level, whoever believes will receive eternal life—one of my favorite themes, remember. Therefore that person will never suffer death *after* death, because he or she will never fail God's judgment.

What Is "The Second Death"?

Chair: Perhaps this is the place to ask what we mean by "the second death," which you refer to, John.

John: Yes—it's quite simple, really. I use the phrase twice (Rev 2:11; 20:6). The "first death" is the one we will all experience, as I've just said: the physical death that occurs at the end of our mortal lives as a result of sin. The "second death" is the counterpoint of eternal life, if you like. It is the death from which there is no return that occurs after the judgment and is the fate of those who have not experienced life in Christ.

Matthew: I think Jesus was saying something very similar in a slightly different way when he said, "Do not be afraid of those who kill the body but cannot kill the soul. Rather, be afraid of the One who can destroy both soul and body in hell" (Mt 10:28).

HEAVEN, HELL, AND THE NEW CREATION

Chair: We turn finally to consider our destination and the destiny of our creation. Let's talk about heaven, hell, and the new creation.

Heaven and the New Creation

Let's begin with heaven. You all, except Jude, mention heaven frequently; but in looking through the many times you speak about it, I see that you rarely ever talk of it as the destination to which Christians are going. That's a bit of a shock, because in popular Christian imagination heaven is going to be our eternal home. Can any of you fill me in a bit?

> **SELECT REFERENCES ABOUT HEAVEN AS GOD'S DWELLING PLACE**
>
> Mk 1:10-11; 6:41; 7:34; 14:62; Lk 3:22; 11:13; 18:13; Jn 1:32, 51; 12:28; Acts 2:34; 3:21; 7:49, 55-56; Rom 1:18; Eph 6:9; Col 4:1; Heb 1:3; 8:1; 12:25; 1 Pet 1:12; Rev 4:2.

John: I can see where that idea comes from. I, for example, remember Jesus saying, "If I go and prepare a place for you, I will come back and take you to be with me that you also may be where I am" (Jn 14:3). This suggests heaven simply because that was where Jesus came from and was going to. It was his Father's dwelling place (see Jn 1:32, 51; 3:13, 31; 6:25-58; 12:28; 17:1).

Matthew: Yes, that's the main way all of us speak of heaven. Heaven is the dwelling place of God, from where he reigns. Therefore I was always writing about "the kingdom of heaven"—thirty-one times, in fact. On one occasion Jesus was quite explicit: "you have one Father," he said, "and he is in heaven" (Mt 23:9).

Luke: Jesus did tell his disciples that their "reward in heaven" would be great (Lk 6:23; Mt 5:12) and that, if they gave to the poor, they would have "treasure in heaven" (Lk 18:22; Mt 19:21; Mk 10:21)—but that's the nearest we get to saying that's the believer's destination; it's simply a way of saying your reward is with God, who will reveal it in due course.

Paul: I don't disagree with that, but the fact that heaven is God's dwelling place means we are "called . . . heavenward," and we rightly belong there too (Phil 3:14, cf. 20). However, if you look carefully at those texts—and 1 Corinthians 15:48-49 as well, which speaks of our being "of heaven" and of bearing "the image of the heavenly man"—you'll see I'm using that to talk about how we live on earth rather than of heaven being our destination. Only at one point do I hint that our destiny is "an eternal house in heaven" (2 Cor 5:1), once this earthly life is over; but the emphasis there is on our eternal home as the gift of God, who lives in heaven, rather than on our going to heaven.

Even in 1 Thessalonians 4:17, where I teach that Christians will rise "to meet the Lord in the air" who is coming down from heaven, I do not say, "and they'll return with him to heaven." I'm using the analogy of what happens when the emperor or other dignitary comes to visit. Citizens would go out to meet him—not so as to return with him to where he's come from, but in order to bring him back with them into their own town.[20]

Peter: People do need to read carefully what we've written, don't they? I write of our inheritance as being "kept in heaven for [us]" (1 Pet 1:4), but that doesn't mean that's where we will go to enjoy it. An earthly inheritance may be kept in a bank, but once you inherit it, it doesn't mean you take up residence in the bank! My greater emphasis, as you must know by now, is on the re-creation of the heavens and the earth.

John: That certainly fits with my vision. I never speak in an unguarded way about believers going to heaven. My vision of the future is one where "the first heaven and the first earth had passed away" and of a new city, Jerusalem, "coming down *out of* heaven from my God" (Rev 21:1; 3:12). That becomes the dwelling place of the redeemed, with God himself at its center (see Rev 21:1–22:5). This is no ethereal, disembodied, nonphysical place

> **THE REIGN
> OF CHRIST'S
> DISCIPLES**
>
> ────────
>
> Mk 10:35-40; Lk 22:30;
> 1 Cor 4:8; 6:2; 2 Tim 2:12.

---

[20]Ibid., 222-24.

populated by spirits we're talking about; this is Eden reclaimed and taken to a new level of perfection. He makes "everything new"—he doesn't write off creation but renews it. That's why in heaven we will serve our God and "reign" over the earth, just as Adam and Eve were instructed to do in Eden (Rev 22:4-5; cf. Gen 1:28; Ps 8:6), although they failed to live up to their calling. There will be plenty of work for us to do.

Chair: So, if I correctly understand what you're saying, our destiny as believers is not to enter some dematerialized spiritual existence, which would certainly be in conflict with what we believe about the transphysical nature of the resurrection, but to serve God eternally in a newly created cosmos.

Paul, Peter, and **John:** Amen!

Hell

Chair: The other side of the coin is hell. Can we say much about the nature of hell?

Matthew: Jesus certainly believed in it and warned people not to end up there. He often described it in terms of Gehenna or Hades. Gehenna was the Valley of Hinnom, where Ahaz and Manasseh sacrificed their sons to Molek by fire (see 2 Chron 28:3; 33:6; Jer 7:31; 32:35). It subsequently became a garbage dump where the fire never died down. Sinful attitudes and actions, Jesus said, would put people on the road to destruction that led to hell (see Mt 5:22, 29-30; 7:13; 10:28). It was worth avoiding, even if doing so involved personal sacrifice, because he believed it to be a place of unquenchable fire (see Mt 18:8-9). Some of the Pharisees had already booked their places there (see Mt 23:15, 33).

Less often, Jesus compared it to Hades (*Sheol* in the Septuagint translation of the Old Testament), which was the realm to which all the dead were consigned and where they lived a shadowy existence in a place of waiting (see Mt 11:23; 16:18).

Sometimes Jesus simply warned of awful judgment (see Mt 10:15; 12:41-42), after which those who were condemned would be "thrown outside, into the darkness, where there will be weeping and gnashing of teeth" (Mt 8:12; cf. 13:50; 22:13; 24:51; 25:30).

Mark: I'd just add to Matthew's comments about Gehenna that Jesus quoted Isaiah 66:24 to describe it as the place "where 'the worms that eat them do not die, and the fire is not quenched'" (Mk 9:48). This confirms that the fires of hell endure over time and aren't to be viewed lightly or as soon passing.

Luke: Just on Hades, remember that Jesus pictured it as more than a place of waiting, at least for some. In his parable about the rich man and Lazarus, he referred to it as a place of "torment" where its residents were "in agony in this fire" (Lk 16:23-24, 28).

OTHER GOSPEL
REFERENCES
TO HELL

Mk 9:43-48; Lk 3:7, 17; 10:13-15; 11:31-32; 12:5; 13:28.

While I have the floor, let me say that the early apostles did not threaten people with hell in their preaching, although they certainly preached the judgment (see Acts 10:42; 24:25). The only reference to Hades comes when Peter says that Jesus wasn't abandoned to rot in "the realm of the dead" but was raised from the dead (Acts 2:27, 31). This was consistent with their constantly emphasizing the message of the resurrection and the offer of life.

The Hebraist: My few references to it fit perfectly with what Jesus taught. Sin leads to death (see Heb 6:1), judgment is eternal (see Heb 6:2), and it is "fearful" because it is a "raging fire that will consume the enemies of God" (Heb 10:27).

Peter: I don't muse on the nature of hell at all, but do stress the reality of a future judgment, as already mentioned.[21]

Jude: Given the terseness of my letter, I mention it quite a bit, but it was germane to my agenda. I threaten those who were endangering the church with the same fate as that experienced by Sodom and Gomorrah, "the punishment of eternal fire" (Jude 7). Then I mention that the "blackest darkness has been reserved forever" for them (Jude 13). That's why true believers should "save others by snatching them from the fire" (Jude 23).

Chair: Paul, you're the theologian; I'm sure you have a lot to say about hell.

Paul: Actually, Chair, I don't. I have a lot to say about judgment but little to say about what happens after that. With others, I see those who are to be condemned at the judgment as already "perishing" (Rom 2:12; 1 Cor 1:18; 2 Cor 2:15; 4:3; 2 Thess 2:10) and heading for "destruction" (Rom 9:22; Phil 1:28; 3:19; 1 Thess 5:3), even "everlasting destruction" (2 Thess 1:9). That last

---

[21]See chap. 10, 234-38.

text is the nearest I get to saying anything about the nature of the destruction and so about hell. It means to be "shut out from the presence of the Lord and from the glory of his might on the day he comes" (2 Thess 1:9-10). So we might see it as essentially an eternal separation from the God who is the source of all life, love, and goodness.

Observer: The reticence of the New Testament writers to elaborate on the nature of hell has led subsequent generations to debate its nature more fully. For obvious reasons, people have traditionally read Jesus' teaching and the frequent use of the word *eternal* as proposing that those who are condemned will suffer never-ending torment in hell forever. The warnings about judgment are terrifyingly awesome.

There have always been some, however, who have questioned whether this is what Jesus and the New Testament writers meant. Jesus was using metaphorical language when he spoke about hell as a fire that never burns out. As some have pointed out, though, he asserted that it is the fire, not necessarily that which goes into the fire, that never burns out. Usually what goes into a fire is consumed. Furthermore, the use of the word *eternal* (which older translations sometimes misleadingly translated as "everlasting") is at least ambiguous. It may mean "unending" but is more likely to mean "belonging to the coming or future age." *Aiōn* is the Greek for "age," and *aiōnios* simply means "agelong" and so "eternal."[22]

The language of destruction might also imply annihilation rather than continuing suffering. There are two forms of the argument for annihilation. One asserts straightforwardly that after condemnation the impenitent will be eradicated. The other, more subtly, takes the form of "conditional immortality." In 1 Timothy 6:16 Paul states that God "alone is immortal." If so, human beings have no automatic access to immortality and can receive it after death only as the gift from a gracious God. The condition for receiving this gift is belief in Christ. Unbelieving sinners who, by definition, fail to meet this condition remain therefore unemancipated from their mortality, on their natural road to extinction.[23]

---

[22]See chap. 7, 145.

[23]The literature on this topic is vast and often quite passionate. For a balanced discussion, see David Hilborn, ed., *The Nature of Hell: A Report of the Evangelical Alliance Commission on Unity*

In addition to reading carefully what the texts say on this matter, theological arguments need to be weighed. Those who believe in hell as never-ending punishment argue that nothing less is merited by humanity's willful sinfulness, and mere annihilation is no punishment at all. Those who believe in "conditional immortality" argue that a morally perfect God would not inflict everlasting torment on his sinful creatures, since the sentence would be unjustly disproportionate to their crimes and would call his moral perfection into question.

Chair: John, time to bring you in. First, let's ask what you say about this topic in your Gospel, as you reflect many years later on the teaching of Jesus.

John: I can be brief. In my Gospel I mention that at the judgment those who do not believe will die or perish (see Jn 3:16; 5:24, 29; 10:28; 11:26); but as you can see from these sayings, I stress that while Jesus was among us his preaching was good, not bad, news because he positively offered eternal life.

My first letter adopts the same approach (see 1 Jn 3:14; 4:17-18; 5:16).

Chair: But you bring the topic to the front of the stage in Revelation.

John: Yes, my agenda in Revelation is different. There I say much more about the eternal fate of those who stand in opposition to God. My starting point is to place everything in the context of the vision of the exalted Christ, "the Living One," who says, "I was dead, and now look, I am alive for ever and ever! And I hold the keys of death and Hades" (Rev 1:18). He proved himself vastly superior to death and unconquered by it, as he rose, "the firstborn from the dead" (Rev 1:5). Death cannot touch him any more. And that gives him the authority to be the Lord who controls the entry to hell.

I assert that destroyers of the earth will themselves be destroyed (see Rev 11:18). The most common image I use comes from Jesus and is that of "the fiery lake of burning sulfur" into which the devil is thrown following in the footsteps of the beast and the false prophet (Rev 19:20; 20:10). Those who worshiped the beast will be "tormented with burning sulfur" (14:9-11), and "the cowardly, the unbelieving, the vile, the murderers, the sexually immoral,

and *Truth Among Evangelicals (ACUTE)* (Carlisle, UK: Paternoster, 2000). For one leading evangelical's consideration of the key texts, see David L. Edwards with John Stott, *Essentials: A Liberal-Evangelical Dialogue* (London: Hodder & Stoughton, 1988), 312-29.

those who practice magic arts, the idolaters and all liars" will follow their heroes into "the fiery lake of burning sulfur" (Rev 21:8).

Doesn't sound like good news for all, does it? But, you know, what's bad news for some is great news for others, for those who have faithfully followed the Master. The greatest good news of all is that "death and Hades" also collapse into this lake of fire and are banished from God's universe forever (Rev 20:14). So they're no longer any threat to the saints. Fundamentally, that's what hell is—being banished from God's presence and permanently on the "outside" of God's new creation (Rev 22:15). What a tragic prospect of eternal proportions for anyone to face when he or she could have believed the gospel, regardless of whether or not hell is everlasting torment.

Chair: Thanks, yes, we shouldn't end on a negative note. To summarize, we've seen that none of you say that Christians are "going to heaven" when they die. We've also seen that, although hell is a terrible reality, you speak of it with restraint and reticence as a destiny that can be avoided. The good news is that, through Christ's death on the cross, God is re-creating "the heavens and the earth." It is this new creation to which Christians are heading and where they will experience something better even than Eden, with God living among his people and with the destructive forces of Satan, sin, and suffering banished from his new creation eternally. That really is good news—good news not just for forgiven sinners as individuals, but also for a broken world that will be fixed at last.

> **Observer:** Michael Bird neatly summed it up when he wrote:
>
> The return of Christ is not a repetition of his original coming, nor an addendum to his earthly work; rather, it is the completion of his work of reconciliation. The divide between heaven and earth is melted down at Christ's second advent. Two worlds collide, and the terrestrial world is changed as heaven is permanently imprinted on it. It is the final stage for God to dwell with his people, in his reign, in his place. As C. S. Lewis said, when the author steps up onto the stage, the play is over.[24]
>
> Then, the good news will be complete! It is finished!

---

[24]Bird, *Evangelical Theology*, 269.

Afterword

The New Testament writers display remarkable creativity in their presentation of the many-sided gospel of Jesus Christ and manage a degree of complexity in handling the different implications of that gospel for their various audiences. They certainly do not simply repeat each other; but based on the trustworthy reports of those who witnessed the life of Jesus firsthand, they explore the meaning of his life, death, and resurrection for Jews and Gentiles, for believers and unbelievers, for individuals and communities, for belief and behavior, for the blessed and the persecuted, for people and creation itself. And they do so bringing their own personalities, gifts, skills, interests, experiences, and agendas to bear on their writings. Given this, it is not surprising that some have sought to identify Matthew's theology, or that of John, Paul, Peter, and the others; but what is more remarkable is the degree of unity and coherence that they exhibit.

The New Testament writers are like instruments in an orchestra playing one glorious and harmonious melody. Each instrument contributes to that one tune. The music that results is that in the coming of Christ, the one who was both fully God and a complete human being, and who was eagerly anticipated by God's people, God acts to put the world back into proper order. He does so by Christ's life, death, and resurrection, by his overcoming of evil and the powers behind it, by his forgiving sinners, redeeming lives, and bringing them into the new community of the church. That church is a great interethnic community that, while still living within the confines of this earth, is a witness, however imperfectly, to the future to be realized when Jesus returns. In the meantime, God has sent his Holy Spirit into the world to continue the work of Christ, both within and outside the church.

On his return, the consummation of God's redemptive work will take place. All evil and all impenitent evildoers will be judged and expelled from his universe, together with all death, suffering, and every other consequence of sin. God will again take up residence among the people he created, redeemed, and loves. Both the physical creation and the people of faith who live in it will be transformed once and for all. Then "every creature in heaven and on earth and under the earth and on the sea, and all that is in them," will join the choir, singing, "To him who sits on the throne and to the Lamb be praise and honor and glory and power, for ever and ever!" (Rev 5:13).

Come, Lord Jesus, come. Amen.

Bibliography

New Testament Theologies for Further Reading

Bird, Michael F. *Evangelical Theology: A Biblical and Systematic Introduction.* Grand Rapids: Zondervan, 2013.

Caird, George. *New Testament Theology.* Edited by L. D. Hurst. Oxford: Oxford University Press, 1994.

Dunn, James D. G. *Unity and Diversity in the New Testament: An Inquiry into the Character of Earliest Christianity.* Philadelphia: Westminster Press, 1977.

Grudem, Wayne. *Systematic Theology: An Introduction to Biblical Doctrine.* Grand Rapids: Zondervan, 1994.

Guthrie, Donald. *New Testament Theology.* Downers Grove, IL: InterVarsity Press, 1981.

Ladd, G. E. *A Theology of the New Testament.* Edited by D. A. Hagner. 2nd ed. Grand Rapids: Eerdmans, 1974.

Marshall, I. Howard. *A Concise New Testament Theology.* Downers Grove, IL: InterVarsity Press, 2008.

———. *New Testament Theology: Many Witnesses, One Gospel.* Downers Grove, IL: InterVarsity Press, 2004.

Milne, Bruce. *Know the Truth: A Handbook of Christian Belief.* 3rd ed. Nottingham: Inter-Varsity Press, 2009.

Morris, Leon. *New Testament Theology.* Grand Rapids: Zondervan, 1996.

Schreiner, Thomas R. *New Testament Theology: Magnifying God in Christ.* Grand Rapids: Baker Academic, 2008.

Other Works

Barnett, Paul. *The Second Epistle to the Corinthians.* New International Commentary on the New Testament. Grand Rapids: Eerdmans, 1997.

Bauckham, Richard. *James*. New Testament Readings. New York: Routledge, 1999.

———. *Jesus: A Very Short Introduction*. Oxford: Oxford University Press, 2011.

———. *Jesus and the God of Israel*. Milton Keynes: Paternoster, 2008.

Beasley-Murray, G. R. *Jesus and the Kingdom of God*. Grand Rapids: Eerdmans, 1986.

———. *Preaching the Gospel from the Gospels*. Peabody, MA: Hendrickson, 1996.

Becker, U. "Gospel." In *Dictionary of New Testament Theology*, vol. 2, edited by Colin Brown, 107-15. Grand Rapids: Zondervan, 1976.

Belleville, Linda. "'Imitate Me, Just as I Imitate Christ': Discipleship in the Corinthian Correspondence." In *Patterns of Discipleship in the New Testament*, edited by Richard N. Longenecker. Grand Rapids: Eerdmans, 1996.

Blackburn, B. L. "Divine Man/*THEIOS ANĒR*." In *Dictionary of Jesus and the Gospels*, edited by Joel Green, Scot McKnight, and I. Howard Marshall, 189-92. Downers Grove, IL: InterVarsity Press, 1992.

Bowman, Robert M., and J. Ed Komoszewski. *Putting Jesus in His Place: The Case for the Deity of Christ*. Grand Rapids: Kregel, 2007.

Brown, Raymond E. *The Birth of the Messiah*. London: Chapman, 1977.

Brueggemann, Walter. *Theology of the Old Testament*. Minneapolis: Fortress Press, 1997.

Bultmann, R. *The Theology of the New Testament*. London: SCM Press, 1956.

Burridge, Richard A. *Imitating Jesus: An Inclusive Approach to New Testament Ethics*. Grand Rapids: Eerdmans, 2007.

Calvin, John. *Institutes of the Christian Religion*. Various editions.

Campa, Roy E., and Brian S. Rosner. *The First Letter to the Corinthians*. Pillar New Testament Commentary. Grand Rapids: Eerdmans, 2010.

Campbell, Constantine R. *Paul and Union with Christ: An Exegetical and Theological Study*. Grand Rapids: Zondervan, 2012.

Clifford, Ross, and Philip Johnson. *The Cross Is Not Enough: Living as Witnesses to the Resurrection*. Grand Rapids: Baker Books, 2012.

Colijn, Brenda B. *Images of Salvation in the New Testament*. Downers Grove, IL: InterVarsity Press, 2010.

Dunn, James D. G. *The Acts of the Apostles*. Epworth Commentaries. Peterborough, UK: Epworth Press, 1996.

———. *Jesus and the Spirit*. New Testament Library. London: SCM Press, 1975.

———. "Methodology of Evangelism in the New Testament: Some Preliminary Reflections." In *New Testament Theology in the Light of the Church's Mission:*

Essays in Honor of I. Howard Marshall, edited by Jon C. Laansma, Grant Osborne, and Ray Van Neste. Eugene, OR: Wipf & Stock, 2011.

———. *New Testament Theology: An Introduction.* Nashville: Abingdon Press, 2009.

———. *The Theology of Paul the Apostle.* Edinburgh: T&T Clark, 1998.

Edwards, David L., with John Stott. *Essentials: A Liberal-Evangelical Dialogue.* London: Hodder & Stoughton, 1988.

Edwards, Jonathan. *The Religious Affections.* Edinburgh: Banner of Truth Trust, 1986 [1746].

Erickson, Millard. *Christian Theology.* 2nd ed. Grand Rapids: Baker, 1998.

Fee, Gordon. *God's Empowering Presence: The Holy Spirit in the Letters of Paul.* Peabody, MA: Hendrickson, 1994.

———. *Pauline Christology: An Exegetical-Theological Study.* Peabody, MA: Hendrickson, 2007.

Fiddes, Paul. *Past Event, Present Salvation.* London: Darton, Longman & Todd, 1989.

France, R. T. *Divine Governance: God's Kingship in the Gospel of Mark.* London: SPCK, 1990.

———. *The Gospel of Mark.* New International Greek Testament Commentary. Grand Rapids: Eerdmans, 2002.

———. *The Gospel of Matthew.* New International Commentary on the New Testament. Grand Rapids: Eerdmans, 2007.

———. *Matthew.* Tyndale New Testament Commentary. Leicester, UK: Inter-Varsity Press, 1985.

———. *Matthew: Evangelist and Teacher.* Exeter, UK: Paternoster, 1989.

Green, Joel B. *The Gospel of Luke.* New International Commentary on the New Testament. Grand Rapids: Eerdmans, 1997.

———. *Why Salvation?* Nashville: Abingdon Press, 2013.

Green, Michael. *Evangelism in the Early Church.* London: Hodder & Stoughton, 1970.

Grenz, Stanley. *Theology for the Community of God.* Nashville: Broadman & Holman, 1994.

Griffiths, Michael. *Cinderella with Amnesia: A Practical Discussion of the Relevance of the Church.* London: Inter-Varsity Press, 1975.

Hansen, G. Walter. *The Letter to the Philippians.* Pillar New Testament Commentary. Grand Rapids: Eerdmans, 2009.

Hays, Richard B. *The Moral Vision of the New Testament: A Contemporary Introduction to New Testament Ethics.* New York: T&T Clark, 1997.

Hurtado, Larry W. "Christ." In *Dictionary of Jesus and the Gospels*, edited by Joel Green, Scott McKnight, and I. Howard Marshall, 106-17. Downers Grove, IL: InterVarsity Press, 1992.

———. *Lord Jesus Christ: Devotion to Jesus in Earliest Christianity*. Grand Rapids: Eerdmans, 2003.

Jeremias, Joachim. *New Testament Theology*. Vol. 1. Translated by John Bowden. London: SCM Press, 1971.

Macleod, Donald. *Christ Crucified: Understanding the Atonement*. Nottingham: Inter-Varsity Press, 2014.

———. *The Person of Christ*. Leicester, UK: Inter-Varsity Press, 1998.

Marshall, I. Howard. *Aspects of Atonement*. London: Paternoster, 2007.

———. *The Pastoral Epistles*. International Critical Commentary. Edinburgh: T&T Clark, 1999.

Martin, Ralph P. *Reconciliation: A Study of Paul's Theology*. London: Marshall, Morgan & Scott, 1981.

McKnight, Scot, and Joseph B. Modica, eds. *Jesus Is Lord, Caesar Is Not: Evaluating Empire in New Testament Studies*. Downers Grove, IL: InterVarsity Press, 2013.

Middleton, J. Richard. *A New Heaven and a New Earth: Reclaiming Biblical Eschatology*. Grand Rapids: Baker Academic, 2014.

Moo, Douglas. *The Letters to the Colossians and to Philemon*. Pillar New Testament Commentary. Grand Rapids: Eerdmans, 2008.

Murray, John. *Redemption: Accomplished and Applied*. Edinburgh: Banner of Truth, 1961.

O'Brien, Peter T. *Commentary on Philippians*. New International Greek Testament Commentary. Grand Rapids: Eerdmans, 1991.

Peterson, Eugene. *The Message*. Colorado Springs: NavPress, 2002.

Rainbow, Paul A. *Johannine Theology: The Gospel, the Epistles and the Apocalypse*. Downers Grove, IL: InterVarsity Press, 2014.

Rosner, Brian. *Paul and the Law: Keeping the Commandments of God*. New Studies in Biblical Theology. Downers Grove, IL: InterVarsity Press, 2013.

Schreiner, Thomas R. "The Penal Substitution View." In *The Nature of the Atonement: Four Views*, edited by J. Beilby and P. R. Eddy. Downers Grove, IL: InterVarsity Press, 2006.

Stott, John. *The Cross of Christ*. Leicester, UK: Inter-Varsity Press, 1986.

Tidball, Derek. "Completing the Circle: The Resurrection According to John." *Evangelical Review of Theology* 30, no. 2 (2006): 168-83.

Tidball, Derek and Dianne. *The Message of Women.* The Bible Speaks Today Bible Themes. Nottingham, UK: Inter-Varsity Press, 2012.

Turner, Max. *Baptism in the Holy Spirit.* Nottingham, UK: Grove, 2002.

——. *The Holy Spirit and Spiritual Gifts: Then and Now.* Milton Keynes, UK: Paternoster, 1996.

Wenham, David. *Paul: Follower of Jesus or Founder of Christianity?* Grand Rapids: Eerdmans, 1995.

Wilson, W. T. *The Hope of Glory: Education and Exhortation in the Epistle to the Colossians.* Leiden: Brill, 1997.

Witherington, Ben, III. *The Acts of the Apostles: A Socio-Rhetorical Commentary.* Grand Rapids: Eerdmans, 1998.

——. *Revelation.* New Cambridge Bible Commentary. Cambridge: Cambridge University Press, 2003.

Wright, N. T. *Jesus and the Victory of God.* London: SPCK, 1996.

——. *Paul and the Faithfulness of God.* London: SPCK, 2013.

——. *Paul for Everyone: 2 Corinthians.* London: SPCK, 2003.

——. *Paul for Everyone: Romans, Part 1: Chapters 1–8.* London: SPCK, 2004.

——. *Paul: Fresh Perspectives.* London: SPCK, 2005.

——. *The Resurrection of the Son of God.* London: SPCK, 2003.

——. "Romans." In *The New Interpreter's Bible*, vol. 10, edited by Leander E. Keck, 295-550. Nashville: Abingdon Press, 2002.

——. *Surprised by Hope.* London: SPCK, 2007.

Scripture Index

Finding the Textbook You Need

The IVP Academic Textbook Selector
is an online tool for instantly finding the IVP books
suitable for over 250 courses across 24 disciplines.

ivpacademic.com